BUS

"Resilience is the core attribute of people who succeed, in business and in life. Sonnenfeld and Ward show what we can learn from resilient people and give us a model of engaged, purposeful leadership that is as critical to dealing with adversity as it is to achieving success. This is a unique and engaging read."

—*Ivan G. Seidenberg, Chairman and CEO, Verizon Communications Inc.*

"As CEO of PepsiCo, I especially enjoyed the role of coaching the waves of rising stars needed to lead the next generation of the Pepsi Generation. The best talent always showed resilience in besting adversity. As in my own career, learning from slipups while in pursuit of big change is far better leadership preparation than cautiously tiptoeing along, trying to avoid missteps. This is the only book I've ever read that captures the importance of setbacks as sources of potential wisdom. I wish I'd written this book myself and surely recommend that all aspiring leaders read it."

—*Roger A. Enrico, Chairman of Dreamworks Animation SKG and former Chairman and CEO, PepsiCo*

"I found the research and wide-ranging examination of how leaders (particularly corporate leaders) have responded to and overcome adversity—in their careers and in their lives in general—to be insightful and helpful. The analyses, as well as the book's recommendations, are anchored in a wide ranging, penetrating examination of individual case histories and an understanding of relevant psychology."

—*John Pepper, Chairman, The Walt Disney Company, and former Chairman and CEO, Procter & Gamble*

"The title says it all. This is a must read for any of us who have or have not been through so-called 'career disasters.' Any adversity that any of us deal with at any time in our lives only serves to make us stronger and better at what we do."

—*Millard Drexler, Chairman and CEO, J.Crew Group*

"Leaders often do not understand that the very traits that lead them to the pinnacle of success can also lead them to the abyss of failure. Many leaders find themselves, often suddenly, confronting previously unimagined and even unimaginable disasters that threaten to derail their careers. Some come back; others do not. No book better describes the attributes leaders need to develop to be resilient in the face of defeat. The book is both for those seeking to stave off disasters and for those confronting them. I plan to make the book a cornerstone of my own course on leadership and of my own leadership!"

—*Bob Sternberg, President of the American Psychological Association and Dean of the School of Arts and Sciences and Professor of Psychology, Tufts Universit*

Firing Back

Firing
Back

How Great Leaders Rebound
After Career Disasters

Jeffrey Sonnenfeld
Andrew Ward

HARVARD BUSINESS SCHOOL PRESS
BOSTON, MASSACHUSETTS

Copyright 2007 Harvard Business School Publishing Corporation
All rights reserved
Printed in the United States of America
10 09 08 07 06   5 4 3 2 1

ISBN 13: 978-1-59139-301-6

Library of Congress Cataloging-in-Publication Data

Sonnenfeld, Jeffrey A., 1954-
  Firing back : how great leaders rebound after career disasters /
Jeffrey Sonnenfeld, Andrew Ward.
      p. cm.
  ISBN 1-59139-301-9 (hardcover : alk. paper)
  1. Crisis management. 2. Leadership. 3. Executives. 4. Success in
business. I. Ward, Andrew. II. Title.
  HD49.S66 2007
  658.4'092—dc22
                                        2006025387

The paper used in this publication meets the minimum requirements of the American National Standard for Information Sciences—Permanence of Paper for Printed
Library Materials, ANSI Z39.48-1992.

Contents

Acknowledgments

This book is about rebounding from catastrophic career setbacks. Over the course of writing the book, and even before the idea for turning our investigation of this type of resilience into a book, we have had the privilege of talking to many prominent individuals from both business and other fields about their downfall experiences. Some of these individuals were able to successfully fire back into new careers, some were not. Some we spoke to after they had regained prominence, some during the darkest moments following their fall from grace. Some were even instigators of the downfall of others. We are grateful to all of them for sharing their experiences with us, reliving what were often painful memories in order to share the lessons they learned. Many of their stories appear in this book, and we give them our sincere thanks. But equal thanks go to the many others who do not appear by name here—those who wished to remain anonymous or were constrained by nondisparagement or confidentiality agreements not to go public with their stories, but who nevertheless provided valuable insights as we undertook this investigation. While we cannot name them even here, they know who they are, and we thank them.

Many of the conversations that provided insight for this work took place at over fifty CEO Summits hosted by our Chief Executive Leadership Institute (CELI). We are extremely grateful to all the past and present staff and researchers of CELI, particularly Joe DeLillo, who has made each and every one of these CEO Summits happen.

Many people helped us personally in making sense of this material in real-life experience, through their love, their wisdom, and their loyalty. Most of them made selfless sacrifices to ensure justice, compassion, and recovery: Rochelle Sonnenfeld, Marc Sonnenfeld, Clarky Sonnenfeld, Ann Sonnenfeld, Sophie Sonnenfeld, Lauren Sonnenfeld, Jeff Ward, Mary Ward, Helen Ward, Sally Ward, Samuel Ward, Thomas Ward, Jo Ann Garrett, Ted Garrett, Bart Garrett, Benn Konsynski, Adam Aron, Ted Killory, Joe DeLillo, Donna DeLillo, George Benston, Andrea Hershatter, Barbara Maaskaant, Bernie Marcus, Patty Marx, Oz Nelson, Jim Kelly, Joe Moderow, Michael Eskew, Leah Soupata, Nell Minow, Jack Duffy, Joe Schneider, Karen Kapler, Terry Donovan, Don Layden, Albert H. Gordon, Carol Herron, George Hornig, Joan Hornig, Arvind Bhambri, Kim Davis, Marty Payson, Ursula Blumenthal, David Blumenthal, John Eyler, Michael Leven, former Speaker of the House Newt Gingrich, President Bill Clinton, President George H. W. Bush, John Seffrin, Jeff Koplan, Bob Hawkins, Frank Louchheim, Al Goldstein, Michael McCaskey, Derek Smith, Marsha Evans, A. D. Frazier, Don Burr, Tom James, Mac Crawford, Warren Bennis, Barbara Babbit Kaufman, Jim Clifton, former Congressman Cynthia McKinney, Jeffrey Pfeffer, Paul Hirsh, David Allison, David Rubinger, Nicole Cipriani, Phil Weiss, Peter Kaplan, Morley Safer, Don Hewitt, Geoff Colvin, Cathy Olian, Alden Bourne, Dan Raviv, Michael Golden, Arthur Sulzberger, Paul Steiger, Joann Lublin, Carol Hymowitz, Steve Forbes, Rich Karlgaard, John Byrne, Peter Applebome, Kevin Sack, Bill Rankin, Adam Moss, Kurt Andersen, Jim Cramer, Mark Hoffman, Joe Nocera, Tom Stewart, Scott Cowan, Jackie Adams, John Porter, Warren Sams, William Brown, Keegan Federal, Michael Bower, Josh Archer, Jagdish Sheth, George Easton, Allen Maines, Jim Rosenfeld, George Easton, Oliver Cooper, Mark Scott, Alan Dabbiere, Jeff Cunningham, Bill Roberti, Tony Cernera, Sandy Climan, Richard Edelman, Stephen Berger, Ed Mathias, Stephen Schwarzman, Chris Nedza, Mark Nedza, Tom Fuyala, Anil Asnani, Jamie Hajj, Paddy Spence, Kate Ellis, Wenda Millard, Tara Whitehead, Ann Mooney, Joel Klein, Jonathan Marks, Phil Lader, Stacy Jolna, Karon Jolna, Anil Menon, Jackie Montag, Tony Montag, Paul Rosenberg, Quinn Mills, Brenda Brayton, Mike Bozic, Stephen Greyser, Rakesh Khurana, John Quelch, Paul Hirsh, Emily Reichman, Bill Crocker, Paul

Lapides, Carlton Whitehead, Andre Delbecq, Joe White, Laurie Kirkwood, Michael Feder, Marc Adler, Doug Dougherty, Rob Hill, Erin Steele, Dan Mullins, Kim Turner, Denise West, Ravi Rammamurti, Ricardo Martinez, Charles Hatcher, Barry Nalebuff, Judy Chevalier, Sigal Barsade, Victor Vroom, Stan Garstka, Joel Podolny, Jeffrey Garten, Diane Palmeri, Bonnie Blake, Benjamin Loebick, Ira Millstein, Dorothy Robinson, Linda Lorimer, Rick Levin, Alan Amason, Beth Auer, Neal Auer, Elizabeth Bailey, Gigi Bair, Todd Bair, Jeremy Beckwith, Sally Beckwith, George Benson, Carol Bishop, Jeff Bishop, John Blackstone, Jill Brown, Ann Buchholtz, Stacy Campbell, Jeff Cohn, Michelle Cummings, Steve Cummings, Rich Daniels, Hal Farnsworth, Daniel Feldman, Scott Graffin, Joe Harder, Anne Henderson, Marshall Henderson, Robert Hirschfield, Chuck Hofer, Cory Jones, Tommy Jones, John Kimberly, Melenie Lankau, Charles Lankau, Peggy Lee, Jon Levy, Ashley Levy, Gideon Markman, Greg Martin, Lori Martin, Karen Napoleon, Bryan Miller, Lisa Miller, Sarah Miller, Alison Norris, Blaine Norris, Mandy O'Neill, Jennifer Pendergast, Kat Raczynski, Kevin Raczynski, Huggy Rao, Tom Reeve, Ruth Reeve, Chris Riordan, Diana Robertson, Carrie Sewell, Eric Sewell, Angela Snapp, Mike Useem, Bob Vandenberg, and so many others.

There were also a great number of people who did a thorough job of digging up the background information and were instrumental in providing the details of our illustrative examples. Our greatest measure of thanks goes to Lindsay Gerdes, who was the most dedicated, enthusiastic, thorough, and altogether wonderful research assistant one could possibly hope for. However, we also benefited greatly from most able research support from Sheldon Baker, Lisa Fryer, Thomas Geggel, Tiffany Mailen, Leigh McCracken, Lorie Nadan, Arathi Narasimhan, Daniela Pedron, Ketna Raithatha, and Amanda Skartvedt.

We have had a great experience working with the folks from Harvard Business School Press. Our editor, Jacque Murphy, has been phenomenal. Jacque has given birth to two children while we were metaphorically giving birth to this book. We're not sure which has been more painful for her, but we know that we caused her undue suffering as she cajoled us toward finishing the manuscript and pushed us to refine it. We know she will make a wonderful mother and that her children will certainly benefit from the character of patience that she has developed from working with us! Thank you, Jacque! Thanks also to Hollis Heimbouch, Marcy Barnes-Henrie, Zeenat Potia, Brian Surette, Christine Turnier-Vallecillo, and the rest of the team at HBS Press as well as Carol Franco, formerly of HBS Press, who all showed tremendous patience and imagination.

Finally, while Jacque and the rest of the folks at HBS Press have certainly gone above and beyond the call of duty in terms of patience with us, the ones that have borne the brunt of this effort on a day-to-day basis are our families, friends, and colleagues, who had to suffer from our lack of attention during the writing of this book. This, of course, is particularly true for our wives and children, Clarky, Sophie, and Lauren Sonnenfeld, and Sally, Samuel, and Thomas Ward, who have given us their total support despite our undeservingness.

This book is dedicated to five personal tutors in the art of resilience who never will have the chance to read this book, namely, Burton Sonnenfeld, Cal Pava, Danny Pearl, Janice Beyer, and Michael Rukstad. We miss them dearly.

CHAPTER 1

The Disappointment of Defeat
or the Defeat of Disappointment

That's life, that's what all the people say.
You're riding high in April,
Shot down in May.
But I know I'm gonna change that tune,
When I'm back on top, back on top in June.
I said that's life, and as funny as it may seem,
Some people get their kicks,
Stompin' on a dream
But I don't let it, let it get me down,
'Cause this fine ol' world it keeps spinning around.

—Dean Kay and Kelly Gordon, recorded by Frank Sinatra, "That's Life"

IN CONFRONTING LOSSES of all types, we are too often faced with various trite prescriptions for squeezing the lemons of life into lemonade. For leaders, however, life's adversity can turn hard-earned assets into monumental barriers to recovery. Leaders can enjoy such resources as great popular recognition, vast networks of supporters, and gushing pools of finances. Yet celebrity, popularity, and wealth do not insulate them from fate.

There is no cruise control for leaders to coast on the momentum of recent triumphs. Today's evidence of good fortune could evaporate with tomorrow's events. As Frank Sinatra reminds us in his ballad "That's Life," one moment we can be on top of the world, and the next, trodden underfoot. What's more, for prominent leaders and public figures, many people, as Sinatra puts it, "get their kicks stompin' on a dream" and enjoy seeing those who have been held on a pedestal get knocked down. Just ask Martha Stewart, should you need convincing about the power of schadenfreude or the delight in the humiliation of those we envy.

This point is dramatized well for us time and time again in the headlines. Whether it is movie or media stars, artists, politicians, business leaders, or even academics, there is a fascination with those who fall from grace, who get knocked off their pedestals either through their own slipups or by external overthrow. For many, the derailment of a career of high accomplishment compounds adversity because their path to date has been so all consuming that so much else was sacrificed in its pursuit. Private dreams became public possessions, which are then cavalierly tossed away by an unappreciative, fickle society. F. Scott Fitzgerald's famous admonition that there are no second acts in American lives casts an especially dark shadow over the derailed careers of leaders and those focused on creative expression.

Nonetheless, some do recover with their careers more ablaze than ever, while others flame out into obscurity. Consider the resilience of John Irving, Mike Nichols, Robert Altman, Carlos Santana, and John Travolta against the retreats of Kurt Vonnegut, J. D. Salinger, Alan Jay Lerner, Judy Garland, and Orson Welles. Some were energized by their losses, while others were forever haunted by the specter of their own early careers. What distinguishes those who stare down setback, determined to rebuild, and those who stare despondently into a void, never able to recapture that spark that ignited the flames of former glory?

In this book, we will consider CEOs—and other prominent leaders whose career paths derail—in a way similar to these contrasting celebrities, showing the resilience of wide-ranging leaders who've lost and regained their footing for even greater triumphs, such as Donald Trump; Jamie Dimon, CEO of JP Morgan Chase; Vanguard founder Jack Bogle;

Home Depot founder Bernie Marcus; Morgan Stanley CEO John Mack; and Martha Stewart. They will be examined as contrasts to talented, fallen CEOs who were once household names but then crashed, never to regain prominent public leadership roles, and largely disappeared from sight, such as Hewlett-Packard's Carly Fiorina; Kodak's George Fisher; IBM's John Akers; Apple's John Sculley; Ford's Jacques Nasser; United Airlines' Richard Ferris; Priceline's Jay Walker; and WebMD's Jeff Arnold.

On June 10, 2004, just days after Coca-Cola CEO Doug Daft was succeeded by Neville Isdell, Isdell announced the exit of Coca-Cola president Steven Heyer with the simple statement: "In discussions over the past week, Steve and I have looked at how he could best realize his personal goals given my election as chairman and CEO of this company . . . We agreed that Steve could best realize his aspirations by pursuing opportunities outside of the company." Heyer, at age fifty-one, was a shining star among U.S. business leaders. He had already served as managing director of consulting firm Booz Allen Hamilton, president of J. Walter Thompson, and president of Turner Broadcasting, in addition to his three years as president of Coca-Cola. He was disappointed by the decision, feeling that his contributions and experience had been undervalued in the blur of Coca-Cola board politics. Just four months later, however, Heyer rebounded, taking over the reins of one of the world's largest hotel chains as CEO of Starwood Hotels, whose holdings include the St. Regis, Sheraton, Westin, and W hotels.

Former president Jimmy Carter challenged a group of CEOs at one of our conferences to consider how they would recover if the American public had fired them. Despite failing to be reelected, Carter continued tirelessly in his humanitarian, public health, and diplomacy missions, heavily promoting democratic reform around the world, and has become revered by virtually all as the United States' greatest *former* president and eventually recognized as a Nobel Laureate for Peace. Leaders should not be measured by how they bask in the gratification of their accomplishments. Rather, they should be measured by how they respond when fate deflates the joys of hard-earned triumphs. How well do they pick themselves up and get back in the race?

Firing Back

This quality of resilience is critical in the lives of creative figures such as leaders and artists. The rise, the fall, and the recovery of both leaders and artists face common stages. Back in the 1930s, Otto Rank was one of the first to link these extraordinary contributors. He suggested that their accomplishments were the consequence of a shared, superhuman urge to create, fueled by a heightened quest for immortality.

Artists and leaders were similarly considered in Howard Gardner's book *Extraordinary Minds.*[1] He proposed a set of traits shared by "influencers"—those truly great historic figures across professions. After studying such creative figures as Wolfgang Mozart, Virginia Woolf, Sigmund Freud, and Mahatma Gandhi, Gardner concluded that rather than raw intellect, lucky circumstances, or even indefatigable energies, these figures possessed powerful skills of (1) candid self-assessment of their strengths and weaknesses, (2) keen situational analysis, and (3) the capacity to reframe past setbacks into future successes. A defeat merely energized them to rejoin the fray with greater ardor. It is not the proportion of their losses that differentiates these influencers from the rest of us, but how they construed their losses.

It is, in fact, wrong to consider adversity a diversion off one's path toward greatness. The subsequent resilience from calamities has been revealed as vital to the character formation and differentiation of heroic figures. Anthropologist Joseph Campbell studied, across cultures and eras, religious and folk heroes such as Jesus, Moses, Mohammed, Buddha, Cuchulain, Odysseus, Aeneas, and the Aztecs' Tezcatlipoca, and discerned a universal "monomyth" of the life stages of these heroes.[2] One stage involved a call to greatness, which led to a separation from one's past to realize superhuman talent. This was followed by a series of continual trials and ultimately profound setbacks that were met with eventual triumph and reintegration back into society.

The apparent losses were reconstructed into assets. These visionary leaders were able to inspire others to join them though their own sagas of redemption. They gained the confidence for transformational leadership, in part, through their stunning transcendence over life's adversity.

Second Thoughts About Second Acts

Ironically, the very same assets of CEOs' past leadership, their renowned reputations and quest for immortal legacies, can become liabilities. Jeffrey Sonnenfeld's study of a generation of prominent CEOs leaving office revealed that reputation or heroic stature and the quest for lasting contribution or heroic mission can become daunting barriers.[3] In his book *The Hero's Farewell*, the loss of heroic stature compounds adversity because private losses are so public for these people. Literary scholar Leo Braudy suggested in his book *The Frenzy of Renown* that society generates a subset of people eager to live their lives in the public eye.[4] They court fame and recognition in grand fashion so that their prominence will allow them greater risk taking. These idiosyncrasy credits come at a price. When a devastating career setback hits such superachievers, they feel greater shame because their loss of self-esteem, their loss of influence, and their loss of self-reliance are so very public.

An examination of two dethroned, prominent, and wealthy fifty-eight-year-old California CEOs, profiled coincidentally in side-by-side articles in the *New York Times*, reveals how differently corporate leaders can confront adversity. One article, entitled "The Afterlife of a Powerful Chief," was an upbeat piece on Hewlett-Packard's former CEO Lewis Platt and his new role, enjoying life as a vintner running Kendall-Jackson Wine Estates despite having a different scale of leadership of a workforce of 1,200 instead of his former 124,000.[5] The adjacent article, entitled "A General Whose Time Ran Out," conveyed the pathetic emotional outcry and frustration of Mark Willes, the former CEO of Times Mirror, over his board's loss of faith in his strategy and their undermining him to sell the entire firm to media competitor, the Tribune Company of Chicago.[6]

Platt, a popular engineer famous for his intelligence and honesty, was a thirty-three-year veteran of the "HP Way," known for his reinforcement of the firm's widely admired core values about people, service, product quality, and citizenship. He had succeeded John Young as CEO and the legendary cofounder David Packard as chairman in 1993. After a great start, however, revenue growth and product innovation were seen as slipping by 1999 due to slow responses to falling PC prices, declining Asian sales, and yawning Internet opportunities. He announced new e-commerce strategies and broad restructuring while suggesting to his own board that he be replaced. In his new role, Platt was enthusiastic about getting his hands dirty with direct product responsibility in the winery, and later went on to serve as chairman of Boeing, stabilizing the firm through a difficult period when two CEOs were removed back-to-back for personal misconduct allegations before Boeing's board recruited GE and 3M alumnus Jim McNerney to rebuild this aerospace giant. Before his death in the fall of 2005, Platt confided to us that his only real career regret was the mistaken selection of Carly Fiorina as his successor and the destructive reign at HP that followed until her own removal in 2005.

By contrast, Mark Willes seemed to many to be at war with the culture he had inherited at Times Mirror when he arrived from General Mills in 1995. He declared unattainable circulation goals and flouted journalistic conventions about the independence and objectivity of editorial versus commercial aspects of the papers. While this sparked a revolt by the *Los Angeles Times'* journalists, ultimately he was undermined by his own chief financial officer, Tom Unterman, who negotiated with the Times Mirror board and the Tribune Company behind Willes's back. He emotionally addressed his employees the day the deal was announced, lamenting the personal disappointment that he was not given the time to prove his strategies.

Fight, Not Flight: Facing Up to the Issue

We have long known that career distress can be one of the greatest sources of life stress. Being fired, for example, has been ranked as number eight among the most stressful events in life—just after death of family members, jail, and personal injury or illness.[7] Loss of title and social role ambiguity are powerful workplace stressors as well.[8] While the psychological and physiological symptoms of chronic stress can have a profoundly corrosive effect, many of the bromides of our therapeutic society are not appropriate stress responses for many creative individuals and leaders. Stress is the perception of helplessness in dealing with serious demands. There is no such thing as objective stress existing on its own. It is a behavior resulting from responses to people, places, and events, where our response is dependent upon our perceptions of the adequacy of resources to deal with the stressor(s).

Thus, since stress is an interpreted phenomenon based on one's feeling of competence and strength, it is unlikely that the vacations and retreats so often prescribed will yield creative individuals the sense of potency and connectedness they require to feel back in control. Research on psychological hardiness in responding to stress suggests that victims must regain control, make commitments to external events, respond to challenges, be willing to take a radical approach, and essentially become blind to their fears.[9] Coping with stress does not mean accommodating and accepting the stress. Often victims are encouraged to reduce the *importance* of stress, through denial, avoidance, projection, and withdrawal, or else to reduce the *effects* of stress, through exercise, diet, meditation, and support groups, but it is also worth examining ways of reducing the *source* of the stress, perhaps through direct confrontation.

Henry Silverman, the CEO of Cendant, was once a Wall Street darling, a dazzling deal maker, building a company called Hospitality Franchising. He assembled such brands as real estate brokerage Century 21, Ramada Hotels, Howard Johnson Hotels, Days Inn, and Avis Rent A Car, to yield 20 percent-plus growth rates and soaring stock prices. The stock jumped from $4 a share in 1992 to over $77 before the scandal hit. Following a presumed masterstroke merger with a direct marketer called CUC that led to the firm's renaming to Cendant in late 1997, his empire and reputation unraveled. A series of investigations revealed massive improprieties in the former CUC that led to inflated earnings of $700 million over three years. The subsequent stock meltdown cost roughly $13 billion in market capitalization.

Silverman, the son of the CEO of a commercial finance company, had been driven to emerge from the shadow of his father's success. "You want to be recognized for what you achieved rather than what your parents achieved."[10] After high-profile work with notorious corporate raiders and gilded investment bankers, Silverman had become a legend through his own empire building as well. In the wake of the CUC scandal, his diligence and management style came under attack. The anger and humiliation ate away at him. For Silverman, the personal toll was heavy. "My own sense of self-worth was diminished," he recalls.

Close friends worried that his anger would consume him. Consider this account: "[Fellow financier] Darla D. Moore recalls a dinner shortly after the scandal broke. She was seated next to Silverman, and as guest speaker Henry Kissinger got up to speak, she looked at her friend, who seemed suddenly quite gray. 'As bad as it seems, nobody has died,' she leaned over to whisper to him, 'but if you don't get some relief [from the pressure], you'll be the first to go.' "[11]

Following suggestions from a psychiatrist he consulted a few times, Silverman found ways to direct his rage. He became a workout enthusiast going to the gym daily, with rigorous aerobics, tennis, and weightlifting. In a year, his bench press weight rose from 65 to 150 pounds. Such sublimation, however, was not sufficient for him, as he was driven by the goal to regain his credibility. He clarified who he believed the villains to be as government investigators began their probe. In the meantime, Silverman replaced all of CUC's leadership and sued its accountants, Ernst & Young, through which Silverman ultimately received some vindication as his efforts helped send several top CUC executives to prison for fraud. To not have to constantly relive the situation in social settings, he and his family curtailed their social life, withdrawing to the comfort of friends such as financiers Leon Black and Darla Moore.

However, this social retreat did not reflect a running away from the problem. Indeed, he put all of his energies into fighting aggressively to save his company. In a private interview we had with Silverman, which we will discuss more in chapter 4, he told us, "It never occurred to me not to stay and try to fix the problem." Silverman sold noncore businesses to repurchase 20 percent of the outstanding shares, to boost the stock price. He began eyeing smaller acquisitions, and, finally, he began to build credibility through alliances with firms like John Malone's Liberty Media, which also drove e-commerce traffic to his service businesses. This approach helped Silverman regain trust and rebuild the enterprise as well as rebuild his self-esteem and reputation. Unfortunately, by late 2005, in the face of soaring gas prices and terrorism, the momentum was still never fully regained; nevertheless, Silverman was celebrated by analysts for his reverse course to break the company back into four pieces.[12]

Recruit Others into Battle: Seeking Opportunity While Maintaining Concern for the Collateral Victims

In addition to feeling the need to redeem himself before shareholders, Silverman felt responsible for the ways his situation affected his family, his coworkers, and his friends. His efforts to bring others into his campaign are not unusual. By enlisting the assistance of others, it is possible to attend to the needs of the innocent bystanders who suffer from the victim's career crisis. This helps to show appreciation for and replenish the resources of one's support system so critical to coping with the stress. This reinforcement from trusted advisers is also of great value for candid feedback. Howard Gardner's observation that resilient exceptional people have a talent for self-awareness is true, in part, because these people energetically use personal networks in both their ascent and their recovery from setback.[13] The trusted advisers the victim consults help through more than consolation alone. They hold up a candid mirror for self-reflection and help brainstorm the range of next steps.

Perhaps no leader's recovery from setback is more inspirational than that of Bernie Marcus, founder of The Home Depot, and his cofounder, Arthur Blank. In 1978, Marcus and Blank were running Handy Dan Home Improvement Centers when Sandy Sigoloff, the CEO of their then parent company, Daylin, fired them. Sigoloff, a tough turnaround manager, was often referred to as "Ming the Merciless." In his book, Marcus explained what motivated Sigoloff:

> *[Sigoloff] really wanted credit for turning Daylin around, saving it from the creditors, saving it for the shareholders, saving it from bankruptcy. But the only Daylin division that had a great cash flow was Handy Dan— my division . . . The day I knew I was finished with Sandy Sigoloff was the day the Daylin board of directors discussed succession. One Sigoloff-appointed board member said, "I don't know why there is any question about succession here, since you have your obvious successor right in this room, Bernie Marcus" . . . A quick glance at Sigoloff's ashen face told me that that was never going to happen. And the very notion that some on the board supported the idea made me a genuine threat to Sigoloff. The situation between us just went from really bad to dire.*[14]

While Marcus believed that he was the prime target of Sigoloff's wrath, when he was dismissed, so were his top lieutenants Arthur Blank and Ron Brill, in separate rooms and in rapid succession. "Ron, like Arthur and me, never knew what hit him." Sigoloff released a statement to the press at Friday afternoon's deadline so that the newspapers would promptly run the story. Marcus explained, "But it was far worse than just the loss of a couple of well-paying, high-profile jobs or a few embarrassing newspaper stories. Sigoloff was primarily after me; for Arthur and Ron, it was more a matter of guilt by association. We all had painful experiences telling our family and friends what happened."[15]

Marcus charged that subsequent to this termination, Sigoloff tried to vilify the victims further by suggesting to the authorities retrospectively that there had been some infractions in a labor-organizing effort. Marcus and Blank say these allegations were trumped up and were never found to have merit by the authorities but were invented to humiliate and wound them sufficiently to prevent them from fighting back. Marcus told us, "He dared me to sue him over his false charges and wrongful dismissal, knowing I didn't have the resources back then to get the true story out at first; but I got to key friends, and later I've gotten to tell it everywhere."

Marcus had his loyal coworkers with him. Another close friend, the financier Ken Langone, joined him, saying, "This is the greatest news I have heard . . . You have just been kicked in the ass with a golden horseshoe."[16] Langone then encouraged Marcus to open the novel sort of store Marcus had dreamed of and offered to help him. Similarly, when Marcus confided in his friend Sol Price, cofounder of the Price Club, he found feedback beyond solace: "Over dinner, I told Price how Sigoloff turned me out. There was a lot of self-pity on my part. Why did this happen to me? I was drowning in my sorrow, going several nights at a time without sleeping. For the first time in my adult life, instead of building, I was more concerned with surviving."[17] Price asked Marcus if he believed he had talent and if he thought that he had "the ability to build something, to create?"[18] Marcus then realized for certain that it was time to get on with his life.

These colleagues and friends believed in Marcus and joined him in battle, encouraging many others to join as well. The stores he envisioned were immense warehouses for do-it-yourself home repair enthusiasts, with greater selection, superior customer service, a highly trained staff, and direct purchasing from the manufacturer. The group relocated from Los Angeles to Atlanta and opened their first store in 1979. By 1990 they had 17,500 employees with sales of $2.7 billion and today, The Home Depot has sales of $82 billion and 345,000 employees. These founders became some of the wealthiest people in the world as they stayed faithful to their motto born in crisis: "We Take Care of the Customer and Each Other."

Rebuild Heroic Stature: Spread the True Nature of the Adversity

Thus, we see that Bernie Marcus did not just take up with sycophantic supporters to assuage his hurt, but rather his friends and colleagues challenged him, inspired him, and joined him. Great leaders acquire a heroic persona that gives them larger-than-life presence. When that is removed, the audience disappears, the coworkers are no longer around, and leaders can lose their identity. They are not comfortable merely being one of the crowd. Great leaders, like great artists, develop a personal dream that they offer as a public possession. If it is accepted, they become renowned, but if it is ultimately discarded they suffer the loss of both a private dream and a public identity. As people rallied around Marcus, they allowed him to regain his familiar role. They rallied because he told them the truth, and they still believed in him and in his heroic identity. When a hero stumbles, the constituents are confused as to how that happened given the larger-than-life presence the hero held.

Just as Marcus took his story to friends, investors, employees, and then to countless readers, so have others who have discovered the need to repair their armor. John Eyler, who became the chief executive of Toys "R" Us and previously was CEO of FAO Schwarz, was terminated at a large clothing retailer on Christmas Eve. He feels what was critical to his resilience was that he did not let the situation define him to others, because if it did, he says, "I might have started to doubt myself as well." Scholars of reputation management have long recognized the value of reputation as a corporate and a personal asset.[19] It is built through experience, performance, and affiliations.

New accounts that one circulates must embrace several critical elements for successful image restoration:

- Clearly denying culpability

- Shifting responsibility for the mishap

- Reducing the offensiveness of the act

- Giving the appearance of reasonable behavior

- Offering acceptable motives

Marcus's explanation of the Handy Dan termination easily satisfies these dimensions.

Another great retailer, Leonard Roberts, the CEO of Tandy/Radio Shack, was fired previously as CEO of Shoney's restaurants. Known throughout his life as a maverick, he married at age seventeen while in high school and became a father at nineteen. He gained several grain patents and a law degree. In 1985, Roberts left as head of the food service division of Ralston Purina to become CEO of the troubled Arby's roast beef restaurant chain. Roberts engineered a profound turnaround there through a combination of team management, aggressive marketing, and new product development. In 1989, he left behind a difficult controlling owner who faced his own legal challenges, to run the $1.5 billion Shoney's chain of sixteen hundred restaurants. Roberts produced dramatic improvements in customer service and franchise relations. Store design, purchasing, and marketing were overhauled quickly. In three years, Shoney's profits went from $15.5 million to over $50 million.

Yet, Roberts was the first CEO to be recruited from the outside, and some see his exit as a political revolt of the old guard against Roberts's style.[20] The *Wall Street Journal*, however, carried a report that some board members felt Roberts had gone too far with his affirmative action efforts just six weeks after Shoney's settled a $105 million racial discrimination lawsuit. The founder, Raymond Danner, is said to have told one manager that he had too many black employees and threatened, "If you don't fire them, I'll fire you." Roberts was unable to offer public comment as part of his $2.9 million severance package, but word of his skills and character got around. Some recruiters thought that his battle at Shoney's made him too controversial. However, when in 1994 Tandy CEO John Roach went looking for a successor, he was so impressed with Roberts's courage, as well as his general management skills, that he made Roberts, a lifelong restaurateur, president of the seven thousand–store electronics retailer. In 1998, Roberts succeeded Roach and went on to pioneer creative store-within-a-store partnerships with suppliers like Sprint, RCA, Compaq, and Microsoft.

Proving Your Mettle: Regaining Trust and Credibility

Artists and performers need their work to be shown, but others often control the display and access to their viewers. Regularly, actors hear that they are too old, musicians that they are passé, and artists that galleries will no longer present their work. Similarly, even chief executives face gatekeepers when it comes to showcasing their skills.

Tarred with the brush of controversy and competing with the ready pool of rising stars, leaders may easily be cast aside as last year's model. After setbacks, they have to demonstrate that they still have the skills that have made them great. Roberts, Marcus, and Silverman all eagerly jumped back into action to prove they retained the talents that built their careers.

The name Trump could easily have gone the way of other real estate titans of the 1980s, such as the Reichmann brothers and Robert Campeau. Donald Trump joined the family real estate business after graduating from Wharton in 1968. In his twenties he was already considered New York's paramount developer, his name whispered in the same breath as the legendary William Zeckendorf. At the age of thirty-six, he put up his Trump Tower, the tallest, most expensive reinforced concrete structure in the city. Trump's name appeared brazenly on his building projects, but by 1990, he was caught in a real estate crunch, with a crushing $975 million debt.

A dozen years later, his net worth was reportedly back to $3.5 billion, his casinos were booming, and he was wheeling and dealing in real estate development just as before. Both he and financial analysts consider the resurgence of his Atlantic City casinos, Trump Plaza, the Taj Mahal, and Trump's Castle as the source of his comeback.[21] In addition to the disposal of personal assets, however, he made his much-derided ego and celebrity a bankable asset. His book *Trump: The Art of the Comeback* in

1997 was a proud follow-up to his audacious book *Trump: The Art of the Deal* of a decade earlier.[22] His celebrity, though, was cemented with his hit television show, *The Apprentice*, which, as NBC's blockbuster series season after season, portrayed him as the witty mentor for a nation of aspiring business leaders. With $11 billion in sales, his empire has continued to grow. He has acquired the GM Building and half of the Empire State Building and built the world's tallest residential building, the ninety-story Trump World Tower.

Even more impressive a comeback is that of the 1980s iconic financier, Michael Milken. Many have seen Milken's life as the essence of American myth. He was born on the Fourth of July, 1946, to a modest California family, and by the mid-1980s, he was a billionaire and one of the most influential investment bankers in the world. He bypassed Wall Street snobs by building the moderate-sized, stodgy Drexel Burnham Lambert into the capital of high-yield (junk bond) debt. By 1987, the value of junk bond debt rose from almost nothing to about $200 billion. However, investigations by the Justice Department, led by Rudolph Giuliani as U.S. Attorney, led to Milken's plea of guilty to six breaches of securities law. He was fined more than $1 billion and sent to prison for two years, his reputation shattered—a lifetime ban preventing his return to the securities business. Many of the institutions holding the junk bonds went into financial distress. This negative press overshadowed the image of the enterprises that junk bonds helped create, such as CNN, FedEx, and MCI. To make matters worse, soon after leaving prison, Milken was told he had prostate cancer and had eighteen months to live.

Nonetheless, Milken is alive and well. His cancer is in remission, and he has written several cookbooks for fighting cancer through diet. He is growing a cradle-to-grave learning company he founded in 1997 with his brother and with Oracle chief executive Larry Ellison. He has a consulting firm called Nextera and funds an economic institute called the Milken Institute. His CaP CURE charity, renamed as the Prostate Cancer Foundation, has raised more than $260 million and provided funding to more than twelve hundred researchers around the world who in turn have helped develop vaccines and treatments to fight prostate cancer as well as create genetic therapies.

Milken was unwilling to wallow in grief, to accept any of the externally imposed constraints on his desire to create and regain prominence. As he returned to demonstrate his business acumen, so did the rush of old and new partners to join him.

Rediscovering the Heroic Mission: Clearing the Past and Charting the Future

The quest for immortality that drives artists and leaders requires that they see a lasting legacy through their work. Even more challenging than the externally imposed barriers that confront exceptional people after setbacks are the self-imposed barriers due to shattered confidence or a lack of replenishment of their ideas and their energy. In many of the cases discussed earlier, this meant lowering their image of where they left off. Marcus and Milken had to start over from scratch. Silverman and Trump had to rebuild their own wrecked empires, while Roberts assumed challenging environments that required learning new skills.

Another retail legend, Michael Bozic, found that a career crisis can be liberating. In 1990, he was thrown out of the chief executive's throne of the Sears Merchandise Group after twenty-eight years at the company. Many believed he had not been given full credit for his innovative triumphs at Sears, such as his Sears Brand Central merchandising concept, and in fact he was assumed to have taken a bullet for his boss, the slow-moving chairman, Edward Brennan.

Following many months of job hunting, Bozic became the CEO of Hills Stores Company, a bankrupt discount retailer in Canton, Massachusetts—quite a comedown from Sears, which at the time was the world's largest retailer. After reviving Hills from near death, Bozic lost control of the company in a wild proxy battle of competing value-investors.[23] Thus, after a successful turnaround there, Bozic left for Florida to lead the turnaround at Levitz Furniture. Bozic left for Levitz with his world-weary wit intact, announcing, "No good deed goes unpunished." In November 1998, Bozic became vice chairman and CEO contender at Kmart.[24]

In the world of communications, Michael Bloomberg has become a near overnight legend. He was fired as a Wall Street broker and went on to build one of the fastest-growing media empires in the world. His TV stations broadcast twenty-four hours a day to forty countries in seven languages. His radio networks, publishing empire, online businesses, and wire service approach a $2 billion empire with four thousand workers. He calls himself the David who challenged the Goliath of financial news. In 1981, Bloomberg was fired by Salomon Brothers, the elite investment bank, where he flourished for fifteen years with the only employer he ever had. The night he was fired, he bought his wife a sable jacket, saying, "Job or no job, we are still players."[25] The next morning, he settled down to work at his customary 7 a.m. to launch Bloomberg with his $10 million of severance.

Finally, no reflections on resilience can be complete without acknowledging the fabled return of Apple Computer founder Steve Jobs. At age thirty-two, two years after being forced out of the firm he had created eleven years earlier, he founded NeXT with five devotees from Apple to build a powerful computer to be used in university instruction. He ultimately sold the company back to Apple for over $400 million and persuaded the then Apple CEO, Gil Amelio, to bring him back as a "consultant" as part of the deal. Jobs showed open disdain for Amelio around the office and derided many of his management team members.[26] After Amelio resigned in July 1997, Jobs agreed to become interim CEO. He cut many of the projects he had inherited and introduced triumphant new products like the iMac, G3 desktops, PowerBook laptops, and the iconic iPod that created a new market and revitalized Apple's reputation.

Not every accomplished creative person can drop back and start anew. In his late twenties and thirties, Alan Jay Lerner wrote or cowrote great Broadway classics like *Brigadoon*, *Paint Your Wagon*, *Gigi*, *My Fair Lady*, and *Camelot*. By his fifties and sixties, he felt his creative genius suffocated by his own creations. "The older a writer gets, the harder it is for him to write. This is not because his brain slows down; it is because his critical faculties grow more acute. If you're young, you have a sense of omnipotence. You're sure you're brilliant. Even if youth is secretly frightened, it assumes an outer assurance, and plows through whatever it is."[27]

It was not his public that held Lerner to punishing standards, it was he, himself. In contrast, many we have profiled take a more optimistic view, adhering to Nietzsche's maxim: "What does not destroy me, makes me stronger." Through heavy life demands, these exceptional people are actually strengthened rather than weakened by firing back from their adversity. The ability to triumph over tragedy rests on these five foundation stones we have just outlined.

While we focus our attention on these paths to recovery, this cannot be done in isolation. We first need to understand the nature of adversity and the substance of the barriers that need to be overcome in order to lay the groundwork for triumph by an in-depth treatise on the causes and consequences of tragedy.

Barriers to Recovery: The Nature of Adversity and Human Resilience

This book examines the often abrupt and unexpected fall from grace of prominent leaders and the process by which they recover and even exceed their past accomplishments with a new adventure. While our primary focus is on business leaders, leaders across all fields face the same challenges and go through the same process in rebounding from setback, and so we also draw from numerous examples across fields ranging from sports, media, and entertainment to politics and social movements.

In chapter 2, we revisit the five levels of resilience from adversity to reveal the solid foundation in research and theory that anchors each of these requirements for recovery. By broadening our investigation beyond the workplace, to embrace victims of natural disasters, war refugees, survivors of catastrophic health crises—those who master grief from a wide range of human cruelties—we can gain some perspective on recovery from career setbacks. At the same time, this chapter reveals how distinctly different traditions of behavioral science research all must be unified in a single comprehensive model of recovery. These include studies on:

- Posttraumatic stress response

- Belonging and the need for affiliation with others

- Attributions of injustice, image restoration, and impression management

- Self-esteem, ego strength, mastery, competence

- Grief, human purpose, and the existential quest for meaning

Up to now, these vital but stand-alone fields of inquiry into resilience yielded important but only partial insights into the total set of requirements. Thus, in addition to compelling testimony from firsthand accounts of survivors, we provide the first comprehensive theoretical model of resilience. On top of this foundation, we will present our interpretations of original interviews with more than one hundred CEOs and case studies of many others; plus analyses of original data on CEO terminations, retirements, and surveys of most of the nation's leading CEO executive recruiters will all follow in later chapters.

Understanding Loss and Adversity

Thus, in chapter 2 we further develop this first integrated model of resilience through wide application to situations of adversity and catastrophe, drawing upon the lessons of multiple disciplines. Rather than telling the breathless war stories of airlines magazines or outlining the narrow hypothesis testing of scholarly journal articles, we hope to generate new, multifaceted insights into the phenomenon of resilience from adversity.

Then in chapter 3 we look more narrowly back at the workplace and, in particular, turn to the challenges of the fallen leader. Here we will consider the unique contributions of the acceptance of failure by supremely successful people, constituent expectations from those who depend on the leader, the double-edged sword of celebrity, and how to learn from pathology.

In some respects, leaders' careers, lives, and even setbacks are far removed from the everyday events and setbacks of ordinary people. Many fallen leaders, particularly business leaders, are amply compensated from a financial standpoint, and so the financial stress imposed by setback, which for many people is the largest source of stress caused by career setback, is largely removed. However, the particular nature of the leader's fall erects certain barriers that must be overcome in order to effect a full recovery.

The scorn placed on those who fall from great heights can erect a substantial societal barrier to recovery. Our society, as reflected in the media, has a tendency to build people up, celebrate success, and place the successful on a pedestal—but then to be quick in trampling on those who fall from grace. This can lead the fallen leader to shy away from the spotlight and seek obscurity rather than facing the long climb back to the next peak in the leader's career.

Failure and setback, although commonly experienced, is still a taboo topic in our modern society, where visible success is lauded. Some of these norms are part of our own defense system for dealing with setback, helping us to avoid wallowing in our own grief and denying that we are in such a predicament. Some are for the protection of our own social identity, striving to maintain an impression of control and normalcy in our relations with others. Yet more are for the social comfort of others. Because of the social taboo of failure, people don't know how to react to the failure of others. They tend to either avoid the person, through some irrational fear that the failure may be contagious, or express the opposite sentiment from that which is appropriate, being abnormally cheery in order to somehow ease the suffering presumed to be caused by the failure.

But the failure to address failure is counterproductive as it stifles the rebound in several ways. First, it is hard to learn the lessons from the setback. Did you make mistakes that could be avoided in the future? What situations, circumstances, or signals do you need to recognize and avoid, or know how to react to better? Second, it is hard to come to terms with the loss emotionally unless the demons are confronted and exorcised. Without this confrontation, they can have a corrosive effect on self-esteem and confidence. Third, the failure becomes an undiscussable white elephant in the room. That is to say, everybody sees the problem, they know of the failure, and they are likely to misinterpret its cause and have trouble talking with you for fear of saying the wrong thing.

Without addressing the failure, it is impossible to use it as a springboard for recovery. A key part of the process of recovery for the leaders we profile in this book is facing up to the reality of what has happened—the catastrophic setback that they have suffered—and reflecting on what that means for their heroic self-concept and how they can overcome this setback to reroute their road to immortality and redirect their heroic mission. This frank addressing of the failure and setback provides a lesson for all who are facing setback, as well as those who are attempting to help others through these catastrophes.

Corporate Cultures as Barriers to Recovery

Chapter 4 moves us from the internal psyche of victims and external expectations for leaders, to consider how the varied work contexts matter. Consider, for example, how the handling of their illicit sex scandals brought down the careers of televangelists Jim Bakker and Jimmy Swaggart, U.S. presidential Democratic front-runner Gary Hart, presidential adviser Dick Morris, or British politician John Profumo, while the comparable sexual scandals of TV sportscaster Marv Albert or Los Angeles Lakers basketball star Kobe Bryant were not fatal to their careers. While the high-profile real estate and hotel tycoon Leona Helmsley virtually disappeared after her seven-month prison term on tax charges, media titan Martha Stewart gained even greater public enthusiasm for her multimedia ventures upon her release from her five-month prison term, much the same way fashion designer and retailer Steve Madden saw his enterprise soar while still in prison for tax charges.

In the preceding examples, one main difference determining the ability to recover is that the value of public trust placed in the clergy or those in public office may be far greater than for those in sports, retail, and entertainment. Therefore, breaking that trust in those worlds may be more damaging than in others where personal and professional lives are more separated. For the clergy or politicians, a sexual scandal is seen as reflecting poor character, which in turn damages the trust in their ability to perform their job, which is based on having a trustworthy character. However, for sports or media stars, personal improprieties are not seen as so closely connected to their ability to perform their job, and so do not have as devastating an effect.

An overlooked factor in career recovery is the type of organization and the sector in which the person suffered the career setback. While the reason may not be obvious, the corporate culture can play a large role in erecting barriers to the leader's recovery. Within career systems theory, firms can be considered along two dimensions: supply flow, which consists of entry into and exit from the firm, essentially governing whether the firm looks inside for leadership talent or accesses the broader labor markets at all levels; and assignment flow, which focuses on the development of employees within the firm, with a focus on creating either functional specialists or generalists who can move from function to function within the firm.

Particularly important to the career prospects of ousted leaders is the dimension of supply flow. Firms and industries that rely heavily on internal development of talent tend to be closed to the outside labor market, particularly at the upper echelons, and thus pose a substantial barrier to reentry for a deposed leader. On the other hand, firms and industries that often rely on the external labor market to fill talent at all levels, rather than developing their own, present a substantially lower barrier to career recovery because they are often seeking to pick up good talent as it becomes available.

Because all the firms within an industry typically follow similar career systems strategies, being ousted from a firm in an industry that has specialist skills, yet is closed to external labor markets, can severely limit the leader's future career possibilities.

Departure Causes as Barriers to Recovery

Subsequently, in chapter 5 we consider whether it matters why the person lost his or her footing. Did it matter if they were a villain or a victim? Can some villains enjoy restitution through acts of contrition, while others are permanently scarred due to the heinous nature of their misconduct? Can some victims restore faith in their weakened aura of greatness, while others will be seen to have permanently lost their competence or confidence during their innocent suffering?

In facing up to failure, and then going on to use it as a springboard for future success, a key part of this reflection is in understanding the reason that the failure occurred. In chapter 5, we develop a typology of failure that covers the spectrum of reasons that leaders fall from grace. Often these failures are not caused by the corruption or competence of the leader, but, as Bernie Marcus's experience illustrates, can be the result of the Machiavellian political machinations of others.

In our research, we find that often those who have been so astute at playing the political game in their climb up the ladder of success often feel that once they have reached the top, they have achieved a status that immunizes them from corporate politics. However, they fail to realize that the political conniving is swirling around them and that indeed they are most subject to its daggers. Like Caesar, they are surprised when they fall to their own Brutus as once-loyal aides slide in the fatal knife. In cases such as these, the dethroned leader's most valuable possession is his or her reputation, particularly among the key gatekeepers who hold the keys to reenter the executive suite. In this chapter, we present original data that summarizes the perspective of these key gatekeepers in the executive search industry and clearly shows how a CEO's reputation is impacted by their departure from the executive suite.

In protecting their reputation, leaders confront the choice that The Home Depot's Bernie Marcus was faced with—to engage in costly feuding behavior to extract the pound of flesh from the antagonist who orchestrated the downfall; or to use it as a springboard, recognizing that political defeat does not reflect on the competence of the leader, and that in fact the other's jealousy of the leader's great ability and potential for immortal success was probably what was ultimately behind the downfall. In such a case, leaders should retain confidence in their abilities to regain their former stature and beyond, and engage in battle only when protection of their reputation is at stake.

Psychological Stresses as Barriers to Recovery

In our final foundation chapter, chapter 6, we return to look inside the mind of the CEO rather than the setting and consider the adverse psychological consequences of job loss, in particular, on a leader's well-being. The unusual need leaders have for creating a legacy and leaving their imprint on the world can pose a substantial psychological barrier to recovery. For many people, this need for a lasting legacy is fulfilled through having children and imparting their values to the next generation, or being involved in an institution that will continue past their lifetime. Leaders, however, suffer from this need to a greater extent than most individuals. Because of this need for immortality, they place an unusually high importance on their career and their contribution and strongly identify with the organization that they lead, even to the extent of being unable to separate their own personal identity from that of the organization. Thus, their forced separation from the organization—which most people would consider a major career setback—becomes catastrophic to the self-image and identity of the leader and more psychologically damaging than the same event would be to others in the organization.

The fallen leader must deal with being a very proud person who has just suffered an enormous loss of self-esteem, the danger of burnout from the emotional drain of energy and spirit, the sudden loss of influence and respect from others in the victim's world, and the frustration of seeing life's opportunities pass by and their heroic mission derailed, as access to the tournament of top-quality career slots may be denied due to a dented reputation.[28] Additionally, the victims must be aware of the impact on their own support system. There is unanticipated collateral damage to the lives of innocent close third parties such as loving family members, loyal friends, and frightened coworkers.[29] While these are potentially valuable sources of support and strength for the subsequent rebound, the damage to them can also represent a barrier to overcome in addition to the direct damage to the individual.

From the Foundations of Failure to Executing Steps for Recovery

Once the barriers to recovery are understood, we move on to examine in more depth the routes to recovery and particularly the five key elements of the recovery process we foreshadowed previously. Thus we will elaborate on each of those elements in chapters 7 through 11, exploring the nature of their contribution to the recovery process. We conclude by recapping in chapter 12, considering those leaders who successfully rebounded from catastrophic setback and those who were overcome by the failure, and what lessons these experiences provide for not only leaders but anyone who is suffering from unexpected setback. Indeed, it is in this ability to recover from a potentially more severe psychological setback that leaders suffer that lessons are learned for all kinds of people suffering setbacks, and thus why we should care about their fate. It is the process of recovery exemplified by these falls from great heights that illustrates the necessary steps to recovery from all setbacks.

Hey, It's Just a Job—or Is It More?

Before closing, it is important to acknowledge that career setbacks through a leader's loss of position are only one category of many of life's disappointments. In fact, even catastrophic career derailment does not compare to the horrors faced by victims of natural disasters and human-caused calamities. At the same time, however, the next chapter will show that there are lessons for leaders to learn from various forms of human suffering. The paths to recovery for attacks on our occupations can be found in the wisdom of resilience from other forms of assaults on our life plan and leadership mission. Thus, our next step is to look deeper into the nature of adversity itself.

When Bad Things Happen to Good Leaders: Thoughts for Future Heroes

It has been observed that if you want to be successful in life, you should first select great parents. Much of life is out of our control. Rising leaders, however, can anticipate that they will experience a wide array of life's adversity. The nature and timing of setbacks will never be convenient. The costs may include derailed career momentum, personal humiliation, the draining of finances, strained personal health, the shattering of personal dreams, and the suffering of innocent family and associates.

At the same time, these occasions of distress are potentially clouds with silver linings. It is through such loss that we often discover what we truly value. It is through such loss that we discover whom we can really trust. It is through such loss that we reveal new dimensions of our own character. The heroic persona is one that emerges only through triumphant battle over sadness and adversity.

As new leaders see that their success spiral has just smacked into a wall, they should step back, catch their breath, and then embrace the obstacle itself as a fresh opportunity to meet unfamiliar challenges. At the same time, they must realize that their mission cannot be accomplished alone. They will need to draw upon the full reservoir of their early career experiences and relationships. Once a devastating crisis hits, it is too late to make friends, too late to establish professional credibility, and too late to build a reputation for integrity. As French field-based scientist Louis Pasteur observed, "Chance favors the mind that's prepared." It is our quest in the chapters that follow to aid in that preparation. We do so by examining the nature of adversity and showing, through the examination of the resilience of prominent leaders and through research across several fields of study, how these five lessons allow triumph to reemerge out of career and life tragedies.

When players walk onto the most hallowed ground in the world of tennis, Centre Court, Wimbledon—the site where careers are made or broken—they are admonished by Rudyard Kipling's words, carved above the doorway leading to that manicured court:

If you can meet with Triumph and Disaster
And treat these two impostors just the same . . .
—("If")

Thus, as Kipling hints, resilience is born from being able to contend with both triumph and disaster, neither succumbing to the mythological Icarus's temptation of hubris in success, nor being forever in despair when life's inevitable failures strike. Here we focus on the imposition of disaster and how triumph is reborn out of these tragedies. We will explain the multilayered elements of authentic comebacks through extensive personal interviews, the accumulated wisdom of decades of scholarship, original quantitative analysis, and powerful case examples. We begin with an in-depth examination of the nature of adversity and how such adversity sows the seeds for future triumph when you have mastered Kipling's conundrum.

CHAPTER 2

Tragedies, Failures, and Setbacks— The Nature of Adversity

We must embrace pain and burn it as fuel for our journey.

—Kenji Miyazawa

IN THIS CHAPTER, we will step away from the world of work, careers, and CEOs to reflect upon lessons drawn from truly horrific human suffering, which puts setbacks in professional lives in perspective. We will show how the five elements of resilience from adversity are anchored in several distinctly different fields of learning: response to posttraumatic stress, need for affiliation, impression management and image restoration, grief and bereavement, attribution theory, self-esteem, mastery and effectance motivation, and existential purpose.

The opening quotation by Kenji Miyazawa, one of the most beloved Japanese authors, was written in the 1920s, shortly before he became popular after his death at age thirty-seven. These words could come from the same spark in five-year-old Rangika De Silva, a Sri Lankan little girl who perfectly sang the English lullaby "Twinkle, Twinkle, Little Star" to entertain her traumatized family, surveying the debris of her former oceanfront home. The adults broke into spontaneous applause. Previously, the adults had gathered around Rangika to hear how she was saved when head-high water engulfed her just days earlier in the tsunami on December 26, 2004. "The sea came and my brother put me in the kotombe tree far up high where I was safe," she recounted. "He carried me above his head with his arms like this," stretching upward. Relief workers observing children playing and laughing were amazed at the resilience of children in refugee camps in the shadows of their ruined homes. Kingsley Wickramaratne, governor of the Southern Province of Sri Lanka, announced that tents were set up nearby destroyed schools within two weeks to resume classes. UNICEF director Carol Bellamy commented after touring the region that "reestablishing routines was essential, that being able to play, that's what children like to do. Going to school. That is the best thing."[1]

Decades earlier, Harvard psychiatrist Robert Coles studied the impact of the civil rights movement of the 1960s on black and white children in his classic *Children of Crisis: A Study of Courage and Fear.*[2] He found that none of the young subjects he studied could have found or afforded psychiatric care—nor to his amazement did any require it! Finding no correspondence between the violence and injustice they experienced, unpredictably, these children grew up as normal, unscarred people. He concluded that the remarkable resilience from adversity challenged the relevance of his own profession: "The vicissitudes of the strong and willful are not adequately described by a language that hopes to document the pains of the ill."[3]

In fact, adversity in childhood actually was a source of inspiration for some of American society's greatest success stories. Media entrepreneur and leading TV host Oprah Winfrey is seen by 25 million viewers in 105 countries and heads her own hugely successful multimedia production company, but to get to this position, she had to overcome some terrible early-life challenges. She spent her first years on a farm in rural Mississippi, raised by her grandmother who taught her to read at a very young age. Reading became her escape when, after age six, she moved in with her mother in Milwaukee, where she was sexually molested by an older cousin and other male relatives. She became pregnant at age fourteen. Seen as wild and incorrigible by her mother, Oprah went to live with her father in Nashville. It was there she found discipline and confidence and ultimately landed the job as a local TV reporter that launched her meteoric career.

Musician, composer, and entrepreneur Quincy Jones was also six when his mother was institutionalized for schizophrenia. Because his father was unable to care for Jones and his younger brother, they went to live with their impoverished grandmother. At age forty-two, after a dazzling career, he was diagnosed with a brain aneurysim, and underwent risky surgery that required freezing his brain. He was not expected to survive, but he recovered to celebrate his own memorial service with friends and then continue a career that earned twenty-nine Grammys, seven Academy Award nominations, an Oscar, and an Emmy.

There are plenty of other examples of successful figures overcoming childhood adversity. It is speculated that President Bill Clinton's vital compartmentalization and drive were a product of living with an abusive alcoholic stepfather during his own childhood. Starbucks founder Howard Schultz credits his own generosity and compassion as an employer with his own searing memories: returning home at age nine to his family's apartment in a New York public housing project, he found his father incapacitated by a work injury with no income, no insurance, and no safety net.

This capacity for resilience from adversity is not a luxury reserved for children. Relief workers in 2005 reported extraordinary community rebuilding in places as devastated as Aceh, Indonesia, where rebuilding began promptly in washed-out communities that were adjacent to villages completely erased from the map. The self-help began immediately, before any of the international relief poured in. Individuals, the Indonesian Red Crescent, military medical teams, local companies, and regional government responded across political and ideological boundaries.[4]

Miyazawa's inspirational words could also have been written by cyclist Lance Armstrong. His own embrace of pain is revealed in his book on his ordeal of battling back from cancer, *It's Not About the Bike*.[5] At the age of twenty-four, Armstrong was ranked the number-one cyclist in the world, but in 1996, the year he earned that ranking, he was immobilized by tremendous pain. The source of the pain was diagnosed as advanced testicular cancer that had spread to his lungs and brain, giving him only a 20 percent chance of survival. Following five months of aggressive chemotherapy, surgery, and dietary changes, Armstrong was back on his cycle in competition.

Nonetheless, he considered this health crisis to be an urgent wake-up call to celebrate his family, his friends, and his health. As he put it, "Odd as it sounds, I would rather have the title of cancer survivor than winner of the Tour, because of what it has done for me as a human being, a man, a husband, a son, and a father."[6] In 2003, Armstrong's comeback was so vigorous, he won his fifth Tour de France. The following year, 2004, he won a record-breaking sixth Tour de France with such staggering vigor, his final stage of the race was considered processional as he was able to ease up to sip a glass of champagne while in the saddle.

In this chapter, we will look at a wide range of extreme adversity, from natural catastrophe and war disaster to terrorist violence and health crises. While the intensity, duration, predictability, and degrees of innocence will vary across these situations, the tools victims relied upon for recovery are remarkably similar and transferable to job dismissals and other career setbacks.

From Hope to Despair

Is Miyazawa's encouragement to embrace suffering a bit misleading? Surely, the determined recovery efforts of Lance Armstrong did not exceed the rigorous treatment and tenacity of countless cancer patients who were less fortunate with fate. Recall, for example, the tragic death of McDonald's CEO Charlie Bell at age forty-four on January 16, 2005, just nine months after he assumed the reins from Jim Cantalupo, his predecessor, who died of a heart attack in office. Bell's colorectal cancer was diagnosed a mere month after he assumed command. Despite aggressive treatment and a tenacious determination to lead McDonald's, he found his medical battle rendered him unable to serve by November, and he died two months later.[7] Novelist Johann Wolfgang von Goethe said, "In all things it is better to hope than to despair," but finding those rays of hope is not possible through a simple checklist of tasks.

Perhaps even the accounts of relief workers and government officials are sometimes selectively optimistic to encourage donors and survivors that the struggle is winnable. We never know the length of that life journey to which Miyazawa referred, nor can we really call for the embrace of the pain suffered by others. An embrace of pain can sound cold and naïve. Even Miyazawa's life was cut very short. In fact, not only is much of the path of adversity unpredictable and often not within our control, but also our suffering is a highly personal experience not readily understood by others offering us advice.

Certainly, as president, Bill Clinton empathetically listened to those who were suffering injustices, suggesting, "I feel your pain," yet he endured relentless teasing by late-night comedians for that earnest mantra. Indeed, one of the authors of this book received a caring personal note from President Clinton while in office saying just those well-intended words. Some argue that a parent can feel their child's pain, while others contend that an observer can never understand the suffering of another. It is only in the eyes of those who have suffered that adversity can be truly understood. Literary scholar Harold Bloom explains, "What matters in literature in the end is surely the idiosyncratic, the individual, the flavor, or the color of a particular human suffering."[8]

The suffering from adversity thus has magnitude and meaning not measurable by external yardsticks. Extensive research on adversity, stress, and psychopathology suggests that the worse the objective ordeal, the worse the posttraumatic stress in what is called a *dose-response pattern*. The greater the oppression, the worse the posttraumatic stress. However, recovery is another matter. People cannot generally choose their crises, because they generally come without prediction.

More importantly, the recovery from that stress will vary by individual.[9] Yes, career distress rationally should be far less traumatic than catastrophic losses, torture, and death. However, it is true that being fired has been ranked by stress researchers at number eight among life's most stressful events, just after the death of family members, jail time, and personal injury or illness.[10] Nevertheless for some, like financier Michael Milken, domestic arts and media entrepreneur Martha Stewart, best-selling author Jeffrey Archer, or fashion designer Steve Madden, even jail time may not be a barrier to personal resilience, professional success, or even public respectability.[11] At the same time, a career derailment may leave another person with devastated self-esteem and loss of direction, making it hard to go on.

Shortly, we will consider the lessons for leaders from the inspirational resilience of survivors and refugees from war and natural disaster, including the Holocaust, the 9/11 World Trade Center attacks, and the 2004

Asian tsunami. Before that, we want to reinforce the concept that the apparent lack of severity of a career meltdown surely appears far less horrifying than fatal natural disasters or the cruelty of war, but the idiosyncratic nature of individual suffering cannot be calibrated. Despair can hit hard regardless of the physical dimensions of the event. Shakespeare warned, "He who has never hoped can never despair."[12] Yet, once hope is shattered, how do we fill the void that becomes despair?

Exactly one month after the catastrophic Asian tsunami, as traumatized nations staggered to rebuild from the loss of thousands of lives, the *New York Times* reported on the suicide of a classmate of one of the authors of this book: Philip Friedman, a fallen prominent political consultant. Friedman, while still a raw Harvard college student, helped guide the major campaigns of such politicians as New York mayor Ed Koch, New York governor Hugh Carey, and West Virginia senator Jay Rockefeller. Thanks to his high fees, he was able to purchase the landmark 55-acre estate of philanthropist Pamela Harriman in 1986. Just a few years later, he encountered financial setbacks, lost his estate with crushing debts, and ran high-profile aborted campaigns in New York for Andrew Cuomo for governor and Andrew Stein for mayor.[13]

An impending loss of pride and self-esteem and the anomic depression of actually obtaining life goals contributed to the death of the father of media entrepreneur Ted Turner. On March 5, 1963, Ed Turner, a very successful outdoor advertising magnate, ate a large breakfast, left his family, went up the main stairway, entered the master bedroom, and shot himself in the temple. After a large acquisition that overextended the firm, a slowdown in the economy, and the rising sentiment to limit billboards, Ed Turner saw a bleak future. According to a close friend and competitor, "Ed was afraid of losing everything."[14]

Similarly, the specter of failure was too much for corporate raider Eli Black, the father of financier Leon Black. Eli Black, approaching age fifty-five, had bought control of United Fruit (now known as Chiquita) and served as chief executive of this firm, which in 1975 was number eighty-four on the *Fortune* 500 list. However, he had run the company into very difficult situations by that year, and attempts were being made to wrest control of the company from him. In January 1975, he smashed through his window on the forty-fourth floor of the Pan Am Building (now the MetLife Building) in New York and fell to his death in the northbound lane of Park Avenue. According to his former vice president of public relations:

> *Black knew he had fallen far short of success in almost every area that mattered to him. The former rabbi was embroiled in bribery and corruption. The great achievement of his business lifetime, United Brands, was a struggle to stay afloat in a sea of debt. His directors were in revolt, his management had lost respect for him, his friends had deserted him, his personal finances were at least as bad as those of the company, his ability to win people's confidence had disappeared, and he had nowhere to turn.*[15]

These extreme reactions to adversity demonstrate that combinations of anxiety and despair can lead people to quit in an effort to no longer feel the pain. Musician Kurt Cobain explained the name of his group Nirvana this way: "Nirvana means freedom from pain, suffering, and the external world, and that's pretty close to my definition of Punk Rock." Perhaps that is what he finally achieved by stopping the music. It has been said that he was overwhelmed by the early success of his band and felt he was losing his way. His suicide note quoted the lyrics of Neil Young, "Hey, hey, hey, it's better to burn out than to fade away."[16]

A Man of Constant Sorrow: "Good Grief" versus Bad Grief

Long before punk rock appeared, music had embraced and tackled the theme of adversity. The classic Appalachian lament "I Am a Man of Constant Sorrow," attributed to blind fiddler Richard Burnett, has been popular in bluegrass and folk song circles for roughly a century. Burnett chants:

> *Oh, six long years I've been trouble,*
> *No pleasure here on earth I found*
> *While in this world I'm bound to ramble,*
> *I have no friend to help me out.*

While the blues standard "I'm Busted" cries out:

> *I went to my brother to ask for a loan I was busted*
> *I hate to beg like a dog for a bone but I'm busted*

My brother said "there isn't a thing I can do
My wife and my kids are all down with the flu
And I was just thinking of calling on you I'm busted!"

Lord I'm no thief but a man can go wrong when he's busted
The food that we canned last summer is gone and I'm busted
The fields are all bare and the cotton won't grow
Me and my family's gotta pack up and go
Where I'll make a livin' the Lord only knows, but I'm busted!

The songs that speak the language of grief are core themes of blues music and country and western music genres that immerse themselves in pain. While grief was common in all the tragic cases described earlier, those who overcame fatal diseases, natural disasters, and the ravages of war managed to keep their losses from moving from normal bereavement to pathological grief. The distress of separation is one that parents and children wrestle with through life stages with the mourning over lost individuals moving through the normal levels of grief. Its manifestations can, of course, include sadness, anxiety, lethargy, insomnia, emotional numbness, intrusive images of death, preoccupation with deceased relationships, crying, dreams, illusions, and anorexia.[17]

The more debilitating pathological grief is what got the better of those individuals unable to extricate themselves from their sense of loss and move on with their lives. It is, in short, a dysfunctional elevation in intensity of the preceding symptoms to an intolerable level. Sigmund Freud was the first to distinguish pathological grief from normal grief in his distinctions between mourning and melancholia, where a person cannot break the attachment to what they have lost.[18] One of those symptoms, strangely, can be the absence of overt grief, with a person thus never achieving a cathartic venting of emotion. More recent research by John Bowlby on stages of grief influenced a generation of therapists and scholars, including the popular work of Elizabeth Kubler-Ross. He identified such symptoms as hyperactivity, the evidence of symptoms of the illness that claimed a lost loved one, genuine new medical illness, furious rage, schizophrenic behavior, social disengagement from close relations, agitated depression, and self-destructive behavior like reckless gambling, excessive drinking, and even suicide attempts.

Sociologists like Robert Merton and Robert Blauner found parallel withdrawal from life in their studies of alienation due to sadness and loss of control.[19]

Losing the Blame Game—Attribution in a Just World

Coupled with the sense of desperation that follows from this self-loathing is often self-blame. The loss of hope is the loss of one of our most intimate possessions that is our life's dream. Such defeat and disappointment is a major source of despair while even the achievement of goals can deprive someone of a comforting sense of direction, leaving a state of anomie or normlessness. Strangely, even at the opposite extreme, a success syndrome can also lead to emotional challenges as those with sudden wealth have found. This was called the "sudden wealth effect" in the era of the dot-com boom and is a notorious feature of the lives of lottery winners.[20] As early as 1897, anomic depression from either crushing defeat or giddy success was identified as one of the primary causes of suicide in population studies of the pioneering sociologist Emile Durkheim.[21]

We wonder whether we asked for more than we deserved or somehow we brought the wrath of fate down upon us, and we perhaps seek spiritual guidance. Sometimes friends blame us for our misfortunes in a desire to see the world in a just order. Several bodies of research come back to ways where we tend to blame the victim and the victim may come to blame themselves. As others hold us responsible for our misfortune, even when it is not our fault, it may start to erode our self-esteem and pride as we start to believe that maybe the world is right and we are wrong.

Studies on psychological attribution suggest that when we fail ourselves, we blame others, but those around us blame us. In short, say that a person walking down the street who trips on their own blames someone or something else, such as the sidewalk paving or someone in their path. An observer, however, concludes just the opposite: that this may be a clumsy person. Researchers Edward Jones and Robert Nisbett found that the miscues get reversed when a person succeeds.[22] Thus if we do well, we'll take the credit, but those around us will have a tendency to think others helped us or we got a lucky break. Some suggest that in competitive environments this is exacerbated. Recall Winston Churchill's comment that Clement

Attlee, his adversary, was "a modest man with much to be modest about" and "a sheep in sheep's clothing."

Forty years ago, psychologist Melvin Lerner's research explained such blaming of the victim as the result of a simplistic framework of justice that stubbornly we carry in our heads, and termed it "the just world hypothesis."[23] The essence is that there is a strong desire for people to see that sufferers are merely getting their just desserts because the world order is fundamentally fair. In experiments where the victim is, by design, completely innocent but still punished, people tend to blame the victim. In fact, the more victims suffer, the more they are blamed, independent of evidence of innocence.[24] Furthermore, people with a strong tendency to believe in a just world tend to be more religious and more conservative.[25] It should not be a surprise, then, that both Islamic extremists like Osama bin Laden and extreme evangelicals such as Jerry Falwell and Pat Robertson would agree that the terrorist attacks killing thousands of innocent victims on 9/11 were the work of God. In fact, on September 13, 2001, two days after the 9/11 attacks, on the eve of a national day of mourning, Falwell appeared on Robertson's "700 Club" television program, asserting that God permitted "the enemies of America to give us probably what we deserve," followed by Robertson's agreement. Later, after public outrage, they both backed off, claiming they did not intend to blame the victims.[26]

Finding Your Way Back

Extensive studies on the survivors of maximum life adversity—such as those victims of human cruelty, like the European Jews who were Holocaust survivors and the Cambodian refugees from Pol Pot's torture, and of natural environmental disaster (e.g., earthquakes) and human environmental disasters (e.g., Chernobyl)—do seem to confirm that the posttraumatic stress impact varied by the intensity of the adversity suffered, more than by the individual differences in background and disposition before the suffering.[27] An obvious difference among types of adversity that matters, beyond the intensity, is the duration of the adversity. Someone suffering exposure to high levels of radiation or fighting a degenerative disease can face continued physical suffering as well as the anxiety of impending losses. Consistent with Abraham Maslow's hierarchy of needs, such concerns for physical safety would generally take precedence over the emotional concerns to attend to once the immediate threat of the storm had passed.[28]

While some can chase the demons out of their lives, others are paralyzed in fear, forever haunted by them. Elie Wiesel has spent sixty years lecturing and writing about the horrors of his Holocaust suffering. The poet Primo Levi chose to take his life rather than to continue to chronicle the comparable horrors he witnessed that continued to haunt him. There are transferable lessons from those who have suffered adversity and conquered it. Eleanor Roosevelt once said, "Learn from the mistakes of others. You can't live long enough to make them all yourself." It is also possible to learn from the successes of others. The five categories of response to adversity that follow are not in an order of importance or a sequence of steps, but they do represent categories of personal fortitude.

1. *Stress and trauma*: Don't adapt to the adversity or fearfully give in, but instead fight it.

2. *Affiliation*: Do not isolate yourself in grief; engage others for mutual support.

3. *Self-esteem, attribution theory, impression management, reputation management*: Do not blame yourself or let others blame you; offer meaning and explanation.

4. *Effectance motivation*: Assert your mastery and competence.

5. *Existential purpose*: Set an anchor in the future that gives you a reason to survive and a purpose in life.

These five challenges naturally correspond exactly to the five elements of recovery for leaders who have suffered catastrophic career setbacks that we discussed in chapter 1. The linkage of these challenges to the elements of recovery are illustrated in figure 2-1. In essence, we have applied the accumulated wisdom of triumphant survivors of adversity in various life disasters to those leaders facing catastrophic career setback.

FIGURE 2-1

Responses to adversity

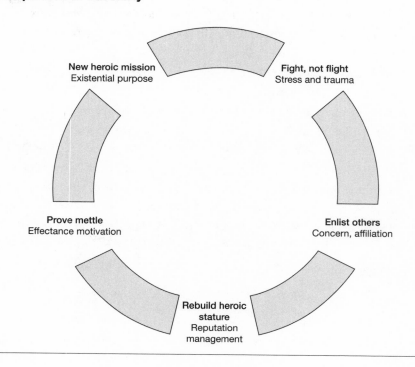

New heroic mission
Existential purpose

Fight, not flight
Stress and trauma

Prove mettle
Effectance motivation

Enlist others
Concern, affiliation

Rebuild heroic
stature
Reputation
management

Don't Adapt to Adversity—Fight It

Forget the breathing exercises on the mats and the secret of your mantra. Folk singer and social activist Joan Baez once said that "action is the antidote to despair." Studies have shown that the shame of defeat can be ameliorated through defiance. Psychiatric research has found that feelings of contempt can therapeutically help minimize feelings of shame.[29] Reflecting upon his termination as CEO of the Gap retail chain after almost two triumphant decades working there, Mickey Drexler, now CEO of J. Crew, told us, "Sure I was angry, and am still angry; that is what helps fuel my accomplishment now."[30] This message is to skip the navel gazing and aromatherapy and go after the source of the problem instead. In July 2006, almost exactly four years after his firing from Gap, Drexler launched a wildly popular $367 million IPO for fashion retailer J. Crew. This followed eight quarters of improved same store sales.

Accordingly, research indicates that accepting stress in coping responses that try to force-fit personality styles to accommodate the stress is not the only approach or even the most effective approach—despite the heavy emphasis on therapeutic programs that offer such accommodation. One major review of the literature on adapting to stress versus reducing it by acting on the source of the stresses concluded, "There continue to be surprisingly few sound empirical studies documenting the assumption that adaptive coping strategies can ameliorate the effects of stressful experiences . . . Perceived self-efficacy in coping may be the most emotionally protective factor in a stressful situation."[31]

Most stress-coping programs actually disenfranchise you from your past greatness by making you, rather than an external threat, the source of the problem. Self-efficacy is often diminished rather than enhanced by making a "patient" out of a victim. Accordingly, if you have been fired, certainly the research confirms that this is a highly stressful event. A vast pool of research also confirms that much of that stress evaporates once new employment is secured.[32] Thus, for many, finding a job may be a more important first step than lengthy analysis speculating over what in their personality may have contributed to their termination.

Similarly, when widely admired business journalist Neil Cavuto was diagnosed with Hodgkin's disease in 1987, he did not concede to this plague. He valiantly battled this form of cancer back into submission through aggressive treatment while continuing to work full throttle. Then, ten years later, a physician examining him antiseptically reported back with no preamble, "Mr. Cavuto . . . You appear to be the unluckiest bastard on the planet. You have MS."

As Cavuto sat in the examining room in stunned silence, contemplating the rapid deterioration of others he had seen suffering this dread disease, "the doctor explained my options. I would have to cut back at work, if I could continue to work at all. My fatigue would steadily increase, and so would the blackouts and stumbling episodes. My form of MS had tentatively been labeled a 'remitting progressive form' of the disease. I understood what that meant: my MS would keep getting worse . . .

There were treatments to slow down its acceleration, but no cures. His cool, almost icy dismissal of my concerns really angered me." [33]

Thus Cavuto sought the advice of national MS experts, began treatment, informed his boss and coworkers. Now, eight years later, he continues to run the business programming of Fox News as well as to master the tremendous pressure of preparing for nightly live appearances on TV for a popular, one-hour live interview show with world-renowned guests from the day's headlines.

Don't Isolate Yourself in Grief; Engage Others for Mutual Support

Cavuto, talking once with us on the set of his TV show in August 2005 about the courage shown by the revelations in his book, said, "I wanted to be straight with people about my own situation, but the real heroes are the others I profile in this book as well as my family and my colleagues at Fox." [34] In fact, Cavuto discussed his efforts to keep his battle with cancer a secret at his prior employment at PBS but found out later that, unbeknownst to him, fellow employees were donating sick time to cover for him. When he began treatment for MS ten years later, he found a caring boss and a great team of colleagues.

"My staff was great. They formed a SWAT team to take care of the details I couldn't. Research on guests for my show was presented earlier. The writing that I routinely handled was quietly done for me. Even my talent back-ups . . . jumped in willingly to be there whenever and wherever." [35]

People have a strong need to belong to their communities and groups for support, as in the Cavuto story. Withdrawal to lick wounds in private is dysfunctional to recovery. [36] In the 1930s, Harvard trait psychologist Henry Murray highlighted the need for affiliation in groups as a core human motivation. David McClelland, also at Harvard, two decades later highlighted this as one of the keys to human motivation. [37] With the shame of defeat, or fear of appearing weak and pathetic, people are often reluctant to deepen the support system or ask for help. [38] In difficult times, top leaders often find themselves increasingly insulated from their board and their management, reluctant to make themselves vulnerable. Ironically, instead of stonewalling their constituents and hiding in difficult times, they badly need to depend upon others.

Do Not Blame Yourself for Innocent Suffering

In addition to relying on groups for support, we turn to groups to create shared meanings of events. We turn to each other to help define even those events we witness firsthand.[39] On July 27, 1996, an anonymous call to Atlanta's 911 number warned that a bomb was about to explode at the packed Olympic Games at the Centennial Olympic Park. At 1:25 a.m., the bomb went off, killing two and injuring hundreds. A band called Jack Mack and the Heart Attacks had just completed a song when the blast went off. We were there then and witnessed the panic in the streets once people realized that the explosion was not part of the stage show.

These long-planned games—with hundreds of millions of dollars invested and the whole country, not to mention the whole world, watching—suddenly were in crisis. A few days later, a half million people nervously crowded back to the park, returning to the bomb site to celebrate the reopening of the park and the continuation of the games. We were there then as well to observe the defiant but anxious crowd of strangers seeking support and meaning from each other. With a stage full of state, national, and city dignitaries, no one seemed eager to speak. The vice chairman of the Olympics, former mayor Andrew Young—a former civil rights leader, a former UN ambassador, and, most significantly perhaps, a former preacher—stepped forward with no notes for what he told us was an extemporaneous address.

After first paying respect to the victims and their grieving families, he shifted to a surprisingly upbeat note:

> *We are here to proclaim a victory. We are here not to wallow in tragedy but to proclaim a triumph—a triumph of the human spirit . . . It is unfortunate that our lives are too often defined by the tragedy of suffering we experience. And yet, it's because of that suffering that brings us to our senses and then we remember who we are . . . You could meet with all the peoples of the world here. We didn't have a single incident, not a single fight, people didn't even get too drunk! We learned to celebrate the joy of humanity. We learned to celebrate that we are all brothers and sisters regardless of race, religion, or national origin . . . Unearned suffering is always redemptive.[40]*

Amazingly, as if on a Hollywood set, the skies that were clouded and misty when he began speaking literally were cleared by rays of sunshine reflecting the rays of hope at the end of Young's remarks. The anxious faces, on the edge of tears, were now filled with smiles as the Olympic theme song was played by Winton Marsalis on a solo trumpet. People left that morning with renewed hope. The only prop Young told us he had was a single 3 × 5 card with the pronunciation of the names of the victims. The rest came to him as the summation of a life of public service and private healing.

Thus, Rev. Young, in contrast to Revs. Falwell and Robertson, turned to spirituality to provide meaning that did not erode self-esteem and divide people through the finger-pointing at victims. Rather, Young explained that were it not for the suffering, all that was wonderful about the entire world sharing athletic contests harmoniously would have been taken for granted.

Similarly, Rabbi Harold Kushner's best-selling book *When Bad Things Happen to Good People* provides a popular perspective on unearned suffering, much like that of Andrew Young's. In essence, he too believes that adversity is not the consequence of punishment for misconduct, but offers meaning through the idea of a spiritual framework that does not blame the victims of innocent suffering. Drawing on the Biblical book of Job, he explains that God did not intend for humanity to understand all suffering to fit our own frameworks of justice.[41] Kushner argues that we should not arrogantly claim we always know the source of our suffering and accept self-denigrating responsibility for our own mishaps.

To Kushner, God's presence is that spark that enables us to go on in the face of the despair of adversity, as we have seen with the immediate community-rebuilding efforts of tsunami victims or the undaunting struggle of 9/11 survivors and Holocaust refugees. Young and Kushner offer ways to overcome the human tendency toward secondary victimization that Lerner's "just world hypothesis" warned about, where victims are blamed for their own misfortunes. Rather than diminish our self-worth as a secondary consequence of adversity, they call for us to celebrate the inspiration to still go on.

Assert Your Mastery for Competence and Confidence

Crushing disappointments and tragedies often leave us with a sense of utter helplessness. Thus, an additional aspect of conquering adversity is the drive to show we can still have an impact on the world around us. Psychologist Robert White labeled this drive for establishing continued mastery as *effectance motivation*—a need to show we have impact on our surroundings and are not merely bystanders to life.[42] This seminal work has influenced forty years of research on the struggle for competence. Lance Armstrong had to get back on his bike, like a fallen cowboy getting back in the saddle at a rodeo, to show he was still able to compete. TV journalist Neil Cavuto's response to his MS diagnosis was to demonstrate for Fox News and his audience that he is still vigorous and competent. Similarly, in the 1990s, CEOs such as Les McGraw of Fluor and Jim Baker of Arvin Industries maintained their leadership while triumphantly battling brain cancer. Both Baker and McGraw have generously contacted us on several occasions to offer their guidance to CEOs we worked with who were facing health crises. In 1996, Intel CEO Andy Grove took the pathbreaking step of sharing his research on the best treatments for prostate cancer for a *Fortune* magazine cover story while he battled that disease. By contrast, Reginald Lewis, chairman of TLC Beatrice International, died of brain cancer just one day after the company disclosed his illness.[43]

Meanwhile, McDonald's CEO Charlie Bell, at age forty-four, and Tenneco CEO Michael Walsh, at age fifty, with the enthusiasm of their boards and colleagues, attempted those same struggles but lost the battle a decade apart. Walsh had been diagnosed with inoperable brain cancer in 1993. The highly respected second-in-command, Dana Mead, confirmed that he closely backed up Walsh in the months that Walsh remained in office as the cancer eroded Walsh's stamina and short-term memory. More publicly, Roger Deromedi, the fifty-year-old CEO of Kraft, was backed up by Altria chairman Louis Camilleri in leading the strategic redirection of this packaged-goods giant as Deromedi focused on his own battle with life-threatening disease. Altria owned 85 percent of Kraft.[44]

An especially compelling saga is that of Carol Bartz, the CEO of Autodesk, who took over a large, fast-growing but badly managed computer-aided design firm. This forty-three-year-old former Sun Microsystems sales manager had emerged to become one of the most prominent women in technology. Soon into the job, she had to overcome a rebellion of programmers loyal to a cofounder determined to humiliate her. One reporter commented, "Worse, Bartz's first major product introduction was a dud, bringing AutoDesk to the brink of collapse and raising questions about her competency."[45] This might have been traumatic enough, but on her second day on the job, she was diagnosed with breast cancer.

At a conference four years later, Bartz told us that she was very conscious of her prominent role as a woman breaking through the ranks of top leadership in technology. Bartz, now fifty-five, said that she never contemplated quitting. "I had made a commitment . . . I think part of that Midwestern farm heritage is that you have to do a job, and you do it. The cows don't wait just because you don't want to milk them that morning."[46] One month after her mastectomy she returned to the office. Her mother died when Bartz was only eight, and she was raised by a no-nonsense grandmother. She rose up the ranks quickly at Digital Equipment Corporation, before leaving for 3M and then Sun. Autodesk's sales are twice what they were when she took office, despite a business downturn in 2001 and 2002. President Bush appointed her to the Council of Advisors on Science and Technology, and she serves on major technology boards such as those of BEA Systems and Cisco. Most importantly, her cancer is gone, and she has remained active with an information network for people with breast cancer.

Just nine days after a mastectomy for breast cancer, Connecticut governor Jodi Rell stepped to the podium to deliver the opening address for the state legislature in January 2005. She was received with wild foot stomping and whooping from this often fractious audience of legislators. The prior year, she had taken over the reins from a scandalized predecessor, and she was determined to deliver an inspirational message. She was admired for her strength and her generosity.[47] Leaders like Rell and Bartz who master such personal crises in a public manner with a goal of modeling courage for others also prove something for themselves. They demonstrate their competence and their determination as unrelenting fighters against life's adversity. This encourages them in their own recovery as much as it helps motivate their constituents.

Clarify Your Mission with an Anchor in the Future

Many times, our despair in the present can be tolerated if we can restore a sense of purpose for tomorrow. One of the greatest challenges of life development that psychologist Erik Erikson described was the struggle between "integrity" or fullness and "despair" or hopelessness. In Greek mythology, the extreme form of punishment inflicted by the gods upon the character Sisyphus was the condemnation to a daily sheer pointless task of rolling a boulder to the top of a mountain, only to see it roll back down again. It was thought there would be no worse human torture than futile, hopeless labor. Existential writer Albert Camus, however, retold the story in a classic 1955 essay, "The Myth of Sisyphus." Here he suggested how the victim endured his fate. For Camus, suffering and awareness of the true meaninglessness of our short lives in the eternity of the universe made despair over our losses seem absurd. Sisyphus, for him, was the hero of the absurd because Sisyphus proclaimed that it is through the scorn of the gods as he descends, free of his stone, that he has reached the heights of the gods and left in triumph: "I leave Sisyphus at the foot of the mountain! One always finds one's burden again. But Sisyphus teaches the higher fidelity that negates the gods and raises rocks. He too concludes that all is well. This universe henceforth without a master seems to him neither sterile nor futile. Each atom of that stone, each mineral flake of that night filled mountain, in itself forms a world. The struggle itself toward the heights is enough to fill a man's heart. One must imagine Sisyphus happy."[48]

Instead of focusing on his lost purpose, he creates one, just as we can recognize that the night is what gives meaning to the daylight. We saw how the daunting personal health challenges of journalist Neil Cavuto, CEO Carol Bartz, and Governor Jodi Rell were emotionally conquered through their public commitments; the larger life mission beyond survival itself is important for giving the victim of adversity and those in the lives of that person a belief in tomorrow.

Too often, overwhelming grief and despair can leave us immersed in a quicksand of sadness and horror. The mission itself serves as a lifeline to a world beyond the present misery. Viktor Frankl's uplifting book *Man's Search for Meaning* opens with a chronicle of personal suffering and eyewitness accounts of the excruciating pain suffered by fellow inmates while he was imprisoned in the Auschwitz concentration camp for five years.[49] Without minimizing the daily torture and the mass murder of loved ones, Frankl observed that those who could emotionally survive their surroundings were those who could imagine themselves free to transcend the suffering and find a meaningful life despite the circumstances. In 1942, Frankl, a young recently married doctor, was arrested with his wife, mother, father, and brother, separated from them at a prison camp, and given a new identity, prisoner 119,104. While he learned after the war that all of these family members were killed, he kept hope alive. While in the prison camp, he secretly worked on a manuscript and imagined reuniting with his family as reasons to struggle onward. Just as important as the prior elements of dealing with adversity, engaging with others, avoiding self-deprecation, and establishing competence and mastery, is the will to create meaning or purpose to fill "the existential vacuum." To survive the horrors, people had to look into the future. "The prisoner who had lost faith in the future—his future—was doomed."[50] Warren Bennis and Robert Thomas have called such horrible events "crucible events" where individuals are tested to create meaning out of difficult life events.[51]

Peter Bell, the CEO of the international humanitarian agency CARE, responds to the grief for the periodic loss of his heroic relief workers by balancing the personal and public missions of his job. Following the devastation of the Asian tsunami over Christmas, he spent the first few weeks of 2005 trying to balance conflicting priorities. The rush of donor generosity and the daunting needs of desperate people requiring food, water, clothing, and shelter created logistical and leadership challenges unsurpassed in CARE's half century of experience in delivering such relief. At the same time, Bell could not turn his back on the ongoing commitments for aid elsewhere: "One of my profound concerns was that our heavy, necessary focus on the devastation in Southeast Asia would drain attention and resources from other places of unfathomable suffering—the hellish camps of Darfur, Sudan, Haitians still struggling to recover from the mudslides of Tropical Storm Jeanne; and the legions of AIDS-ravaged villages throughout most of sub-Saharan Africa."[52]

That is not the only suffering he had to balance in his response. He also had to attend to the mourning of the CARE organization itself as a family because the CARE country director for Nepal, Robin Needham, drowned in the tsunami while visiting Thailand. One of Bell's first stops was to help comfort Needham's family in Kathmandu.

Unfortunately, this instance of personal grief was not unique for Bell and his courageous team. Margaret Hassan, a woman of Irish and English heritage, married an Iraqi and ultimately became head of the CARE office in Baghdad, where she worked for three decades to improve the quality of life of Iraqis. After the bombing of the UN headquarters there, it became clear that little distinction was being made by the insurgents between those who came to bring humanitarian relief assistance and those who came for war. In the fall of 2004, she was kidnapped on her way to work and threatened with death. Her torture and grisly execution was recorded on video by her captors.

"Over the couple of decades we have probably lost more than a hundred CARE workers who have been caught in the crossfire. This is the only case where a member of our staff was singled out and targeted precisely because of her humanitarian commitment. Margaret was just extraordinary. She had a heart of gold but at the same time had a spine of steel."[53]

As Peter Bell explained to us in December 2004, CARE had closed its Baghdad office during the war for just four days. When Margaret Hassan returned from the countryside, she encountered an Iraqi with a rifle loading cans of paint from CARE's warehouse into a truck. She told him to stop, and he threatened to shoot her. She stood her ground, defiantly saying, "No, you are not; those paints are headed for a hospital in Baghdad. What god told you you could take that paint?" The gunman put the paint back. Recounting this story while choking back tears in his conversation with us, Bell commented, "Margaret, in her last meeting with her staff, said, 'Life is not about surviving, life is about living with passion.' "[54]

When other CEOs meet this dedicated man at our CEO Summits, they often wonder, how does Bell go on, so often surrounded with such sadness and danger? He answers them by describing the gratification of returning joy and hope to the lives of people who often saw little but despair and loneliness previously. In his own words, "We calculate the good that we are able to do in terms of saving lives and reducing suffering against the risks our people run . . . We rely most importantly on the close relationships between the people of CARE and the people we help. We work with tens of thousands of the world's poorest communities."[55]

Another answer, however, is revealed in a comment he offered the *Wall Street Journal*, following the tsunami. "We hope to work ourselves out of business, toward a time when extreme poverty and loss of this magnitude are distant memories."[56] A business goal of irrelevance is easily achieved by some CEOs, but not this one with so daunting a mission. The brilliant founder of Eastman Kodak, George Eastman, took his own life in his seventies, leaving a suicide note reading, "My work is done, why wait?"[57] Like the artist whose canvas is never done, Bell will never be able to look at a map of the Earth, let alone the daily news reports, and say with anomic emptiness, "My work is done, why wait?" For people like Bell, the mission continues into the future, coupled with hope and progress.

Adversity

Adversity can be the cruelest thief in the world. It can steal our confidence, our reputation, our pride, our most cherished relationships, our feeling of control, and our sense of purpose in life. Those who do not prevent this robbery of all that we most treasure in life often surrender their will to live. Those profiled in this chapter who survived and triumphed over adversity did so by instinct, the advice of others, or trial and error. The devastating life circumstances described here are not conditions any of us anticipate ever happening to us.

How, then, can a leader be expected to deal with adversity any better than anyone else? Plenty of nonleaders are heroic, and plenty of leaders have missed moments to be heroes. Those leaders who triumphed over adversity recognized that greatness was thrust upon them by opportunities they did not seek. In this second chapter, we have taken the five elements of overcoming adversity and looked at the distinct deep psychological traditions from which each is drawn, including posttraumatic stress response, the need for affiliation, self-esteem, attribution of justice, competence motivation, and existential purpose. Perhaps the best way to summarize this chapter is to profile someone who instinctively applied all five of these elements for overcoming adversity.

Jimmy Dunne is a charming, caring, honest person. He is a great parent and humble but accomplished financier with a cunning street savvy. He was not, however, trained as a crisis manager, a grief counselor, an IT engineer, or a media spokesperson. Yet as the CEO of Sandler O'Neill & Partners, he, in one day, had to master all those skills while looking for real estate, setting up benefits funds, and other details too numerous to re-count. The maverick investment banking firm Sandler O'Neill provides financial services for small and medium-sized banks around the country and had its headquarters on the 104th floor of the south tower of the World Trade Center. The firm employed 171 employees on September 11, 2001. Eighty-three made it to work in the office that morning but only seventeen came out alive. The forty-five-year-old managing part-ner, the only surviving senior partner, stepped up to the plate and took charge. Thus he went about a leadership journey that taught his firm, himself, and all of us a great deal about recovery. We can organize his ac-tions around the lessons of this book.

First, he did not capitulate in despair, but *immediately engaged in battle against adversity*. Dunne commented to us tearfully, "They attacked my firm, they killed sixty-six of my people, they killed my friends."[58] He set up a makeshift trading floor staffed by employees from other offices, friends, relatives, and volunteers. Steve Crofts reported on the firm's re-covery battle on CBS's *60 Minutes*:

> *There had been discussions about selling or liquidating the firm but Dunne made it his mission to try and keep it alive—for the 100 parents who lost sons and daughters, for 46 widows or widowers, and their 71 children under the age of 18, the work helped deaden the pain, made them feel relevant. Within four days of the attack they had already moved into temporary quarters—a customer service center given to them by Bank of America—but the firm's phone system, computer network, corporate net-work, and virtually every piece of paper had been destroyed along with the people who knew most all about them. A list of all their clients had to be reconstructed from memory. Entire departments were wiped out. Almost all of the bond and stock traders were killed. But Jimmy Dunne wasn't about to give up.*[59]

At our CEO Summit in December 2003, Dunne explained how he jumped into battle two years earlier: "Sometimes it's easier when your back is against the wall. It was easy in that it was obvious as to what we had to do. I knew exactly what we had to do. We had to do everything possible to take care of those families, to do everything we could possi-bly do to fight back with every fiber in our bodies. And if I died of a heart attack seven days into it, that would have been just fine . . . Whether or not everyone liked me then or likes me now, no one thought I was a coward."[60]

Second, rather than retreat from his traumatized employees, he knew he had a responsibility *to show empathy, compassion, and interdependence with colleagues*. In fact, many of the people who had also been the firm's core assets helped him repair this shattered firm. His empathy to his colleagues was shown through public demonstrations of mourning, through discussions, counseling, tears, and financial support. Dunne posted a giant spreadsheet in the lobby with the names of all the deceased employees and made sure that someone went to every funeral. He gave roughly a dozen personal eulogies himself. About a third of the firm's assets were put into a fund for the families of the victims. Salaries and bonuses were paid through the end of the year based on the best year employees had enjoyed. Family benefits were promised through 2006, and an office was set up to process insurance claims for employees' families. Even now, the photos of all sixty-six employees appear on the Web site in tribute as well as on the desks of many employees.

Third, he did *not look for targets of blame*. Dunne led the firm through a celebration of survival with none of the finger-pointing over suspected injustices that other hard-hit firms at the World Trade Center endured. Accordingly, not only did competitors throw business their way along with space and technical assistance, but most importantly, clients remained loyal. At one point he wondered whether more would have survived if the firm had had an evacuation plan, but in calling around he learned that Morgan Stanley, which lost only six of its thirty-seven hundred employees in the twin towers, had no plan. Dunne found it reassuring that Morgan Stanley people just ran.

Fourth, Dunne knew, despite the loss of brokers, traders, systems, and entire departments, he wanted to prove that they *still had the competence to be a viable enterprise*. Dunne instinctively knew that people had to believe that Sandler O'Neill would be in business with every other financial institution when the market reopened—and it was ready for business when the stock market miraculously opened six days later. Jimmy Dunne had never done an interview in the media before. However, when a cable news channel erroneously reported that the firm had gone out of business, as most predicted it would, he went on CNBC, proclaiming its revival. Dunne explained on air that the employees were acting with the skills they had: "We don't write songs. We don't write novels. We are going to respond as we know how."[61] A week later, the firm closed its first investment banking deal since the attack and began hiring. The next few weeks were shaky, but in two months, the firm was profitable and is now a full third larger than it was before the attacks.

Finally, Dunne locked *on a mission implanted in the future.* He gently pushed the firm to balance grieving for lost friends and colleagues with moving away from defining itself by the deaths and losses. Instead, he retired the old phone numbers and refused to consider any new hires as replacements for lost colleagues. In fact, in a *Fortune* interview, he said that he asked a superstar young investment banker in a job interview what he might like to do if hired. "I want to replace Chris Quackenbush [Dunne's deceased senior partner]," came the reply. Dunne reported, "When he said that, I felt like I wanted to vomit."[62] Needless to say, they passed on hiring that applicant.

Just as the sum total of Andrew Young's career was called upon to help with his rare skills as a diplomat, an orator, a clergyman, and a municipal leader when it came to the Olympic Park bombing, Dunne, too, felt that his past experience had prepared him for this horrible test of adversity. Dunne reflected to us in April 2006, "There were some nights at four o'clock in the morning when I sat there and thought someone had reached down my throat and ripped out my heart . . . I think I trained my whole career to do this. I honestly believe that everything that's happened to me was leading to this."[63]

In short, these five elements of resilience allowed these victorious survivors to thrive again despite the corrosive effect of secondary victimization due to losses from alienation from others, diminished self-esteem, shattered respect of others, eroded feelings of mastery and control, and cynicism replacing optimism for the future. The powerful stories of seizing triumph from the jaws of defeat were not examples of just good fortune. These figures showed tremendous tenacity, but they also had to make difficult choices when the options often seemed unclear and the outcomes unknown.

CHAPTER 3

Societal Barriers to Recovery

You can see all the stars as you walk down Hollywood Boulevard,
Some that you recognize, some that you've hardly even heard of,
People who worked and suffered and struggled for fame,
Some who succeeded and some who suffered in vain . . .
Everybody's a dreamer, everybody's a star.
Everybody's in showbiz, it doesn't matter who you are.
For those who are successful, be always on your guard,
For success walks hand in hand with failure, along Hollywood Boulevard.

—From "Celluloid Heroes," by Ray Davies and the Kinks

HAVING EXAMINED MORE DEEPLY the psychological foundations for our lessons from conquering adversity in the previous chapter, we now will look at lessons from failure in particular. The core challenge here is to understand how society's infatuation with success often blocks open discussion of failure. We are entranced by tips for success, but the preceding song by Ray Davies and the Kinks reminds us that we tend to get caught unprepared for failure.

When prominent people fail, they find that success is a double-edged sword because the comebacks can be even more difficult given the impact on self-esteem and the constant scrutiny, if not schadenfreude, or celebration of failure. Such street-savvy CEOs as Disney's Michael Eisner,

AIG's Maurice Greenberg, and Hewlett-Packard's Carly Fiorina so believed their own manufactured press, they seemed completely unprepared for their predictable falls from grace. We all tend to fixate on the climb for success and rarely prepare for the slide back down. Mountain Rivera, the fallen prizefighter in Rod Serling's *Requiem for a Heavyweight*, lamented, "Every punch on the way up just slides right off, you don't feel a thing, but on the way down, they all come back to hurt you . . . sometimes so bad I can't stand it. It's the bill you pay for success."

The Quest for Success: The American Dream and Self-Help Mantras

Twenty years after the Kinks' ballad was released, we still see the frenetic quest for success as epitomized in the TV audiences of up to 50 million people watching each episode of Donald Trump's *The Apprentice* on NBC to gain tips on obtaining a lifestyle of luxury. This is matched by his best-selling books with titles like *Trump: Think Like a Billionaire*, *Trump: How to Get Rich*, *Trump: The Art of the Comeback*, *Surviving at the Top*, and *Trump: The Art of the Deal*, which are perceived by many in the media as a unique social phenomenon of unparalleled fixation on a glittering image of achievable wealth.[1]

In fact, *New York Times* columnist Frank Rich applauded the show as a welcome relief from CEO corruption, labeling it as "more palatable than the corporate shenanigans that have been in the spotlight on the public stage in recent years."[2] At the same time, others have criticized this television phenomenon for its elimination game or musical chairs–like celebration of success at the expense of coworkers as well as the danger of winning at any cost.[3] Nonetheless, despite frequent media criticism and the crowded genre of "reality TV shows," Trump's *The Apprentice* has flourished, going into a fifth record-setting season. This has been juxtaposed with setbacks in his own casino and resort businesses.[4] In fact, in conversations with us about his own business reversals amid the glistening image of success, he would diminish the notion of bankruptcy, saying, "Oh, you mean the 'B' word [bankruptcy]? Big deal! What people don't understand is that it's just a restructuring with the banks."[5]

Trump actually emerged from this bankruptcy quickly—with the company actually saving roughly $98 million a year in interest payments as a result of the restructuring. Trump, dropping his TV persona, has also confided to us that one of his most poignant lessons was not from the model of a successful person but from a failure. "I always had admired the postwar residential developer Bill Levitt, who built Levittowns around the nation and sold the enterprise to the conglomerate ITT. They made a mess of it, and Levitt, bored in his wealth, living in a chateau in southern France, bought the company back for what he thought was a bargain. Soon after, he'd lost everything. I went to a party and saw a lonely old man sitting in the corner—it was Bill Levitt. I went over to sit with him and his painful story of overextending himself taught me a great deal about knowing where the edge really is, knowing what you can and can't do—some of my most powerful learning."[6]

In fact, the unabashed celebration of the attainability of success long predates Trump as a key pillar of the American psyche. As far back as 1732, Benjamin Franklin published his hugely popular maxims for success in his *Poor Richard's Almanack* series, with such now familiar aphorisms as "Early to bed and early to rise, makes a man healthy, wealthy, and wise," "Haste makes waste," "Love your neighbor, yet don't pull down your hedge," and "He that lies down with dogs, shall rise up with fleas." Biographer Walter Isaacson has shown that few of these proverbs were original to Franklin but were cleverly adopted and sharpened for pithiness and impact.[7] The much echoed phrases became ingrained in later self-help literature and also have been the subject of jokes. Groucho Marx lamented in his memoirs, "Early to bed, early to rise, makes a man you-know-what. This is a lot of hoopla. Most wealthy people I know like to sleep late and will fire the help if they are disturbed before three in the afternoon . . . You don't see Marilyn Monroe getting up at six in the morning. The truth is, I don't see Marilyn Monroe getting up at any hour, more's the pity."[8]

Franklin's model of upward mobility was reflected a century later through the work of a Yale-trained economist named Thorsten Veblen. Veblen's influential 1899 book, *The Theory of the Leisure Class*, introduced the concept of "conspicuous consumption," whereby social class is indicated by the extravagance of consumer purchases.[9] In short, people, like Donald Trump and his apprentices, display their acquisitions as a source of pride, similar to the way the seventeenth-century Puritan ethic became distorted when people tried to indicate through wealth that they were among the divinely elected. Veblen also introduced the concept of "pecuniary emulation," in which instead of resenting the wasteful extravagance of the wealthy classes, people aspire to be like them. Veblen suggested that, to chart our progress, we engage in what today we might term "keeping up with the Joneses," such that people keep score of their successes through material benchmarks, or what Veblen called "invidious comparison."

Two other American apostles of the religion of success were born around the time Veblen published his analysis. Dale Carnegie and Norman Vincent Peale were the founding fathers of twentieth-century self-help philosophy and were both born in humble settings at the close of the nineteenth century. Their words are echoed in the self-empowering perspectives of contemporary self-help figures like Stephen Covey. His 7 *Habits of Highly Effective People* echoes the tips of his predecessors like Carnegie and Peale with new language for a new generation ("think win/win," "be proactive," "empathic listening," etc.).[10]

Dale Carnegie's suggestions—"Believe that you will succeed and you will" or "Take a chance! All life is a chance. The man who goes furthest is generally the one who is willing to do and dare"—represent the positive spirit of his 1936 *Poor Richard*–like self-help classic, *How to Win Friends and Influence People*.[11] Carnegie, a poor farmer's son, became a superstar salesman for Armour & Company before becoming an author and motivational speaker, drawing on the positive-reinforcement theories of Harvard psychologist B. F. Skinner's operant conditioning. He argued that 15 percent of success was based on knowledge, while 85 percent was based on communication and attitude.

Similarly, Norman Vincent Peale's popular broadcasts and his 1952 book, *The Power of Positive Thinking*, echoed the Benjamin Franklin/Dale Carnegie spirit with maxims like "Change your thoughts and you change your world" or "Empty pockets never held anyone back. Only empty heads and empty hearts can do that."[12]

Failing to Anticipate Failure

Such folk wisdom about success did not insulate these authors from ex-periencing their own setbacks. Norman Vincent Peale's infectious opti-mism grew from his pulpit to inspire 20 million readers through a book that ironically almost did not get published due to his own despair. Peale did not write the book until he was in his fifties. Demoralized by the re-jection of publishers, he tossed it in the trash, but his wife rescued it and surreptitiously took it to a publisher.

More dramatically, Benjamin Franklin, the self-made wealthy Philadel-phia printer, popular writer, and self-taught scientist-philosopher, became a great statesman only out of his failure forty years after the *Poor Richard's Almanack* series. He was rebuffed in his quest to be accepted as an aris-tocratic gentleman back in class-conscious England. Historians have de-scribed his passionate radicalization as an advocate for the American Colonies and a brilliant revolutionary statesman as arising from his per-ceived humiliation by the British Empire. Enamored of the sophisticated English upper-class life, he was also a devoted imperialist. By 1776, when Franklin was seventy, his personal disillusionment with his ambitions to join English society had converted him into a fierce supporter of Amer-ican independence. In that cause his diplomatic skills were crucial to the war effort and the health of the new government that emerged.[13]

At least Peale and Franklin were able to transcend their failures and were mobilized for healthy recovery. The name Horatio Alger is virtu-ally synonymous with the epitome of business success, but he was actu-ally a commercial and personal failure. Alger was the presumed author of "rags to riches" stories of poor boys who, through lucky breaks and per-sonal loyalty, enjoyed moderate middle-class comfort. He was actually a former minister from Brewster, Massachusetts, who was a fugitive from several charges of child molestation. In mid-March 1886, he fled to New York City, where he failed as a newspaper writer. He enjoyed brief fame as the author of the book *Ragged Dick* but then slid backward working as a private tutor, eventually dying impoverished at age sixty-seven.[14] The aura of success posthumously attached to the Horatio Alger name was actually the result of a hoax carried out by a crafty magazine editor who fed a nation at war an image of a triumphant author who profiled success in others.

Similarly, self-promotion of success seems to actually breed failure. We are surrounded with recipes for success in leadership. Far-ranging media outlets map out seemingly accessible paths to the top. Despite these inspirational tales of triumph, the real-life sagas are steeped in hardship. Such boastful autobiographies of chief executives such as *Mean Business*, by Al Dunlap, then leading Sunbeam, and *Odyssey*, by John Sculley, then leading Apple, were published just on the eve of their great falls from office.[15] No sooner had these books been shipped off to the bookstores than the hidden debris that derailed these leaders began to surface.

This phenomenon, often referred to as the "curse of the *Sports Illustrated* cover," seemed to come to life when Major League Baseball Hall of Fame member Ted Williams was featured on a 1996 cover, only to trip over his dog and break his hip. When *BusinessWeek* put Enron CEO Jeff Skilling on its cover in 2001, he left office abruptly six months later, and twelve months later the firm descended into scandal and went bankrupt. That same year, *Forbes* selected Charles Schwab Corporation as its company of the year, but within two years the firm's stock had fallen from $35 to $7, and a third of its employees were laid off. Two years in a row, Tyco's Dennis Kozlowski was anointed by *BusinessWeek* as one of the twenty-five best CEOs of the year, but eighteen months later, he was fired and on trial for plundering $600 million of his shareholders' wealth.[16]

Two economists, Ulrike Malmendier of Stanford and Geoffrey Tate of the Wharton School at the University of Pennsylvania, systematically studied 566 CEOs between 1975 and 2002 to compare the high-profile award-winning CEOs to matched peers and found that the award-winning CEOs were more likely to have fluffy self-promotional books written about them and enjoy higher compensation but produced worse performance.[17] In short, the celebrity CEOs commanded 39 percent increases in salary versus 18 percent for the noncelebrity CEOs. Meanwhile, the return on assets for the firms of award-winning CEOs deteriorated steadily for the three years after the recognition, while the less-celebrated CEOs showed increased performance.

This research suggests that the celebration of success can lead to distraction and ultimately failure. Perhaps also sustained high-performance given the pressure of "regression to the mean" hurts the celebrity CEO due to initially stronger firm performance. Similarly, this research may disguise the easier repairs of "low-hanging fruit" sorts of problems in the firms of the noncelebrity CEOs. Finally, it is possible that some CEOs just handle celebrity better than others, such as Henry Ford, J. P. Morgan, John D. Rockefeller, GE's Jack Welch, Intel's Andrew Grove, and The Home Depot's Bernie Marcus.

Regardless of why the celebrity CEOs fail, we are far more interested in their success and our own success, thus ensuring a lack of preparation for our missteps. The maverick low-cost airline People Express went from a cold start-up in 1981 to $1 billion in revenues by 1984, with four thousand employees serving over one hundred cities. Through overexpansion and an ill-conceived acquisition, the company strained employees and systems, while encroachment on core routes of the major trunk line carriers led entrenched competitors to retaliate and drive this highly spirited firm out of business through predatory pricing and biased computerized reservation systems. In the heady days of early success, founder Don Burr graced the covers of *Forbes*, *Fortune*, *BusinessWeek*, and *Time* magazines. He later commented, "The press can really get to you—it can be intoxicating and you start to believe it yourself. In fact, even my mother started to believe we were geniuses." Burr took the loss of his pioneering firm hard and retreated from the limelight for years, working on private investments and eventually building some small aviation technology service firms. "I see now that my own hubris had become as big an obstacle as was our competitors' unfair edges. There were danger signs I just missed."[18] Nonetheless, twenty years later, Burr got back in the cockpit to launch Pogo Air, an air taxi business capitalizing on a new class of efficient very light jets and flexible schedules, with his one-time adversary, former American Airlines CEO Robert Crandall, as his chairman.[19]

In April 2005, twenty years after the demise of People Express, we brought Don Burr together for a surprise lunch with David Neeleman, the founder of the tremendously successful five-year-old airline JetBlue. The sixty-two-year-old Burr and the forty-five-year-old Neeleman had great respect for each other's history and continued creative edge and had traded wisdom years earlier. Now Burr generously commented, "If I'd have failed earlier in life like David did, it might have saved me a decade. I just wasn't ready for it."

Neeleman had experienced failure having had one travel business from his youth fail and then, soon after selling his successful Morris Air to Southwest Airlines, being fired by Southwest's flamboyant CEO Herb Kelleher over stylistic clashes. Neeleman was bored and restless with a desk job, feeling underutilized and chafing at long meetings. He said, "When Herb told me they needed someone just like me at Southwest, I assumed it would be a lovefest when I got to Dallas."

Reflecting on getting fired, Neeleman said, "I was shocked, humiliated, and angry. I wasn't ready for this and I cried at first, but then got back in the game." His wife of twenty-one years suggested that with the $20 million he left with from Southwest, he didn't need to work, but Neeleman said, "I had something to prove to Southwest and others." He first created an airline reservation and revenue management system called Open Skies and sold it to Hewlett-Packard for $22 million. Then, in February 2000, at age forty, once his noncompete term expired, he launched JetBlue, a carrier with concepts he adapted from his own Morris Air, as well as from People Express, Southwest Airlines, and Virgin Air.[20] Five years later, he had over $1.3 billion in sales, over seventy-five hundred employees, seventy-five planes, and one of the highest market values in the industry. Neeleman, who continues to work as a flight attendant one day each week, has found ways to prevent the infusion of hubris that became a problem for Burr and People Express.

Why Leveraging Failure Remains a Mystery

It is seems strange that the intricacies of failure are not examined with the same intense scrutiny that we invest in dissecting the sources of success. When failure is studied in scholarly and popular literature, it tends to be matched with insights on avoidance of failure rather than in truly understanding its dynamics. For example, the classic 1974 psychological study of longitudinal career success by Douglas Bray, Richard Campbell, and Donald Grant, entitled *Formative Years in Business*, revealed that the importance of a good early start through supportive supervision and appropriate early assignments could lead to a self-fulfilling success syndrome.[21] Such momentum, in fact, described the tracks for long-term success studied in the disguised firm we now know was AT&T. As people's careers soared through good politics, their once great employer, a protected monopoly, was atrophying and unprepared for collective failure.

Rarely is failure portrayed as a liberating event or an enabler of life change. But we often look at the factors that derailed a successful fast-track career. Almost twenty years ago, the Center for Creative Leadership conducted pathbreaking studies on how swift-rising executives fell off the success track.[22] An excellent examination by Dartmouth's Sydney Finkelstein revealed a similar set of factors for how prominent intelligent business leaders lost their footings.[23] The pathological behaviors he noted included arrogance, presumption that their firms controlled their surroundings, the conflict of a complete merging of their personal interests with the company's interests, the thin-skinned determination that others see them as faultless, and the ready regression to inappropriate past strategies from earlier parts of their career. Political pundits examine the factors that led to the defeat of public figures, but mostly we merely shake our heads in amazement over the resilience of some, like presidents Richard Nixon or Bill Clinton, dismissing them as "comeback kids."[24]

Nonetheless, there are at least nine reasons why we do not see a more enthusiastic embrace of the phenomenon of failure.

Stigma of Failure

First, our society so worships success that we are afraid of associating with a possible carrier of failure, for fear of contagion. The natural response to this fear is to always appear successful, or else people will distance themselves from us. Whistle-blowers who challenge the system often find themselves out of work as they become associated with the problem they helped identify. Even *Time* magazine's 2002 People of the Year, whistle-blowers Sherron Watkins of Enron, Cynthia Cooper of WorldCom, and Coleen Rowley of the FBI, found their careers blunted due to their association with scandal.[25] University of Pennsylvania sociologist Erving Goffman referred to this as the concept of "stigma," which referred to any trait or behavior that symbolically distanced the bearer as "culturally unacceptable" or inferior, with associated shame, guilt, and disgrace.[26] The resolution of ostracism due to being stigmatized is to conceal the source of shame.

Shattered Self-Esteem

A second reason we do not explore our failures is that we have so injured our self-esteem that it is too painful to acknowledge the defeat. A lifetime's personal dream and the aspirations of others in your life may seem to have ended. People can feel lost with no career road map; a sense of anomie or a lack of direction and powerlessness can lead to withdrawal and depression.[27] Consider the emotional toll taken on Michael Fuchs, a brilliant, widely admired media executive who is best known for his positioning of the popular Home Box Office cable channel.

Home Box Office had been a promising but troubled enterprise when Cablevision entrepreneur Charles Dolan sold it to Time Inc. in 1973. The ingenious and tenacious long-term Time executive Michael Fuchs built it into a powerhouse of both financial strength and creative programming, eventually even successfully taking over the contentious Warner Music after the merger with Warner Communication by the time he was fired on November 16, 1995. Some thought he was fired due to sparring with the heads of Warner Brothers films, while others thought he was fired by a threatened boss, CEO Jerry Levin, since he was seen as a potential strong successor. Regardless of the reasons, he was badly winded after the fall. A dozen years ago, he reflected that his business ferocity may have been, in part, fueled by the sense of determination and injustice he felt in caring for the mother whom he adored through her early onset of debilitating Alzheimer's disease while he was still only a high school student. He felt robbed that she did not have the chance to see him as a successful media titan. Consider this reporter's account, however, of how the fight was taken from him when he was fired in 1995 after eighteen years on the job: "He was addicted, as he put it, to the 'metronome, the urgency' of his huge job—and then, all of a sudden, at the age of forty-nine, he was out of work. 'You walk into the building on a Thursday a master of the universe and walk out that night a man without a country,' Fuchs explained to me. 'I didn't realize what it would be like to wake up the next day with nowhere to go . . . It was incredibly disconcerting.' "[28]

Initially, he thought that some other media giant would enlist him to run their entertainment business, but no one offered him a job. "People were afraid that I'd come in and change things and move the furniture around, and that was probably true . . . but people were always more afraid of me than they should have been. I was never that much of a killer. I was just outspoken and I wasn't afraid of anyone." [29]

Ultimately, Fuchs gave up the hopeful waiting, no longer anticipating a return to the big time. "I spent about a year waiting for something to happen, waiting to run another media company, and then it dawned on me that I'd never really be able to run a big machine again . . . After a year, I decided I never wanted to be back in a corporation. I decided that life wasn't for me." [30] Fuchs then went on to invest in several highly successful Broadway shows and magazines as well as some Internet businesses, with checkered results. The dream still lingered, however. "I get a few pangs. I still get up in the middle of the night and think of what could have been." [31]

The Risks of Rage and Revenge

Reasonable people can become understandably enraged when they feel a great injustice has befallen them. Kenneth Langone, the fiery financier and cofounder of The Home Depot successfully fought back against an action of the NASD enforcement division. On March 3, 2006, a NASD hearing panel concluded that its own enforcement division was wrong when it found in 2003 that Langone and his brokerage firm, Invemed Associates LLC, had illegally shared in their customers' profits on hot initial public offerings in 1999 and 2000. While Credit Suisse and other investment banks paid fines of tens of millions of dollars for such charges, Langone told us in 2005 that he refused to "quietly take his lumps." He has likewise defiantly stood his ground in defending his role as head of the board compensation committee of the New York Stock Exchange. New York Attorney General Eliot Spitzer has charged that Langone misled the board in awarding former NYSE chief Richard Grasso $190 million and violated New York State law over non-profits guiding reasonable compensation. Langone not only refused to discuss settlement, as the judge in the case suggested, but, in a March 8 CNBC interview, cautioned his friend Grasso to continue to fight on as well, warning, "If he [Grasso] settles the case I can tell you right now, his friendship is over with me." Langone reminded us in a 2005 discussion: "People go to war over honor." [32]

Such feistiness is not always victorious. One of the most feared and widely admired executives in the financial universe for almost four decades, Maurice Greenberg had built up a once-obscure property casualty firm into one of the world's leading financial service firms, with revenues of almost $100 billion from businesses in 130 countries. But the stormy end to Greenberg's legendary reign as CEO of American International Group (AIG) was hastened by the pressure by Eliot Spitzer and Greenberg's own hostile confrontations with even once-friendly board directors while he was under regulatory scrutiny for possible financial fraud. When we met with him in September of 2006, we could not help but be impressed by Greenberg's tremendously sophisticated visions of global diplomacy and continued profound influence, but also his continued anger over moves by the AIG board.

When long-term friends who were also directors questioned government allegations of improper accounting that could restate company assets by several billion dollars, he shot back with a spirited self-defense. As reported in the *Wall Street Journal*, Greenberg "called and yelled at several directors, including longtime friends Frank Zarb, former chairman of the National Association of Securities Dealers, and retired attorney Bernard Aidinoff, for 'turning' on him and leading a 'boardroom revolt,' the people say. Shortly after the probe began, he complained about the 'McCarthyistic' legal and regulatory atmosphere that he believed attacked him unfairly."[33]

When Zarb convened a meeting of other such distinguished directors as former U.S. secretary of defense William Cohen, former U.S. ambassador to the UN Richard Holbrooke, and Harvard economics professor Martin Feldstein, according to this *Wall Street Journal* account:

> *Mr. Greenberg called in periodically on a speaker phone, where he was connected from his boat in Florida . . . "You couldn't even spell the word insurance," he said to the group, according to people familiar with the situation. Later he called again, this time from the corporate jet, to criticize Mr. Zarb and others for being led around by lawyers, the people say. As the meeting wore on, a consensus developed that Mr. Greenberg could be a stumbling block in resolving the regulatory issues if he continued as chief executive.*[34]

By mid September 2006, most of the charges against Greenberg regarding improper accounting were dropped by Spitzer, and while no criminal charges were expected, the civil court battle raged on regarding alleged accounting deals which disguised underwriting losses. Meanwhile, in February of that year, AIG reached a settlement with the Attorney General, with the firm paying a record fine of $1.6 billion to settle state and federal charges of securities fraud, bid rigging, and failure to pay proper contributions to state workers' compensation funds. Greenberg felt that he had been personally betrayed and that his board had capitulated, sacrificing him along the way, before they understood the situation.

Similar outrage was targeted at directors once friendly to fallen HP CEO Carly Fiorina that she became furious even when constructive advice was privately offered. "She would not accept suggestions from anyone that didn't match what she wanted to hear," one former supporter on the board told us. Richard Hackborn, a skilled power broker on the HP board, was an enthusiastic supporter of Fiorina's and willingly stepped in with her as chairman, allowing Fiorina to push out the beloved Lew Platt, her predecessor. Although one of her most staunch defenders of the ill-fated Compaq merger, Hackborn was angrily rebuffed by Fiorina over his private concerns about the continued poor performance of HP and high executive turnover during her six years.[35]

Fiorina's own side of the conflict was revealed in her 2006 revenge book entitled *Tough Choices*. She claimed that Hackborn, along with Tom Perkins, George "Jay" Keyworth, and Dick Hackborn, were all board members with longtime ties to HP who loved to debate technology but when they wandered into other areas, they were disruptive and "they didn't know what they didn't know."[36] Fiorina admitted that she rebuffed a reorganization prescription suggested by the board, saying "From my perspective, their suggestions came out of left field and were half-baked," but was outraged to see a report in the *Wall Street Journal* that clearly showed that someone from the board had leaked her action to the public.

Meanwhile, the tragic saga took on new Shakespearean twists when Keyworth himself was quietly asked to leave the board for his alleged role in leaks continuing into 2006. Angry over this treatment of his friend Keyworth, Perkins himself quit, slamming down his briefcase as he exited. Months later, he launched an outraged public campaign protesting not only the treatment Keyworth had been subjected to but also the controversial, if not illegal, *pretexting* techniques used by investigators to obtain the phone records used to identify Keyworth as the accused leaker.[37] His primary target of vengeance was then board chairman Patricia Dunn; the results included Dunn's resignation from the board, which he haddesired, but also plenty of fresh humiliation for all—the resignation of Keyworth along with the exit of several senior HP executives, criminal charges by the State of California, Congressional investigations, and an SEC review, not to mention great damage to the image of the firm he loved at a time when its market performance ironically was soaring. Having addressed the board ourselves, we know this saga was not a straightforward Biblical morality story. Unlike the corporate scandals of the early part of the decade, this ordeal was not driven by anyone plundering shareholder wealth through financial fraud. Misguided execution of perhaps inconsistent good intentions, as well as spiraling fury and revenge, created plenty of losers and no winners.

There is a disappointment and forceful sense of righteousness that often leads imperiled executives to fail to reinforce the bridges to allies who can help them. Driven by indiscriminate rage, they fail to distinguish between those whom they can trust in an inner circle and those who are genuine threats to their survival. Unbridled rage can resemble a childlike response to frustrations with realities and lead to dysfunctional consequences.

Debilitating Shame

A fourth reason we do not embrace setbacks is that the victims feel ashamed. They may feel liable for the losses to their family and to those coworkers they feel they have let down. They believe, often correctly, that without their business card, they are worth less to others around them. They view failure as a personal deficiency and not an injustice in the workplace.

When TV's Fox News business anchor Neil Cavuto was diagnosed with multiple sclerosis, his thoughts quickly turned to how to deal with his wife, Mary:

> To this day, I don't know what thoughts went through Mary's head when I was first diagnosed with cancer, or what she thought when we first learned about my MS. All I kept thinking was that Mary was once again getting the ever-short end of the marriage stick. When the priest said "in sickness or in health," I don't think she knew what she was signing up for![38]

Next he thought of what to say to his boss, Roger Ailes, reflecting that despite their friendship,

I was still very worried. MS was another matter entirely and business was business. As CEO, Roger had responsibilities that far outweighed our friendship and understandably so. It was easy to understand why it would be in the best interests of Fox for Roger to let me go. His cable channel was successful, but only a year old, building but not yet established, with a start-up's inherent risk of failure. Why would he want to stick with me? I couldn't think of any good business reasons. Treatments alone would take me out of work from time to time. And after I'd finished them, the progressive, degenerative nature of my illness would make my absence more frequent, and my symptoms more visible and debilitating—on daily television.[39]

Cavuto thus thought, "Just don't tell them at work—don't tell anybody. They'll be none the wiser."[37] However, his "panic-stricken" memories of how badly this worked previously at PBS in 1987 when he fought Hodgkin's disease in secrecy led him later to share his plight with Ailes, who turned out to be a very understanding, supportive boss.

Denial and Diversion

A fifth pitfall for victims of failure is that they wrongly believe that they can disguise their defeat by superficial wordsmithery. Does anyone really believe that the intensively competitive and ambitious former Enron CEO Jeffrey Skilling actually quit six months into the job to "focus on family matters"? Similarly, two weeks before being ousted as HP's CEO Carly Fiorina met with journalists at the World Economic Forum in Davos, Swizerland, claiming that relations were good with the board and that "since the merger of Compaq Computer and HP in 2002, our competitive position has improved in every dimension."[40] While competitors like Dell and IBM soared in market share, new products, and market value, HP was mired in dissension and a stock price that was half what it was when she arrived six years earlier. In fact, when HP dramatically missed its own fiscal projections for the third quarter of 2004, Fiorina fired three top executives rather than blame herself.

Research suggests that people with high self-esteem often display a self-enhancement bias in that they believe they excel at many things, and they are determined that others recognize the fine qualities that they believe they possess. These higher-self-esteem people tend to want to showcase their good points and their strengths, to stand out from others. People with lower self-esteem are more likely to present themselves in less flattering ways, focusing on weaknesses and failures. Ironically, lower-self-esteem individuals are sometimes better prepared for failure because they are more likely to have expected adverse events and even to have prepared by perhaps devaluing the opportunity.[41] Higher-self-esteem people, however, are more focused on augmenting the perceptions others have of their strengths and will use more self-enhancing language that often attempts to deny failure. When the language explanations used by fallen high-self-esteem individuals is not credible or convincing, they are surprised and frustrated.

Thus the persistence of the proverbial and always unconvincing "resigned to pursue other interests." Victims of failure may believe that they can control speculation or that no one else really knows what happened. Even in situations of burnout and plateauing, this desire to sweep the obvious facts under the carpet is common.[42] No one is fooled by these desperate impression management efforts to bury the truth. Nonetheless, victims cling to the pathetic hope that if they hide under the covers, perhaps the monsters will go away. Friends may encourage this inadvertently by suggesting, "Why bring attention to this? Fewer people know than you think." The reality is that those you may most fear knowing about the setback will either know already or become immediately aware the moment you are a candidate at their doorstep.

The Embarrassment of Others

Frequently, those around a victim do not know how to respond, and the victim feels they must do things to help the well-wisher cope with the situation. Thus, ironically, rather than assist the victim with his or her suffering, they actually add to it. Twice one of us saw close friends struggling with brain cancer receive well-intended visitors soon after surgery. Each time, the patient found awkward friends assuming unwelcome roles as cheerleaders offering annoying platitudes on recovery that minimized the challenges before the victim. Banal comments like "You look better already" or "You'll be out of here in two weeks" rang hollow and seemed to do more harm than good. In fact, one especially maladroit visitor, the boss of one of these cancer victims a decade ago and the dean of a business school, had the misguided thought that he should tell the sufferer of a plan to raise money from the patient's associates, in the name of the patient, for an endowed chair to support fellow junior faculty members with common interests in technology management! Needless to say, the patient, hoping to win the painful battle for life, was not flattered by this plan to immortalize his name by drawing on the generosity of his wealthy friends.

Friends and associates of victims frequently practice face-saving techniques similar to impression management in the use of personal denial statements, as described in the previous section. As psychologist Erving Goffman found forty years ago, it is often more comfortable not only for the victim to maintain a front that denies the reality but also for others around the victim.[43] Hence, they commonly advise victims of distress to practice avoidance tactics, which rarely repair the problem. They offer diversionary recommendations with Polonius-like clichés such as "Move on! Don't wallow in your misery!" Such personal advice surely hampers the victim's attempt to analyze what has happened, to plan appropriate next steps. Similarly, they say, "Take a vacation. You need a break from the stress," while in reality the victim rationally may need to understand and even confront the source the stress.

Time Warner co-CEO Nick Nicholas was sabotaged by his colleague Jerry Levin while away skiing in Vail. The aspiring Levin cleverly approached the other co-CEO, Steven Ross, the former Warner Brothers CEO, who owned a large share of the combined enterprise. Ross was dying of prostate cancer and concerned about his legacy. By exacerbating the friction between the two CEOs, Levin maneuvered to have Nicholas fired and to take his place. First he secured Ross's support, thus gaining twelve of the twenty-three directors.

On February 19, 1992, a Time Warner director called Nicholas in Vail to tell him that his twenty-eight-year career was over. A decade later, Nicholas was still astounded at how smoothly Levin, with only half the votes behind him, convinced supporters of Nicholas that it was a done deal. Dick Munro, Nicholas's predecessor, reflected recently that when Levin came to him for his support, "I remember being stunned. It was done. It was over. He wasn't looking for my approval; it was just a courtesy call." Munro added, "I've often reflected on what I should have done or could have done. There are times when you wished you had behaved differently and that was one of those times: I have always felt deep down in my soul I should have done something to save Nick. But it was too late; it was over." [44] As we visited with Nicholas in his office in early 1993, we witnessed several of these directors, including the revered Jewel Tea CEO Don Perkins and Munro, call in, complaining how poorly Levin was performing and how much they missed having Nicholas. Nicholas thanked them with sincere-sounding appreciation. Nicholas then smiled to us as he hung up the speakerphone and commented in a bittersweet tone, "Thanks, guys; where were you last year?"

Lack of Resources for Battle

Ironically, sometimes the more humble a person's origins, the easier they find it to assemble the resources needed for battle. A campaign for image restoration can soak up a great deal of financial and emotional resources. It may require the direct courtship of skeptical investors, amassing legal armament, convincing influential political forces, affiliation with credible third parties, or having the personal courage to start over. Ironically, those born to wealth or prominence often feel this weakness especially keenly, compared to "self-made" people accustomed to tenacious battle. Not having scraped for crumbs of support before, they may be fearful of taking risks now that may leave them hungry. People like media and domestic arts entrepreneur Martha Stewart who have climbed a ladder of success from humble beginnings are more confident of starting over if they lose their footing.

Accordingly, the roller-coaster career of former AOL Time Warner president Robert Pittman seemed to help prepare him for future challenges. Pittman, the son of a Mississippi Methodist preacher, lost his eye at age six when he was kicked by a horse that threw him. He suggested that this loss made him work harder to be accepted. "If you have an artificial eye, you're different. The dream of every kid is to fit in and be like all the other kids." [45] Thus, to prove himself, he pursued interests that relied on good vision, like fly fishing and aviation. He even earned a waiver from the Federal Aviation Administration allowing him to fly despite his artificial eye. Moving from a local radio station as a highly spirited disc jockey, he took a job as a DJ in Pittsburgh, which led him to the become program manager of WMAQ; he lifted it from twenty-second place to third in its market. At age twenty-three, he then moved to WNBC as program director and made it the nation's number-one radio station. By 1981, he had launched the pioneering MTV cable network, modeled on radio programming, as part of Warner-Amex Satellite Entertainment Company. He then tried independent production, backed, in part, by Warner's Steve Ross. When that failed, he returned to the Warner family, and after the 1990 merger with Time, he ran Time Warner Enterprises, where he persuaded Ross to buy the Six Flags theme parks. Undaunted by the challenge of running the theme parks and related stores, Pittman once called us asking for a tutorial on such basic retail terms as *the cost of goods sold* and *SKUs*.

During a partial divestiture of that business, Time Warner CEO Jerry Levin and president Dick Parsons fired Pittman. By 1995, the former wunderkind was now forty-two years old and unemployed. He then took over as CEO of residential real estate company Century 21 before moving over within a year to America Online as president. Improbably, he again joined up with Levin and Parsons as co-COO following the AOL Time Warner merger in 2000. After being pushed out again two years later, Pittman spent roughly a year in seclusion with his family before emerging to relaunch his career, running the Pilot Group, a private equity fund targeting small media properties. Always the optimist, he retained a good deal of Time Warner stock, believing that Parsons would make the enterprise work. As one of his friends commented to author Nina Munk, "When it rains, this boy says it's sunny."[46]

The Double-Edged Sword of Celebrity

The more career successes someone has and the more prominent they become in their profession or their industry, the more widely known will be their setback. As we mentioned earlier, financial researchers Ulrike Malmendier of Stanford and Geoffrey Tate of Wharton have concluded that celebrity CEOs are likely to suffer diminished performance three years after winning awards from magazines and appearing on their covers.[47] Fame can actually morph into infamy. The abrupt transition often hits accomplished people especially hard. Literary scholar Leo Braudy wrote in *The Frenzy of Renown* that many people seek or endure public recognition in the belief that fame will liberate them from the shackles of conventionality and the dangers of powerlessness.[48] No one ever called Alexander III of Macedonia Alexander the Great until he coined the label himself and created a false lineage to Achilles and Odysseus. In the mid-1960s, psychologists called a leader's right to a buffer from conventionality "idiosyncrasy credits."[49] Whatever coveted cushion of material comfort there may be in attaining celebrity status, the fall from great heights is only more painful. The recovery process is more complicated as well.

One challenge for celebrities is the envy of others. When Martha Stewart was sentenced in the summer of 2004, a feeding frenzy of critics, ranging from the *New York Post*'s Christopher Byron to the *Wall Street Journal*'s Charles Gasparino (now at CNBC), vociferously but wrongly continued to proclaim her firm's imminent demise. The intensity of their antipathy came off as a bit of schadenfreude, or gloating over her misfortune.[50] In fact, on Friday, July 16, 2004, the day after Stewart's sentencing, seven cable TV shows and three network shows devoted their evening coverage to this event. The most hostile panel that night appeared on CNN's *Paula Zahn Now*. People such as journalists Gasparino and Byron (the fortunate author of the hostile but underwhelming book *Martha Inc.*, published in 2002) and self-described brand expert Robert Passikoff all gleefully pronounced her demise and the collapse of the company, having predicted it in their earlier writings.[51] It often seemed as if ad executive Jerry Della Femina and we were the only believers in the firm's recovery. The more her company and her career rebounded, the angrier some critics seemed to become. By the time Stewart was released from her five-month prison term in February 2005, the company's stock soared fourfold, she announced the launch of two major TV shows picked up by networks as a series, and her business was resurgent. While magazines ran mea culpa covers like *Newsweek*'s entitled "Martha's Last Laugh: After Prison, She's Thinner, Wealthier and Ready for Prime Time," it is no surprise that her most strident but now disappointed critics neglected to address their fateful predictions.[52]

Similarly, with each public career misfortune, Jim Cramer—the highly successful former hedge fund manager, financial journalist at CNBC, and founder of TheStreet.com—attracted flocks of gloating peers. As he suffered a series of injustices, gleeful antagonists seized the opportunity for condemnation, regardless of the facts. Once, when he wrote for the magazine *Smart Money* on "orphan stocks," the editors neglected to print his customary disclosure of related stock holdings. Cramer was condemned by rivals even though his editors admitted their error, even though he did not sell the stocks in question in any sort of "pump and dump" scheme, and even though he was exonerated in an SEC investigation of this matter.[53] In 2002, a disgruntled former employee who had been terminated for poor performance authored a scandal-mongering book that inspired a vocal chorus of long-standing adversaries, such as a reported early-career abusive boss of Cramer's and the short-lived editor of a competing journal.[54] Once again, the critics' voices were silent when the red-faced publisher of the book, Harper-Business, had to recall thousands of printed copies in the first month and destroy them, acknowledging the book's false accusations.[55]

The Myth of Self-Reliance

Fifteen years ago, Harvard leadership scholar John Kotter revealed that a critical element of great leadership is acknowledging interdependencies through embracing and aligning your reliance upon others.[56] In his book *Organizing Genius*, leadership scholar Warren Bennis also critiqued American society's misleading focus on rugged individualism.[57] He identified the critical nature of the interdependencies between great leaders and great groups while studying the golden days of the original animation team at Walt Disney Studios, the scientific energy of the Manhattan Project, the creativity unleashed by Lockheed Martin's legendary maverick Skunk Works, and other such endeavors:

> *The myth of the triumphant individual is deeply engrained in the American psyche. Whether it is midnight rider Paul Revere or basketball's Michael Jordan in the 1990s, we are a nation enamored of heroes—rugged self-starters who meet challenges and overcome adversity. Our contemporary views of leadership are intertwined with our notions of heroes, so much so that the distinction between "leader" and "hero" (or "celebrity," for that matter) often becomes blurred. In our society, leadership is too often seen as an inherently individual phenomenon . . . And yet we all know that cooperation and collaboration grow more important every day.[58]*

In reality, this collaborative approach to overcoming adversity is not new to the American success saga, it has just been underappreciated. In TV shows from *Dallas*, with its J. R. Ewing, to Donald Trump's *The Apprentice*, the emphasis is on the triumph of the individual gunslinger. The actual spirit of American success celebrates courageous entrepreneurs who push the frontiers, but also the enthusiastic supportive group when things go wrong. From the courageous wagon trains of settlers driving westward, to the Grange movement's agrarian cooperation in farm life, to the bootstrapping successes of ethnic urban ghettos, all celebrate the collective triumph over adversity.

Many prominent figures do not like the uncomfortable position of being on the receiving end of advice, as opposed to giving advice. Rather than happily deciding they are now receiving payback after a career of giving to others, they often believe that seeing or accepting advice, borrowing credibility, and accepting financial support from other parties makes them look and feel weaker. Relying more on the generosity of others, they need to shift from familiar power bases like formal authority or positional power, coercion through influence, or the control of valued resources to power bases such as past earned respect and legitimacy, referent power, the sense of obligation of friends, and the identification and empathy some will have for your suffering.

Fallen HP CEO Carly Fiorina, for example, clearly saw it as a sign of weakness to ask for help from her troops and to accept the advice of concerned and supportive board members as her performance faltered and her control slipped. When we warned the brilliant co-CEO of Time Warner Nick Nicholas about the likely unwieldy and destructive "monarch-like" motives of his aging, ill, and forceful co-CEO Steven Ross and the need to fortify his board relations, he laughed, saying that a smooth succession process was in the works, relying on good faith and merit to win the day.

By contrast, Roger Enrico assumed the reins of PepsiCo following his early-career marketing triumph of the Pepsi Challenge against Coke and after completing a masterful turnaround in the Frito-Lay snack foods division. He soon began preparing to divest the restaurant group, which had been assembled by one of his adored mentors, of such chains as Taco Bell, Pizza Hut, and KFC while also discovering massive ethical and operational problems in their international business. One of Enrico's first moves was to call on Craig Weatherup, a rival for the CEO job who was preparing to take an early retirement, and ask him to help lead the international cleanup because he and Pepsi desperately needed Weatherup's legendary quiet integrity and balanced leadership skills. Soon after Weatherup's great results on this project, Enrico rewarded Weatherup with a genuine CEO position as head of the newly spun-off Pepsi Bottling Group, with his own headquarters in Somers, New York, not under the shadows of PepsiCo in Purchase, New York.

Anne Mulcahy took the helm as CEO of Xerox in 2000, at the lowest point in its history, following dramatic market share losses, obsolete core product technology, and scandalized predecessors admitting to revenue recognition inaccuracies that caused multibillion-dollar financial restatements. She said in conversation with us in January 2005, "By the time I was made president of Xerox in 2000, everything was coming unraveled at once, revenue was declining, we were losing major customers, cash was shrinking, we were told we had $120 million but couldn't find it, employees were discouraged and leaving, our stock price was cut in half, and we had a widespread SEC investigation . . . I should say that when one takes over the top job, you should say this was the fulfillment of a lifelong dream. I wondered if they gave it to me because no one else wanted it."[59]

Mulcahy's turnaround of Xerox began quickly, with strong cash flow by the end of 2001, $1 billion in profits after racking up hundreds of millions of dollars of losses in the prior year, billions of expenses cut (including one-third of the workforce) with market capitalization now up $7 billion, debt cut in half, and a surprisingly strong return to innovation with now over two-thirds of the products under five years old—all this in a compassionate, nonarbitrary way. "As a twenty-eight-year Xerox employee, I knew I needed help from industry analysts, bankers, investors, customers, and employees. We needed honest and direct data so we needed to be good listeners. Often we learned that the more obvious problems obscured more fundamental issues."

Rather than indulging in the vanity of hobnobbing with fellow CEOs and giving slickly orchestrated formulaic presentations at celebrity-drenched events, she rolled up her sleeves to learn, ask for trust, and share her vision. To obtain the "quick accurate assessments" she sought, she began a commitment of traveling one hundred thousand miles a year, visiting every major Xerox facility (roughly two hundred locations), and each week seeing at least a half dozen major customers. Her honest descriptions of problems won her worried employees over. In one location, a worker on the manufacturing floor spoke up in front of the crowd to compliment her bad-news discussion, saying, "It is so good to hear that *you* know how bad things are around here." Mulcahy said credibility was key to her ability to resurrect Xerox, and this would not come about through misleading pep talks that "did not ring true."

As she traveled, she made mistakes and admitted them. For example, in October 2000, five months after she became president of Xerox, she admitted to Wall Street analysts that the company's core business model was "unsustainable." While she moved on to explain the restructuring plan to shift technologies and avoid bankruptcy, analysts focused only on her unfortunate term "unsustainable," and almost immediately the market value fell by 60 percent. Mulcahy told us, laughing at herself, "This was not my finest hour!" She has since learned to be careful with her terms but still does not compromise her directness and integrity. Accordingly, the stock rebounded quickly.

Reputation Restoration: Learning About Failure to Rebuild Success

Leadership books abound with simple recipes for success. They flaunt titles featuring everyone from the *Star Wars* characters to Attila the Hun and the many bromides from successful sports figures. As the TV shows fade away and the records of the sports figures slip, the titles disappear from bookshelves, only to be replaced with new cliché-drenched success pronouncements. True transformational leadership is enhanced through experience with adversity. In fact, many venture capital firms search for this experience with failure in people's backgrounds. Yet, the popular writings, breezy self-help business books, and general teachings on leadership seem to largely underplay this insight.

A long-standing best-selling Harvard Business School case study of the visionary transformational airline entrepreneur Don Burr of People Express has all but disappeared from classrooms after his pioneering enterprise was forced to sell out in distress. The firm had made a few bad calls in finances, postmerger operating challenges, confronting competitors' technological leaps, changing consumer preferences, and possible predatory competitive pricing. The lessons of this great social enterprise are all the more valuable now—not because we do not know what led to an unchallenged success, but because the limits of the system were tested. Unfortunately, these lessons are ignored by most business schools.

Accordingly, one of us found it nearly impossible to teach the great Ibsen play *An Enemy of the People* to success-oriented Harvard MBA students because the hero challenged the system, and then . . . *failed*. After the hero revealed that the town's water supply for spas was polluted, this news destroyed the town's revenue base—its medicinal natural spas—and his own neighbors forced him out of town. The lessons of recovery are hard to locate because of our discomfort in looking into the phenomenon of failure.

Reputations can be rebuilt only after we know the source of failure. Reputations include elements of external image and personal identity, and their repair requires the examination of each.[60] Genuine folk heroes achieved their greatness not through unbroken chains of success but rather through reflections on failure that give rise to the needed directions for resilience. The anthropologist Joseph Campbell has provided us with the core building blocks of robust recovery and written stories of folk heroism. Whether the leader was Moses, Jesus, Mohammed, Buddha, Odysseus, Aeneas, Cuchulain, or Tezcatlipoca, the great folk heroes were of humble origins. They then followed a dream to slay some dragons and were rewarded with a series of glorious missions that led to a chain of success, thus overcoming devastating setback. This is what led to their celebration as transformational or heroic leaders.[61]

More recently, Howard Gardner's study of great historical figures, *Extraordinary Minds*, similarly identified a set of common qualities that described his "influencers."[60] Gardner did not believe that core intelligence, lucky breaks, or even an untiring spirit were the factors that made a difference. Instead, he suggested that the great figures he chronicled possessed a candid appraisal of their own strengths and weaknesses, were effective at keen analysis of unique situations, and mastered the capacity to reframe past setbacks into future successes. The crushing nature of defeat did not deflate them but rather energized them to reengage with even greater gusto for their adventures. In addition, it was not the magnitude of the setback that set these people apart. It, instead, was how brilliantly they managed to reconstrue their losses.

Historical business figures such as Ross Perot, Edward Land of Polaroid, Henry Ford, and Thomas Edison remind us of the catalyzing force of failure. Ross Perot endured a great loss in 1974 when two Wall Street investment houses he owned collapsed—yet his greatest political, technological, and financial triumphs still lay in the future. Both of Henry Ford's first two automobile ventures, the Detroit Automobile Company in 1899 and the Henry Ford Motor Company in 1900, were market and financial failures. Polaroid founder Edward Land once told us how bitterly he fought crushing patent infringements by Kodak several times in his career. Even the brilliant wizard Thomas Edison had been profoundly outmaneuvered by tycoon Jay Gould. Edison lost the rights for substantial telegraphic inventions.

The later history of such business failures shows that such setbacks could be empowering rather than paralyzing events in the lives of these storied leaders. In this chapter, we have considered how our fascination with success leads us to avoid an understanding of how to learn from failure. We also looked at the common barriers to examining failures. These were largely dispositional—that is, something about the character of the suffering victim. In the next chapter, we will look more at the context of failure, helping to answer the question, Is the fault within me or is it "them"?

The great circus aerialist Karl Wallenda said in 1968, "Life is being on the wire, everything else is just waiting." He loved the thrill of his death-defying show. Wallenda fell to his death in 1978 at the age of seventy-three in downtown San Juan, Puerto Rico, walking along a seventy-five-foot high wire. Shortly afterward, his wife eerily reflected, "All Karl thought about for three straight months prior to this walk was not falling. It was the first time he'd ever thought about that, and it seemed to me that he put all of his energies into not falling rather than walking the tightrope."[63]

CHAPTER 4

Corporate Cultures as Barriers to Recovery

You don't understand: Willy was a salesman. And for a salesman, there is no rock bottom to the life. He don't put a bolt to a nut, he don't tell you the law or give you medicine. He's a man way out there in the blue, riding on a smile and a shoeshine. And when they start not smiling back—that's an earthquake. And then you get yourself a couple of spots on your hat, and you're finished. Nobody dast blame this man. A salesman is got to dream, boy. It comes with the territory.

—From "Death of a Salesman" by Arthur Miller

IN THE PRIOR CHAPTERS, we first outlined, in chapter 1, a model for overcoming adversity, with examples of successful leaders who employed these approaches. In chapter 2, we examined the psychological anchoring of the five elements of this model, looking at decades of studies into the nature of adversity and human behavior. In chapter 3, we looked at how Western society's fascination with success and fear of failure leads us to miss the lessons of setbacks. Now, in chapter 4, we will continue to move from within the individual psyche, where we began, to more fully consider conditions in the external context of careers that make comebacks so difficult. In particular, chapter 4 considers how, in the corporate world, industrial and professional subcultures create distinctly different challenges.

The preceding reflections on the life of Willy Loman, a fictional burned-out sixty-year-old salesman who committed suicide in Arthur Miller's celebrated 1949 play *Death of a Salesman*, provide a chilling vantage point on the specter of failure that can haunt a career salesman. Loman took his life after struggling with a faltering career of missed opportunity and living in Brooklyn far from the soaring dreams and striving he had since his youth. Now frustrated with his lack of success and the under-achievement of his once promising adult sons, he felt tremendous defeat. Only his loyal wife, Linda, seemed to appreciate his emotional quicksand:

> *I don't say he's a great man. Willy Loman never made a lot of money. His name was never in the paper. He's not the finest character that ever lived. But he's a human being, and a terrible thing is happening to him. So attention must be paid. He's not to be allowed to fall into his grave like an old dog. Attention, attention must be finally paid to such a person.*

Such lack of attention was not Miller's lament himself. By the time of his death over a half century after this play, Miller had written twenty-five plays—several, such as *The Crucible*, earning almost equal recognition to *Death of a Salesman*, winning three Tonys, Emmys, and the Pulitzer Prize—along with influential essays and major film scripts. Long before his death at age eighty-nine in 2005, he was widely recognized as one of America's greatest playwrights, along with Eugene O'Neill and Tennessee Williams.

At the same time, as with virtually all creative figures, he was still haunted by the specter of failure. The prosperity of his early childhood ended in the stock market crash of 1929, which wiped out his father's clothing business. Miller's family left their spacious Manhattan apartment for a crowded flat in the Gravesend section of Brooklyn similar to the setting of his great play. As with characters in his plays, his academically gifted elder brother sacrificed his educational dreams in a futile effort to save the family business. Miller's initial efforts in the theater were not successful. His first six plays were rejected. In 1944, his first Broadway production, ironically titled *The Man Who Had All the Luck*, was canceled after only four performances. In 1947, Miller's final stab at a life in the theater, his play *All My Sons*, enjoyed an extended run. Throughout his career, Miller's writing continued to reveal the destructive side of the American Dream, but paradoxically, as the son of an Eastern European immigrant, he modeled the promise of that dream. In fact, to some, his iconic marriage to film star Marilyn Monroe symbolized the attainment of that dream.

While he remained productive through his last full year of life, the momentum was not sustained. As one prominent and enthusiastic theater critic commented,

> *Few of his later plays met with critical or popular favor. After his success with "Sons" and "Salesman," Miller was attacked by conservative writers for his politics in the '50s and abandoned by most of the critical establishment . . . As with most major American writers, high regard gave way to a period of critical neglect and hostility, which—in Miller's case— roughly coincided with the same arc in the career of his contemporary, Tennessee Williams.*[1]

A *New York Times* obituary summarized the reason Miller resented critics throughout his career:

> *Mr. Miller's antipathy was understandable. At one moment he was hailed as the greatest living playwright, and at another as a has-been whose greatest successes were decades behind him. Even at the height of his success, Mr. Miller's work received harsh criticism from some prominent critics. Eric Bentley, the drama critic for* The New Republic *in the 1950's, dismissed "The Crucible," writing, "The world has made this author important before he has made himself great."*[2]

It may seem inconceivable that so prominent a literary figure as Arthur Miller could ever be burdened with the yoke of public assessments, but the fleeting nature of fame is especially fragile in the "What have you done for us lately?" sense of immediacy for such worlds as the arts and entertainment. Actor-director Orson Welles could never reprise such youthful contributions as his *Mercury Theatre on the Air* triumph "The War of the Worlds" and his historic film *Citizen Kane*. Most of the world never heard from J. D. Salinger for the next fifty years of his life after he wrote the coming-of-age classic *The Catcher in the Rye*.

Similarly, in his late twenties and thirties, Alan Jay Lerner wrote such Broadway classics as *Brigadoon, Paint Your Wagon, Gigi, My Fair Lady*, and *Camelot*. By his late fifties and sixties, he had almost become resentful of his early career success because it had come to suffocate his creative genius. He felt his chief competitor and censor was the lingering image of his younger self: "The older a writer gets, the harder it is for him to write. This is not because his brain slows down: it is because his critical faculties grow more acute. If you're young, you have a sense of omnipotence. You're sure you're brilliant. Even if youth is secretly frightened, it assumes an outer assurance and plows through whatever it is."[3]

There are many fields, such as entertainment, the fashion industry, new technologies, and consulting, where success is also defined far more in the present. In many other occupations, such as the management of large, more stable industries, early career accomplishment leads to a fast-track trajectory and legacy that continues to pay back in later-life rewards.

Occupational cultures vary widely. Comebacks in all industries are possible, but the challenges vary by the leadership norms of each industry's culture. Fallen retailers have different comeback challenges than software executives who stumbled. Despite comeback efforts and tearful contrition, disgraced televangelists like Jimmy Swaggart and Jim Bakker never regained the forceful pulpits they were forced to abandon. Meanwhile, other clergy, such as Charles Stanley, have survived public controversy and turbulence in their personal lives. Some retailers, like Bernie Marcus of the The Home Depot, Tom Stemberg of Staples, and John Eyler of Toys "R" Us, made it back for even greater triumphs, while others, like Kmart's Joseph Antonini, never resurfaced after their dismissals. The careers of Continental's Frank Lorenzo, Eastern's Frank Borman, United's Richard Ferris, and Delta's Ron Allen were grounded, while David Neeleman of JetBlue, Don Burr of People Express, and Hollis Harris of Continental found new routes to success in aviation. The reason why some were able to come back while others floundered is that comebacks were possible when the failures did not destroy the distinctive leadership qualities of the culture of an industry. In this chapter, we will look across industries ranging from financial services and media to transportation, retail, and manufacturing to reveal how the culture of an industry often defines success, career mobility, failure, and recovery in very different ways.

Defining Success by Corporate Culture

In some occupational cultures, those who move across many employers are considered lost, peripatetic, opportunistic job hoppers unable to make a commitment. By contrast, other occupational cultures may consider a stable, long-service employee to be stagnant, plateaued, obsolete, or deadwood. The same person can be glowingly classified as the proverbial "brilliant rocket scientist" in one culture but a "self-absorbed showboat" in another. Corporate culture is surely one of the most overworked and trivialized business terms when used in common parlance. But when anthropologists study culture, they look at the physical artifacts, the underlying norms and values, and the fundamental assumptions and beliefs about how things should work. Underneath all this, anthropologists look at how membership in a given society is determined. It is on this cultural dimension of membership that we will focus.

The artifacts of culture give us clues about what is most appreciated and valued. When we wander into an office building, we can learn a great deal by the interaction encouraged by the use of common spaces like egalitarian cafeterias open to all or elegant executive dining rooms for private sessions. Office arrangements such as who merits the window views, how open the space is, and the location of different departments can convey notions of status and interdependence. At United Parcel Service (UPS), for example, there has never been a private executive dining room since its founding in 1907. The CEOs and top leadership eat sitting side by side with all other employees daily in the same cafeteria in a low-key setting that straddles a natural stream. The building is nestled in a forest and sits quietly below the tree line on the northern edge of Atlanta. By contrast, at the center of the same town, Coca-Cola's top brass enjoy a luxurious private dining room that offers unobstructed views overlooking the city and is perched atop their office tower (which is adorned by a huge lit Coke logo), with the employee cafeteria thirty stories below them.

Norms and beliefs are studied through informal methods such as reading the literature of a culture, charting its history, and listening to its myths as well as through formal methods like looking at rewards systems and promotions processes. Thus, we can look at corporate annual reports, hiring materials, and promotional media for clues to the culture. What does the firm proclaim in its mission statement, and which objectives seem to drive the business? Who seems to get ahead through what career tracks? Are short-term objectives given heavier weight in performance reviews and incentives than longer-term goals? Second-guessing your boss in the military is a risky business because obedient respect for the chain of command is critical for execution and safety. At Wal-Mart, a boss who learns that his employee has circumvented him with a complaint taken to the boss's boss is taught to not only avoid vindictiveness but to go out of his way to thank and praise the employee for their concern.

Underlying assumptions can be best studied by living in the culture through what anthropologists call *ethnographic studies*. There you can see what the fundamental theories of justice and the timetables for measuring results may be. While a TV broadcaster measures success by daily viewership based upon recent programming decisions, a forest products company or pharmaceutical company might be more oriented toward the payout of longer-term investments, given the time it takes to grow a tree or develop a new drug.

The leadership cultures of firms across industries can be classified into four rough clusters determined by where we get people and how they are given assignments and training. The flow of leadership talent through organizations, then, is driven by two questions: where does an employer find the talent (*supply flow*), and what does an employer do with job assignments once they locate the talent (*development flow*)? The first question revolves around the classic "make versus buy" trade-off. Some firms tend to look within their enterprise to find talent as a preferred course, while others prefer to find fresh outside candidates for leadership roles when they become available. Economists would question whether the firm was relying upon an internal or an external labor market for leadership talent.[4] The second dynamic, development flow, considers whether job assignments are the result of company-sponsored movement led by mentors and central plans or self-initiated moves led by a tournament style of advancement, where a winnowing pool of internal competitors rises to the next round of contests.[5] Those with sponsored movement more often tend to reward loyalty, seniority, and group contributions over time. These cultures produce generalists. Firms with tournament-like approaches produce specialists. These firms focus on more immediate individualistic accomplishment and meritocratic measurement, such as sales figures, patents, and credentials, which are attributes of an individual rather than a group or the total enterprise.

These two dimensions, leadership supply and leadership assignment, can be squared off to create a four-cell typology, as depicted in figure 4-1.

The top-right quadrant is *baseball team*. These highly competitive businesses are constantly scouting the outside labor market for the hottest, freshest talent. Their strategic objective is to be a prospector for new ideas because they fundamentally sell novelty, new ideas, fads, fashion, and fast-breaking technologies. Research has classified most firms in industries like entertainment, advertising, investment banking, consulting, biotech, software, and law as often showing elements of baseball team cultures.[6] Baseball team–like firms must excel at recruiting the hottest new talent and tend to invest less on internal training and grooming. As Microsoft founder Bill Gates said to us in April 2005, "We are constantly looking for the best new ideas and bring that talent into the company."[7] Strategy researchers Raymond Miles and Charles Snow have termed such firms *prospectors*.[8]

FIGURE 4-1

A typology of career systems

	Fortress	Baseball team
External	Human resource orientation: retrenchment	Human resource orientation: recruitment
	Strategic model: reactor	Strategic model: prospector
	Typical competitive strategy: cost	Typical competitive strategy: focus based on human skills
	Club	**Academy**
Internal	Human resource orientation: retention	Human resource orientation: development
	Strategic model: defender	Strategic model: analyzer
	Typical competitive strategy: noncompetitive	Typical competitive strategy: differentiation

Supply flow

Generalist ◄————————————————————► Specialist

Assignment flow

Given the risk-seeking culture of these edgy enterprises, disappointments are a way of life. Indeed, these firms have by far the highest turnover.[9] In fact, when people leave a baseball team firm, 85 percent of them return to the excitement of another baseball team. When careers hit walls or when companies fail, it is considered normal in baseball team firms rather than classified as the failure it might be perceived as elsewhere. With a strong emphasis on educational credentials and measurable personal contributions—from sales volume to research patents—there is a belief in meritocracy. The goal of a person who fails is to show that their narrow professional expertise is still fresh and on the frontier of their field so that failure is attributed to rapid external changes in technology, the anxiety of uninformed financial backers, or the fickle interests of customers rather than internal know-how. When leaders slip up in a baseball team, this must be conveyed as a temporary setback from taking worthwhile risks that did not pan out in a highly uncertain environment.

In the top-left box we refer to *fortresses*, those firms whose strategic mission is a struggle for survival. They may be in an acute state of distress, such as bankruptcy. They may be in a highly competitive industry with high costs and diminished margins, such as airlines. Alternatively, they may be in industries with implicit volatility from cyclical or structural changes, such as retailing or extracting natural resources like forest products or metals. Miles and Snow have termed such firms *reactors* because they have little control over their context.

These firms recruit generalists as outside hired troubleshooters but do not expect long service following a successful turnaround. Given the risks of turnaround, someone who fails in this context can recover from a career setback by demonstrating competence in their broad portfolio of skills. Furthermore, it is important to show that the failure was not due to a lapse in personal integrity. Given the contentious trade-offs made in the fortress context, there are frequently hostile constituencies, including creditors, customers, employees, and shareholders. Trust is a vital attribute that must be demonstrated to convince various stakeholders that decisions were reached through a just process. Our research on Harvard MBAs ten years after graduation shows that when executives leave a fortress, many (roughly 40 percent) will actually choose to return to a fortress because they have become comfortable with the turnaround culture.[10] Thus some, as turnaround specialists, have even made the experience of failure an asset since they can demonstrate that they are not afraid of adversity and have found their way back. This can be reassuring to investors and employees.

Academies tend to recruit early-career for "entry-level" positions and promote from within along functional pipelines. The turnover in academies is far less than at baseball teams and fortresses. These firms value expertise, but of a sort that tends to be more company-specific wisdom. This creates a distinct competitive edge for the firms in industries such as consumer products, electronics, and pharmaceuticals. Academies have more than a third less turnover, with complex career ladders of expertise and departmental boundaries. This allows for a strong reliance upon internal labor markets as in firms with highly competitive tournaments for promotion. These firms tend to offer far more internal training to their executives, and their alumni often populate the leadership of other firms. Thus, firms such as General Electric, Procter & Gamble, IBM, Johnson & Johnson, and the *Washington Post* are examples of academies that have served as training grounds for many great leaders. In fact, at one point in their careers, GE's Jeff Immelt, Microsoft's Steve Ballmer, eBay's Meg Whitman, and AOL's Steve Case all worked for Procter & Gamble.

Nonetheless, people's careers can get in quicksand in that cross-functional moves become more difficult over time. A critical challenge in overcoming adversity in an academy is to recognize that your career has possibly been sidelined. This used to be called "the penalty box" at IBM. Those leaving an academy must convincingly show that their skills are generalizable beyond what worked back at GE, IBM, Pepsi, P&G, and so on, and show that they are not just dependent on past "house knowledge" or the particular unique elements of their old culture. Trying to replicate their old lost culture is a common trap for such leaders. In particular, those who leave for leadership roles in a feisty baseball team or a struggling fortress will need to demonstrate skills of self-reliance since they will not have the same depth of support structures they enjoyed in their world.

Clubs have traditionally offered relatively secure career trajectories. They cultivate the humble, devoted service of functional generalists willing to move across departments laterally in a firm throughout their career. It takes a great deal for someone to fail in this context since there is often a more forgiving culture. Clubs often seem to tolerate performance failures because there is very low turnover. In reality, those who seem to have failed are "put on the shelf," with little chance of reentering the faster track of promotion. Recovery can be very difficult because people have trouble shaking the active memories of early-career missteps. People can become typecast. When someone is compelled to leave a club, reentry into another club is difficult. In fact, in our longitudinal study of Harvard MBAs a decade after graduation, only 25 percent of people leaving a club tended to return to another club.[11] Most (64 percent) who leave these age-graded firms tend to race toward the faster-paced world of a baseball team, where there are more chances to prove yourself, even if there is far less job security.

Lessons from Baseball Team Cultures—Can You Still Knock Them Out of the Park?

Baseball teams employ what researchers have referred to as a prospector's strategy in a search for novelty. They are so focused on discovering "the next new thing" that they often must buy talent rather than patiently develop it from within. In fact, it is hard to groom the talent from within because these firms often do not know what skills and backgrounds they will need in the future. The wildly successful TV producer David Salzman, who created such hits as *Dynasty, The People's Court, The Jenny Jones Show, The Fresh Prince of Bel Air*, and *Mad TV*, said, "The one-hit-wonder, as ephemeral as it may be, is essential for driving the creativity in the television and movie business."[12]

As George Hornig, COO of the mergers-and–acquisitions (M&A) boutique Wasserstein, Perella and Company, told us, "Ten years together is quite amazing," referring to the creative genius of founders Bruce Wasserstein and Joseph Perella, the company's CEO and chairman. The two had led a defection of some twenty investment bankers from First Boston's M&A group through that "amazing" period. "We expect stability," Hornig continued, "but you're always going to have a superstar who comes along with forty clients who want to join and you can't resist. There will always be that talent market around."[13]

While that interview was in 1988, Hornig says he still agrees with that view on the fluidity of talent in his business. Not only has he gone off to senior leadership roles since then at four more firms, including Deutsche Bank and back to First Boston (now known as Credit Suisse First Boston), but even Bruce Wasserstein and Joseph Perella have moved on to other opportunities, with Wasserstein now the CEO of Lazard, and Perella at Morgan Stanley until leaving during the assault on the troubled leadership of Philip Purcell. Hornig adds as an update, "If I thought the gypsylike movement of talent was a key challenge in 1988, I never realized how easy I had it back then."[14]

Indeed, there are strong external networks because executives at baseball team firms identify with their particular profession more strongly than with a given employer. The turnover across these firms tends to be quite high, and thus failure can be buried in the normal trajectory of a high volume of job moves. In fact, it is in such industries where we often find folks recovering from setback so easily that they appear to "fail upward." What is critical is that to recover from failure in baseball teams, victims of setbacks must prove the freshness of their expertise.

Accordingly, in March 2005, Bill Gates hired Ray Ozzie, the CEO of Groove Networks, to help lead the next-stage development of Microsoft Office and Windows. Gates had once called Ozzie "one of the top five programmers in the universe."[15] Ozzie's career is typical for someone in a baseball team culture. Ozzie was an early enthusiast of online community experiments in the 1970s as a systems programmer on the PLATO project at the University of Illinois, where so much of the Internet was hatched. He launched his corporate career at Data General in Boston, developing workstation operating systems. Soon thereafter he joined Dan Bricklin, the pioneering codeveloper of VisiCalc, the first electronic spreadsheet, at a firm called Software Arts. He extended the products to interface with Microsoft and got to know Bill Gates and Steve Ballmer well in the early 1980s. By 1984, he had obtained financial backing by Lotus Development Corporation founder Mitch Kapor to launch a company called Iris, which developed the hugely successful Lotus Notes. When Lotus sold out to IBM in 1995, he stayed on for a few years. In 2001 he founded Groove to continue to advance network software to help far-scattered executives collaborate online.

Despite the fact that PLATO, VisiCalc, and Lotus Notes may not be widely known as lasting triumphs to rising generations, no one would consider Ozzie a failure, let alone a has-been, in this swift-moving field. In fact, as one Groove employee put it, "Everybody knows Ray's track record. Most of the original people at Groove literally didn't know what the project was when they accepted the job. They just wanted to work for Ray Ozzie." [16] Surprisingly, the survival of a company is less important to the reputation of an executive in the baseball team culture than the survival and freshness of their ideas.

Next we move from technology to finance. Dan Levitan had been responsible for some of New York investment bank Schroder & Company's biggest deals, such as the underwriting of Starbucks. Nonetheless, in January 1997, a large merger he had spent six weeks trying to close dissolved, along with his marriage, while his job situation deteriorated. Stunned by the bad news at work, he was interrupted by his assistant's determined knocking at the door. As he answered, in walked the courier to ambush him with divorce papers from his wife. Weeks later, at age forty-one, he quit and traveled to Africa to climb Mt. Kilimanjaro with his brothers and think. [17] Eventually, he realized that he had a facility for funding budding companies and left New York for Seattle to join his old client and Starbucks founder Howard Schultz, to create the venture capital firm Maveron. Schultz told us he originally selected Levitan over the fancier firms with larger teams since Levitan was the only investment banker who asked questions and listened. Schultz had hoped Levitan would join him earlier, but Levitan needed the liberating event of failure to make a break with his past success spiral.

Their investment skyrocketed, with early investments in companies such as eBay and Drugstore.com. He not only reinvented himself personally but met and married an art dealer and began a new family life, settling in to an idyllic home alongside Lake Washington.

Jack Bogle is another financier who is an example of how the baseball team world can accommodate failure as long as the victim can demonstrate character and competence. Instinctively, Bogle knew that this would be a key challenge as he set about the task of creating Vanguard, the nation's first index mutual funds company, right after being fired as the CEO of Wellington Management Company in 1974.

Sparks began to fly when the Wellington Management Company, which included the Wellington and Windsor Funds (which Bogle created), merged with Boston-based Thorndike, Doran, Paine and Lewis in 1965 to bring research and investment talent together with a reputation for conservative management. Hostility grew over contrasting management styles, with Bogle being more detail oriented and his new Boston partners more consensual. Meanwhile, Bogle's heart was failing, and he lost valuable time in treatment, receiving a pacemaker and eventually a heart transplant. By a vote of ten in favor and two abstentions, the board fired Bogle. His response was to bypass the management company and appeal directly to the underlying boards of directors of Wellington's various funds. They broke from tradition and asked Bogle to remain as their president to handle the administrative services that became Vanguard. The name was selected because it was the flagship commanded by Lord Nelson in the famed British victory over the French in the Battle of the Nile in 1798.

In his book *Character Counts*, Bogle explained the challenge in his revolution in mutual fund governance with the concept of no-load fees:

> *While most of our directors shared my sympathy for a no-load system, all were aware that it could be seen to abrogate the charter restriction. They also were properly concerned about whether we had the skill to make it work (the no-load business was then but a small part of the fund business) and whether any brokers, having sold Wellington shares, wouldn't persuade their client to redeem them leaving our firm in a risky no man's land. But determination carried the day.*[18]

Vanguard is now one of the world's largest investment management companies, with 18 million institutional and individual shareholder accounts and $750 billion in U.S. mutual funds. Meanwhile, Bogle has become the leading voice of moral authority over the U.S. mutual fund industry.

Having the courage to accomplish this was no easy feat, but he told us this confidence came from his childhood experience in mastering adversity. Despite his glistening Princeton credentials, his family lost their modest fortune in the stock market crash in 1929 and even lost the family home. He worked as a newspaper boy and ice cream server at the age of ten. Unfortunately, his broken father developed a drinking problem, lost his job, and left his mother. Bogle said this inspired him to begin a quest to restore the family's honor through a return to his financial conservatism. As he stated it: "Truth be told, I could write a book on adversity—growing up, family 'issues,' lack of money, academic travails, getting fired from Wellington, first heart attack in 1960, awaiting a transplant—all this taught me patience and persistence. When I left Wellington Management, I was fired and there would be no Vanguard. I did not expect this to happen twice in my life. Life has a lot of reverses and difficulties. You must just take on life with enthusiasm."[19]

Another financier, John Mack of Morgan Stanley presents an equally breathtaking tale of comeback—although he refutes the term 'vindication.' A North Carolina grocer's son, Mack soared up the ranks of the bond trading division of Morgan Stanley, becoming president twenty years after he joined. Following the 1997 merger with Dean Witter Discover & Co., Mack agreed to take the number two role behind Phil Purcell. Then in 2001 he was pushed out after it became obvious that Purcell wouldn't let him ascend to the top job as was the original intent during the merger. After a three-year term, Mack stepped down in a political battle as CEO of Credit Suisse First Boston (now renamed Credit Suisse). Following the spring 2005 meltdown of Purcell's command at Morgan Stanley, however, the board swallowed its pride and courageously brought the immensely popular Mack back as CEO.[20]

The cold, crisp world of finance provides many other compelling tales of financiers who have achieved tremendous personal comebacks. Robert Lessin was the youngest-ever partner at Morgan Stanley when he jumped ship to become vice chairman of Smith Barney. By his late thirties, however, while in top form as a major investment banker, he suffered a near-fatal stroke as a result of a rare blood disease. In 1997 he was completely paralyzed on one side and expected to be hospitalized for nine months. But after two months, he was back on his feet, ready for adventure.

Lessin no longer looked at finance the same way, however, and in the spring of 1998 said farewell to his boss, Jamie Dimon of Citigroup, to become one of the nation's premier venture capitalists of the Internet through Dawntreader Ventures, which he still chairs while also serving as vice chairman of the investment bank Jeffries & Company. He told us that it was the love of his family, the drive to be with his children, his access to medical knowledge, and his fierce determination that brought him through the nightmarish period. When he returned with a new mission, his financial skills and sterling network of relationships kept him in high demand since he had never taken a leave of absence.

Several months later, in the fall of 1998, Lessin's former boss, Jamie Dimon, also had a major disruption in his career. On November 1, 1998, Dimon, as president of Citigroup, was summoned to a management conference center in Armonk, New York, and fired by co-CEOs John Reed and Sandy Weill. Dimon had first met Weill as a college student at Tufts when working on an economics paper on the takeover of Shearson, an investment bank where Dimon's father and grandfather had worked. Weill, a social friend of Dimon's father's, was the mastermind of the merger. Weill liked Dimon's paper so much that he hired him for a summer job.

Years later, after graduating from the Harvard Business School, he joined Weill as his assistant. Shearson was by then part of American Express. When it became clear that Weill would not be succeeding James Robinson as CEO of American Express, Weill and Dimon left together and, using the Baltimore-based Commercial Credit, rebuilt a financial giant. They briefly took the name Primerica, which was one of their acquisitions that previously acquired Smith Barney. Dimon became president of Primerica by age thirty-five. In 1993, they bought the Travelers Group and assumed that name. History was made in 1997 when they bought the legendary Salomon Brothers and led the shattering of the Glass-Steagall Act with their purchase of Citibank—the first major recombination of an investment bank and a commercial bank in over sixty years.

As the stock continued to soar, the relationship between Dimon and Weill began to unravel, resulting in Dimon's dismissal. Some attributed his termination to sparring with John Reed, who entered with the Citibank acquisition, while others attributed it to a clash of styles that peaked when Weill's daughter, Jessica Weill Bibliowicz, left the firm, complaining that Dimon had thwarted her potential career moves.[21]

When Dimon brought the news home of his termination by Sandy Weill after serving sixteen years at his side, Dimon's eight-year-old daughter asked whether they'd be living on the streets. His ten-year-old daughter asked whether she'd no longer be able to attend college. His twelve-year-old asked for his cell phone.[22] Since Dimon had left with a $30 million severance package, his family did not face hardship and spent much of the next sixteen months reading and traveling. When we spoke with him in the fall of 1999, he said that he was still not interested in making a commitment to any particular institution just yet but was reviewing options. Later that fall, he actually sought out Weill for lunch and even encouraged his mother to resume her friendship with him.[23]

Dimon commented on initiating this ice-breaking event:

It was close to the one-year anniversary, and I had mellowed by then. Sandy wasn't going to call and I knew it was time. I was ready to say thank you for what he did for me. I also knew that he and I should talk about what happened. I wanted to get this event behind me so I could move on. Part of me said I had spent sixteen years with him. Twelve or thirteen were pretty good. You can't just look at one side and not the other. I made my own mistakes, I acknowledged I was partly to blame. Whether I was 40 percent or 60 percent to blame really didn't matter. I felt very good about my meeting with him.[24]

Three months later, in March 2000, Dimon was announced as the new CEO of Bank One, the nation's sixth-largest bank. Its stock price shot up 90 percent under Dimon's leadership. In 2004 it merged with JP Morgan Chase, with Dimon to become the next CEO of the merged institutions. This $58 billion purchase of Bank One by JP Morgan Chase was, according to *Fortune*, in part to gain the leadership of Dimon. In fact Dimon has been labeled "the most watched, most discussed, most feared banker in the world today."[25]

Lessons from the Academies

The two challenges of academies are, first, to know when to leave the comfort of these relatively stable and often paternalistic cultures, and, second, to be able to prove that your skills are portable to another firm without trying to transplant or clone the same practices. Since people are terminated less often in academies and clubs than in baseball teams and fortresses, the definition of *failing* is more subtle. Often, it may merely mean that someone's career has been sidelined. In the 1960s and 1970s at IBM, historically if someone fell off the traditional eighteen- to twenty-four-month promotion cycle, they were considered plateaued or "in the penalty box." The perception in such firms, whether it is true or imaginary, is that once people are missing certain "heats of competition," they will become excluded from subsequent tournaments for future promotion. On other occasions, they may see a gulf emerging between their personal values and that of the larger company and realize that they may have traveled as far as they can with this firm.

Bill George, the hugely successful former CEO of Medtronic, reflected on this recently in explaining how he saw "the handwriting on the wall" that it was time to leave prior employers. Under Bill George's nine-year leadership, the Microwave Division of Litton Industries battled successfully against appliance industry giants like GE and Whirlpool to become the leader in the consumer microwave oven market, gaining a 33 percent share, growing the business an average of 55 percent a year, and becoming the parent company's most profitable division.[26] Nonetheless, George was discouraged; he considered Litton to be a growth company without a mission, much like the old ITT. It grew from a single military components business to 133 disparate divisions. "As president of its rapidly growing microwave oven division, I had complete autonomy . . . Eventually Litton became victim of its own complexity and Litton industries itself was sold in 2001 for . . . the same value the company had thirty years before."

George happily was long gone by then. Despite his successful record at Litton, he knew it was time to leave when he overheard a conversation between the CEO and the head of their oil exploration business. George recalled the CEO saying, "Charlie, the audit committee is very upset about your audit report. I know you have to do what you have to do to get the business, but if you ever put it in writing again, you're fired." To George, "The message was as clear as a bell: its okay to make payoffs; just don't get caught. That incident convinced me that I was working for the wrong company."[27]

Years later, George again hit a fork in the road while working successfully inside an "academy." After several promotions, he was heading nine divisions of Honeywell and leading eighteen thousand employees.

Nonetheless, he felt that he had "hit the wall" and was typecast as a turnaround expert. In his words, "I was out of sync with Honeywell's slow-moving, change resistant culture. I also found myself becoming more concerned with appearances and my attire than with being myself. Reluctantly, I faced up to the reality that Honeywell was changing me more than I was changing it. I had 'hit the wall' but was too proud to act on it. I felt I was in a trap from which I couldn't escape."[28]

Rather than grieve, he moved on—and succeeded. George took off in 1989 to run Medtronic, a much smaller outfit he once thought was not enough of a challenge. When he arrived, the company had annual sales of $755 million with a payroll of four thousand employees. When he retired just over a decade later, it had annual revenues of $5.5 billion and twenty-six thousand employees. Medtronic was consistently rated by *Fortune* magazine as one of the best companies to work for, and its shareholders enjoyed a market capitalization jump from $1.1 billion when he joined to $60 billion a decade later—a yearly compound return of 35 percent.

Thus, one lesson for recovery from setbacks in an academy is timing—knowing when to leave. Another lesson is how to enter elsewhere. It is critical that leaders from academies demonstrate that they are broader than any single functional area and can move beyond the company-specific approaches of their own training. Sometimes the timing of questions about diminished internal opportunities for promotion is not subtle. Naturally, this is most obvious when leaders are passed over for promotion, as, for example, when Jeff Immelt was named as Jack Welch's successor at GE. Immediately, the two close finalist candidates, Robert Nardelli and James McNerney, departed to lead other great firms. Nardelli moved off to continued greatness at the helm of The Home Depot, while McNerney led 3M through a dramatic revival and then, after five years, moved to lead Boeing back to strength.

Both Nardelli and McNerney have shared candid disappointment that they did not succeed Welch despite dedicated careers of roughly a quarter century each, skillfully rising up the ranks of GE. McNerney reportedly took the bad news in stride and had already been talking with other firms about backup options. Nardelli was stunned and demanded, "I want an autopsy." Although Welch called Nardelli "the best operating executive I've ever seen," he said he had to "go with his gut" in bypass-ing Nardelli.[29]

Nardelli, the son of a GE factory worker, described the meeting with Welch at the Albany, New York, airport on a miserable, sleeting Sunday evening in November: "I went with my heart in my throat. How do you describe this? It's something you strive for for 30 years. You're hanging on to every word. You're focused on his mouth, and the final words, 'I've elected to give it to Jeff.' And you're like, 'Did I really hear it right?' You've got to tell me why. Tell me what I could have done better. Tell me the numbers weren't there, the innovation, the talent development, the relationship with the Street. Give me a reason." Asked years later if he still wants an autopsy, he replied, "Absolutely! Let's exhume the body."[30]

Nonetheless, Nardelli got past his shock as GE board member Ken Langone, the founding financier of The Home Depot, brought Nardelli an opportunity with exactly the same advice he gave to Home Depot co-founder Bernie Marcus twenty years earlier—"You've just been kicked in the ass by a golden horseshoe"—and encouraged him to take the reins at The Home Depot. This $46 billion home improvement retail dynamo's annual growth of 30 to 40 percent a year had fallen to 17 percent, and the stock price had tumbled by 42 percent. A decline in home sales, inven-tory management problems, and inefficiencies in the system were blamed. The solutions that Nardelli brought, however, were heavily crit-icized. With the quality reengineering tool of Six Sigma as his gospel at GE, Nardelli came under harsh criticism during his first two years that his effort to force manufacturing-like processes onto retailing was leaving stores out of stock in key areas, and service levels were declining as its use of part-time sales associates soared to 50 percent, compared with 20 per-cent at their leading competitor.[31] While his board was patient and sup-portive, Nardelli has since acknowledged that some of the tactics imported from GE were a less than perfect fit, and he revisited them. After another two years, Nardelli could look back on sales increases of 60 percent to $70 billion and earnings increases of 105 percent, with promising new urban outlets and international expansions.

Similarly, Jim McNerney, as the first outside leader in 3M's century-old but innovative culture, had to prove that he was not just mindlessly transplanting practices from GE when he took over in December 2000.

He introduced many near-deified GE practices, such as the Six Sigma production rationalization practices, workforce reductions, and a leadership development institute modeled after GE's Crotonville. He was often the only person to show up at meetings without a tie. His blunt, probing questions were jarring to some—especially when he talked about commercializing innovation.[32]

McNerney saw that he was hitting some cultural walls and worked with his senior management in off-site retreats to reformulate 3M's core values—adding a sense of urgency. In meetings with McNerney and his top team two years into the job, we heard that he was keenly aware of his need to avoid trying to reinvent GE at 3M. He was given great credit for his sensitivity to the unique strengths of the old 3M culture and was careful to not take charge with an army of GE soldiers to help him lead an attack. In fact, he said, "I think the story here is rejuvenation rather than replacement . . . We're world class at the front end of the innovation process. If I dampen our enthusiasm for that, I've really screwed up."[33] In June 2005, he left to take over the scandalized aerospace giant Boeing. After four and half years at 3M, he had left a big imprint, with its stock price up 17 percent and net income up 24 percent over the year.[34]

Lessons from the Clubs

In a club, personal setbacks through health, family matters, executive slipups, and even less than perfect strategic choices can be forgiven, as long as an executive displays candor and selflessness. The vast grassroots network of dedicated volunteers and committed professionals represents many of the selfless virtues of long service, loyalty to a noble mission, and breadth of responsibilities that help define a clublike culture.

A major challenge of overcoming setbacks in a club is that memories are long. People who stub their toes midcareer—or even early-career—find that they can be continually haunted by a prominent setback. At UPS, virtually all top executives have worked their way up the system from within, most beginning as unionized hourly workers, with careers that often spanned functions ranging from driving trucks to operations, HR, engineering, marketing, and even legal. A talented rising UPS star who brilliantly mastered senior positions in engineering, marketing, and operations led a high-profile international partnership in the early 1990s but was unable to shake his reputation as having trouble with "the chemistry" in his relations to superiors over the years and went off to work for a competitor.

Similarly, in 1989, Horst W. Schroeder was removed as president of Kellogg by William E. LaMothe, Kellogg chairman and CEO, with a failure of management "chemistry" as the reason offered. Schroeder began at Kellogg in West Germany as a controller and later managed Kellogg's European operations, where he achieved noteworthy results. In Battle Creek, Michigan, however, Schroeder's colleagues described him as stubborn, forceful, and even imperious and autocratic. This style was in stark contrast to Kellogg's patrician small-town Michigan family culture, which emphasized teamwork, employee involvement, and sharing credit with others. The conflict between Kellogg's paternalistic culture and Schroeder's leadership style was too great to overcome, especially when the performance of the firm began slipping.[35]

The unseating of Ford Motor Company CEO Jacques Nasser a decade later repeated a very similar story to that of Kellogg and Schroeder. Nasser was fired in October 2001, following numerous rollover accidents with the Explorer, its flagship four-wheel-drive sport utility vehicle, that resulted in two hundred deaths. As the company slipped into its first series of consecutive quarterly losses in a decade, Nasser's removal was further hastened by his draconian performance reviews and ruthless human resource practices, leading to multiple lawsuits and Ford's sinking employee morale. The Ford family, which controlled 40 percent of the firm's voting power, saw an assault on their paternalistic concern for the workforce. They acted by giving the CEO position to family member William C. Ford Jr., already the chairman of the company. In September of 2006, Ford returned to the chairmanship, bringing in thirty-six-year Boeing executive Alan Mulally as CEO. While Nasser has not returned to lead a major public company, he has become reflective on lessons learned and gone on to board roles at Polaroid, Allianz, and British Sky Broadcasting and to other advisory roles.[36]

Returning to UPS, even as second-in-command, Oz Nelson seemingly suffered a major strategic setback in his goal of leading UPS's rapid globalization. Just months after forging partnerships with a dozen European package couriers in early 1987, Nelson reversed course and UPS withdrew, leading an initiative to purchase a competitor, DHL. A few months later, that plan was scrapped just moments before the public announcement of the deal. Nelson was not punished for this false start but in fact was promoted to CEO. It was Oz who killed his own acquisition plan when he learned more about some troubling DHL global business practices that would not be consistent with UPS's values. The courage to make the right call did not weaken him but in fact fortified his reputation. Once in office as CEO, he then showed the courage to promote a former fellow contender for the CEO position, Don Layden, and gave him the power to build the global business the right way.

Within five years, UPS moved from its base in the United States, Canada, and Germany to serving as many nations as the United Nations then recognized. This great success was not the product of flawless plans but due to the firm's ability to learn from setbacks. Nelson and Layden learned how to openly share frustrations with their colleagues so that problem solving was shared. In fact, they had a history of working closely together a decade earlier when they helped lead a postmortem team after a prior effort at European expansion had failed. Similarly, Nelson's successors Jim Kelly and Mike Eskew worked closely to weave together a tightly integrated, seamless global system of high-margin supply chain logistics services.

At the same time, some setbacks in a club are not forgivable. Individuals' indiscretions that violate institutional trust can be unforgivable. A senior executive who enjoyed a noteworthy UPS career was terminated promptly when it was proved that he had padded a single travel reimbursement with false car rentals. Similarly, five years later, suspected conflicts of interest in lining up a major new business partnership with a service vendor resulted in swift investigations and top-level terminations.

The lesson here is that people can overcome honest mistakes in a club environment, despite the long memories, if the situation is approached with humility and outreach to colleagues to share in the problem definition and efforts at recovery. That is, unless the slippage is one of shattered faith in character. The club's belief that people can learn from their mistakes is tenable if the mistakes are considered to be honest ones.

When someone's integrity is eroded, they will have lost their credibility and will never be trusted again.

Consider how this is demonstrated in the sad saga of William Aramony—a man who once headed the nation's largest community philan-
thropic organization. United Way of America was severely traumatized
when its leader violated the core pillars of integrity and humility. Under
the long reign of the flamboyant Aramony, United Way created various
shady side businesses to facilitate self-dealing. Following the 1992 revelations of fraud and misdirection of funds to support a sordid personal
life, Aramony was forced to resign. He was convicted three years later
and sentenced to prison for spending $1.2 million of the nonprofit's
money on vacation, travel, and perks for himself and friends. Aramony
served a seven-year sentence.

In the years since his 2001 release, he has not made any return to public life—nor is one likely.[37] Baseball teams can find homes for fallen stars,
even when they return from prison, such as for convicted designer/
entrepreneurs Steve Madden and Martha Stewart, if society feels that there
has been proper contrition and if their skills are still sharp. Despite Aramony's suffering, apologies, connections, and knowledge, in the world of
clubs, his character has made him a permanent "untouchable."

By contrast, consider a failure and termination from another club culture, where integrity was never in question. Clubs can terminate promising executives for reasons other than breeches in integrity or failures to
collaborate in problem solving. Sometimes, despite high degrees of job
security, not fitting in can be a problem, as Horst Schroeder of Kellogg
learned. Southwest Airlines competes in an industry dominated by
fortresslike major trunk line carriers operating in distress, with draconian
layoffs and service reductions in a battle for survival. By contrast, Southwest Airlines, with its lower labor costs and point-to-point operating system, has flourished. According to its cofounder, Herb Kelleher, the real
source of its success is its culture and not merely a favorable cost structure.
He has stated,

*We're not looking for blind obedience. We're looking for people who on
their own initiative want to be doing what they're doing because they consider it to be a worthy objective. You are careful that people don't preoccupy
themselves with cosmetic things like offices and titles. If you take a genuine*

interest in the well-being of your people, outside as well as inside the workplace, you eventually create trust . . . Our real accomplishment is to have inspired our people to buy into a concept, to identify with the company—and then to execute.[38]

This trust has been nourished through unrivaled job security:

Certainly there were times when we could have made substantially more profits in the short term if we had furloughed people, but we didn't. We were looking at our employees and our company's longer-term interests.[39]

In addition, the airline encourages various cross-departmental activities through lateral job-swapping programs and training in how to work as teams. Cockpit crews, reservation agents, flight attendants, mechanics, and administrative staff all take such classes.

Nonetheless, in 1993, several months after being acquired by Southwest Airlines, Morris Air entrepreneur David Neeleman found this "groupiness" to be suffocating, and he complained of a decline in Southwest's legendary innovation. Neeleman was thirty-four years old and had received $22 million in Southwest stock. He was stunned when Kelleher fired him five months later because he did not fit into the Southwest Airlines hierarchy. Neeleman told us in April 2006, in reflecting, "I didn't see it coming. The day I was fired, I was in tears. I wondered, how did this happen? I was angry and determined to get back into what I love doing. I was determined that we would do something better than Southwest. With nine kids at home, my wife thought there was no need to get right back in."[40]

A five-year noncompete term in his severance agreement kept him from starting another airline, so he launched related aviation services. In 2000, at age forty, as soon as he was contractually able, Neeleman launched discount airline JetBlue with the simplicity of the operations of Southwest, and its spirited culture, but with more customer service innovations, such as satellite TV on individual screens in each seat. Forging a new club, roughly 80 percent of its workers are shareholders and fiercely loyal to the company. Virtually all of its reservationists work from their homes, and, as in many clubs, the firm has a no-layoff policy.

When people fail in a club, it is generally due to their character and integrity or their lack of adherence to cultural norms. While Neeleman's integrity and competence were never a question, he failed in a club and was determined to prove that he still understood and admired the values of a clublike system, even if he did not fit in at Southwest. He wanted to "out-Southwest" Southwest Airlines. Neeleman managed to show that he could still embody the values of the club by creating a culture of strong affinity and few status distinctions.

Lessons from the Fortresses

Fortresses are high-turnover cultures since they both clean house through sweeping survival-driven cost cutting and then hire from the outside as a primary source of talent. Each of the major, old line truck carriers today is led by entire management teams from the outside, including their CEOs. When they seek turnaround strength from the outside, they do not emphasize narrow functional expertise as much as they seek generalists with flexibility to migrate swiftly to where problems arise each day. Fortresses typify business imperatives such as financial brinksmanship with creditors, divestitures for needed cash and focus, operational cost cutting, business process reengineering, head count reduction, human resource peacemaking, market repositioning, and reworking of the fundamental building blocks of a business.

Bill Roberti of Alvarez and Marsal, who, in prior CEO roles, turned around Brooks Brothers, the Plaid Clothing Group (Burberry), and Duck Head Apparel Company, told us, "I always look for people who can execute like soldiers and give it their all—even if the battleground switches from the plan in the war room."[41]

Roberti took on an especially challenging assignment when he and his turnaround firm were hired to revamp the St. Louis school district. He became superintendent of schools in June 2003 with a mandate to make the distressed school system financially and operationally efficient. Almost immediately, they discovered that the projected budget surplus from the prior superintendent was actually a deficit of $35 million, which later turned out to be a deficit of $90 million. Furthermore, the school district spent $12,000 per student, more than 40 percent above the national average, but only 5 percent of high school juniors could read at a proficient level. Tens of thousands of students were leaving for the suburbs and for private schools.

The remedies were not popular. Over howls of anger, they closed sixteen schools and sold forty properties while also outsourcing some school services, such as transportation, food services, and custodial support, laying off two thousand employees—none of them teachers.[42] They eliminated $72 million of the district operating funds, and the schools moved closer to receiving full state accreditation, with outside educators applauding improvements. As Roberti explained his mission to us, "This is not a jobs program. This is a school system that is supposed to teach kids, not to provide jobs to the community. I think that the public has a right to the same level of expertise in management whether it is a school system or any kind of business that's public and trades stock. People should be held accountable."[43]

Nonetheless, at some public forums where Roberti shared the results at the end of his assignment a year later, some community members broke into applause over his exit. This did not mean public officials concerned about national education did not recognize the improvements. The following year, Roberti and his firm were invited into Louisiana for a statewide version of their assignment for the city of St. Louis. Other cities, such as Washington, D.C., began to discuss adapting elements of Roberti's mission.[44]

These turnaround missions are rarely ones where the external acclaim is universal, as Michael Bozic found out while president of Sears Merchandise Group. He ran the retail business at the core of what, briefly, became a misguided conglomerate under CEO Edward Brennan. Bozic revived the sluggish retail enterprise with new concepts such as Sears Brand Central. In an effort to appease shareholder pressure for change in the aftermath of the company's first loss, Brennan pushed out Bozic, taking over the head merchant job himself, rather than sell off the disjointed businesses ranging from Coldwell Banker in real estate to Allstate Insurance and Dean Witter in securities. This setback, after his decades at Sears, did not cut short Bozic's career, because fellow retailers knew the source of the problem and saw Bozic as part of the solution.

He was quickly recruited by bankrupt Hills Department Stores and turned the company around successfully, taking it out of bankruptcy and rebuilding market share. However, by 1985, the cash that he was now generating for the firm was tempting to those who wanted to sell the firm and strip those assets, and an investment firm bought enough shares to win a proxy battle. Bozic then left to become CEO of Levitz Furniture until he was recruited as vice chairman of Kmart under Floyd Hall, with the enticement that he would succeed Hall as CEO. When Hall retired in 2000, several board members concluded that Bozic, at fifty-nine, was too old and they needed someone younger, so they recruited thirty-nine-year-old Charles Conaway from the CVS drugstore chain. Two years later, Conaway resigned in disgrace, later facing criminal charges, while Kmart slid into bankruptcy.[45] Bozic commented to us, "I was happy doing what I was doing, with employees, shareholders, and competitors recognizing what we had done in each enterprise, but it seems that in retail, no good deed goes unpunished."[46]

For some, leaving office due to the right financial timing can still leave a haunting sense of a leadership mission that is not complete. The closing of a $6.6 billion sale to a consortium of investors on Thursday, July 22, 2005, transformed the huge Toys "R" Us retail chain into a private company. As part of the sale agreement with Bain Capital, Kohlberg Kravis Roberts, and Vornado Realty Trust, CEO John H. Eyler agreed to step aside to allow the new buyers to consider strategic alternatives without being in the shadows of Eyler's impressive repositioning of the brand.

Eyler took over the helm of Toys "R" Us in 2001 after being courted by the great half-century-old giant toy retail chain for a decade. Previously, he tripled the revenues of the privately held legendary toy store FAO Schwarz. That opportunity had come along after Eyler was fired, by surprise, on Christmas Eve as president of a large menswear retail chain. Eyler led a strategy at Toys "R" Us to bring improved merchandising to the beaten-down, gray-toned big-box discounter through well-stocked shelves with the hottest items through holidays and exclusive toys, as well as energized service, with in-store demonstrations, friendliness, and the pizzazz of a marriage of toys, games, style, and entertainment. Eyler remodeled hundreds of stores each year, with the company's new great growth in Europe and with Babies "R" Us stores. Nonetheless, competing against Wal-Mart, where toys were often used as loss-leading bait to draw in shoppers, Eyler saw a chance to help the company escape the short-term pressure of financial markets while it regrouped by endorsing the buyout by deep-pocketed financial firms.

At the same time, it was not easy to just step away from a mission in which he so deeply believed. Five months after the sale of the business, Eyler told us:

> I went into a Toys "R" Us store the Monday after Thanksgiving and there were problems. If my mother was walking through this store I would not have been proud of that store. It was not refilled from the Thanksgiving weekend, which was not appropriate. The staff was not working the crowd appropriately. Not giving the right kind of service. When you have a portfolio of 1,600 stores you can always find a store that does not meet your standards. But I was not very happy with that store. That store on that day was lousy. I sent this feedback to the current leaders.[47]

The same sort of attachment to the turnaround mission is shared by others in fortress cultures outside of retail. For example, Henry Silverman of Cendant was tremendously proud of the lodging and travel colossus he had built by weaving together the businesses of Ramada Hotels, Days Inn, Howard Johnson Hotels, Avis Rent A Car, and Century 21 to forge Hospitality Franchising, only to see share price crumble following the ill-fated CUC merger to form Cendant. While he was once the shining star of Wall Street, the defeat was personally humiliating and frustrating. He told us, "I felt that my self-worth was sharply diminished." He soon began counseling and developed a plan to seek justice. While he never again managed to become the darling of Wall Street, the massive financial fraud in the overvalued CUC assets led him on a crusade to get the truth out regarding his unscrupulous CUC partners. He told us in 2004,

> When we announced in mid-April 1998 what we had discovered at CUC, our attorneys urged me to avoid the "f" word: fraud. Their view was that once we stated we had found fraud, all our defenses under the Securities Acts were moot—and the only thing we could argue about with the inevitable class action litigation would be the amount of damages. I rejected their point of view. I felt if I wasn't totally honest with all my constituencies, I might be perceived to be part of a cover-up. It never occurred to me not to stay and try to fix the problem.[48]

Silverman was determined to show that material information had been concealed, while initially his attorneys tried to contain the problem by suppressing the full truth. Eventually, with government assistance, the auditors paid a heavy fine, and a CUC executive—former Cendant vice chairman Kirk Shelton—was sentenced to ten years in prison.[49]

Ironically, just a few years earlier, one of Silverman's hotel groups, Days Inn, was embroiled in scandal before he bought control of the chain. In 1989, Days Inn was purchased by Stanley Tollman and Monty Hundley, the chain's largest franchisees, with Mike Leven as CEO. Soon after the purchase, Leven noticed shrinking cash balances and began hearing complaints from vendors such as builders and telephone companies that longstanding bills were not being paid. Although the new owners quickly redirected the CFO to report to them and not to Leven, the CEO, Leven discovered that they were essentially stripping assets by not paying their own franchise fees and the mortgage payments they owed.

Leven confronted Tollman and Hundley and then resigned with no severance. When they retaliated by launching threatening litigation, Leven was thrown for a loop. Having built the chain tenfold with huge franchise expansions into Europe and Asia, he had also pioneered progressive personnel practices, hiring the homeless and the elderly to provide new opportunities for those on the fringes of the nation's economy. Ironically, when the *CBS Evening News* ran a previously researched piece on Leven's work in securing employment for the homeless, he too had been without a career home for months, unbeknownst to the show's producers.

A year later Days Inn ran out of cash and filed for bankruptcy, and it was bought by Henry Silverman's company. In 2004, Tollman and Hundley were convicted of defrauding lenders of $100 million. Leven, meanwhile, began to get psychological counseling, as he described to us, "I walked in and the psychologist took one look at me and asked, 'Who died?' I told him no one had died. But he asked me again and then I started talking about Days Inn. I realized it had been my baby, the place I loved, and leaving was very hard."[50]

Leven later became president of Holiday Inn Worldwide, where he launched a powerful new campaign to build the brands of the various Holiday Inn divisions (Holiday Inn, Crowne Plaza, Holiday Inn Express) and led an operational overhaul to enhance the quality of the services. In 1997, he created his own hotel franchise chain, called U.S. Franchise Systems, which included Microtel Inns & Suites, Hawthorn Suites, and Best Inns.

The lessons for these leaders in fortresses is that—despite the crisp, analytic tools required for turnaround work, frequently moving across firms—there is a deep personal and emotional consequence to public failure. So much of their personal identity is wrapped up in their resilient, fix-it roles. Their setbacks take place within a context of distress and with legal culpability and frequent character-damaging finger-pointing. A key task of those who fail in fortresses is to be able to separate their personal identity and character from that of their fiery business context.

John Hancock, the former CEO of British furniture retailer MFI, who also had a disagreement with his board when leading the newsstand giant WH Smith, explained to us that this struggle is often hard to have in a public company: "As the CEO of a public company, with all the pressures that come from investors, analysts, and the press, the forces are in place to keep you trapped. You are not a free agent in managing your own exit. In order to survive, you have to maintain a fine line distinguishing yourself from your job, so that you are not entirely defined by that role." [51]

Those who succeeded in recovering from setbacks in fortress cultures managed to draw this line of demarcation.

Conclusion: Career Setbacks and Corporate Cultures

Clergy ensnarled in publicized sex scandals will likely see their careers dissolve, while entertainment figures may not only recover, but their careers may actually be enhanced through the infamy. While one culture values trust, another profession values celebrity.

In finance, the values are character matched with competence, where professional expertise is critical. The visionary institutional builder Jamie Dimon was pushed out of Citibank—an enterprise he helped create as president under Sandy Weill—and soon resurfaced as CEO of Bank One. Similarly, Herb Allison, as president, helped lead Merrill Lynch into the digital age but was pushed out by David Komansky, his CEO, only to resurface soon as the CEO of the huge mutual fund enterprise TIAA-CREF. John Mack, the CEO of Morgan Stanley, was pushed out by Phil Purcell of Dean Witter in a merger designed to retain them both as leaders. Years later, even after being pushed out of office again, this time at Credit Suisse, John Mack returned to retake the throne from Purcell amid cheering throngs of professionals in a scene reminiscent of King Richard the Lionheart's return to oust the sheriff of Nottingham.

Is culture the simple explanation for these situations? Well, it is certainly part of the answer. The implication is to know what cultural barriers surround you when you experience defeat. In fact, the very notion of defeat is defined differently by culture. But then, how do we even define culture? The catch-all term of *corporate culture* often leads to the shrugged shoulders of "so it just all depends?" Just as generals are criticized when they wrongly apply the lessons of the last war to very different circumstance in new warfare, surely one of the most widely used and abused words in business parlance is the term *culture*. Unsure of how to define it, amid a collision of uses, the cautious editors of the *Harvard Business Review* even refused to publish articles on that topic in the 1980s.

Beyond the corporate connotation, some complain that the term has such wide use, it risks losing its meaning. In this "postmodernist" world of cultural relativism, the "when in Rome" connotations of culture have led some to suspect judgment and action. In the famed writings of philosopher Michel Foucault, practices offensive in one culture were presumed to be acceptable in another, and hence universal standards were questioned.[52]

In fact, as far back as the 1950s, the great anthropologists Alfred Kroeber and Clyde Kluckhohn tabulated over two hundred common academic definitions of culture![53] By the 1970s, however, some common agreement had emerged on levels of culture, which distinguished material aspects of culture—such as tools, rituals, and architecture—from symbolic aspects of culture—such as beliefs, meaning, assumptions, and values.[54] Thus, we have come to see culture as predominating traits, behaviors, and attitudes that help define a group, a nationality, or even a corporation. In this chapter, we have seen that part of the struggle for recovery of leaders has to do with how well they embody the ideals of the culture of their occupation or industry. Those whose failure showed they defied the values of their occupations had great difficulty overcoming their setbacks.

Thus, to help define the ways culture can be defined and then to consider how success and failure at work may be differently defined within those cultures, we have suggested a typology of cultures. In particular, four sets of corporate cultures were drawn from our original research over twenty-five years of study. The four categories of culture are determined by how much they rely on outside staffing and the degree to which they cultivate specialists or generalists. We can see fundamentally different leadership values that follow these material choices.

Firms that greatly value specialized expertise and celebrity reputations are labeled as baseball teams. These gypsylike cultures have highly mobile workers who are expected to turn over often. They are driven by the wizardry of their profession more than by loyalty to a given employer. As with the baseball athletes these players resemble, performance is judged by highly individualistic metrics. In companies ranging from software firms and biotech firms to advertisers and media firms, individuals can excel even while their employers fail. Ray Ozzie's Lotus Notes may not have been enough to save the Lotus Development Corporation, but that firm's disappearance into IBM did not diminish his star power as he was eagerly sought by Microsoft's Bill Gates. Internet pioneer Vint Cerf suffered little in reputation cost as his employer, MCI, collapsed in the WorldCom scandal. External associations, leagues, and professional networks, along with credentialed performance, are critical elements of recovery.

Firms that also put a premium on expertise and individual performance but that groom more from within are called academies, which place their emphasis on internal training. As with great electronics and consumer products firms, they tend to develop their own talent and nurture institutional wisdom or house knowledge. Failure often happens when leaders do not realize that they have hit a wall due to narrowed functional tracks and must move on. The successful recoveries of GE alumni such as 3M's Jim McNerney or The Home Depot's Bob Nardelli show that they have portable skills and will not just try to re-create identical practices that helped them succeed in a prior academy culture. John Sculley's inability to make that shift hurt his career move from Pepsi to

Apple. The challenge to recovery for leaders from a world that values house knowledge is to demonstrate that they can accommodate a new context and not try to re-create past success.

A third type of corporate culture is represented by the clubs. In these firms, partnership-like interdependence builds so that interpersonal trust and dependability often matter more than the technical wizardry of always being correct. When JetBlue founder David Neeleman, a conservative-lifestyle Mormon, was fired by Southwest Airlines CEO Herb Kelleher, a freewheeling, whiskey-guzzling chain-smoker, he had to prove that his impatience for what he felt were endless meetings at the "groupy" cohesive Southwest did not indicate any imperial traits in his own style. UPS CEO Oz Nelson began his tenure having to unravel his original plan for globalization, while his successor, Jim Kelly, had to try different paths to resolve a massive, nationwide Teamsters strike the month he took over. In neither case did anyone within the firm doubt for a moment that their leaders would help the firm learn collectively from any missteps along the way. Nelson triumphed by launching a huge global reach for this great firm and transforming the culture from an operations and execution orientation to a customer-driven one. Kelly rewove the social tapestry of the firm and led UPS to become a multifaceted leader in technology, taking the firm public in what was at the time the largest IPO in U.S. history. Both helped lay a path for their successor, Mike Eskew, to build a smooth global logistics enterprise with a mix of acquisitions and organic growth, still learning as it grew. Due to careers invested in building trust, they could in times of crisis draw on that banked credibility. Amid the 1997 strike, for example, reporters interviewed UPSers to find out how the sophisticated CEO, Jim Kelly, a former truck driver himself, had modeled the basic humility and common touch to be able to comfortably talk with any driver on a loading dock or in any boardroom in the nation.

A final type of corporate culture is the fortress. The peril of a firm in trouble can lead to a siege mentality where survival is a critical objective. The successful leaders must prove themselves to be tough and persuasive like IBM's Lou Gerstner, instead of appearing tough and abusive or unreliable, like Sunbeam's "Chainsaw Al" Dunlap. The temptation to abuse workers and cheat partners is high when this survivor ethic prevails. As we saw with Cendant's Henry Silverman or Days Inn's Mike Leven, it was critical for them to prove their sterling reputations by legally drawing lines in the sand that separated them from the misconduct of partners.

In short, heroic actions in one culture could be deemed as insufficient, inappropriate, or even villainous in another culture. Each culture helps create the heroes it needs because those heroes provide a code of conduct—or a fundamental set of aspirations and values—for that culture to follow. Anthropologist Richard Dorson and historian Dixon Wecter have shown how changing social aspirations in folklore over different periods of American history led to the celebration of different occupations in our folklore, from frontiersmen, lumberjacks, and cowboys to warriors, social activists, inventors, and business tycoons, depending on where the nation's greatest uncertainties were manifest.[55]

Thus, those who followed the prescriptive path for greatness as defined at a certain time, for a given occupational culture or societal expectations, were more likely to regain their footing after a major misstep. The role of context loomed large in assessing the effectiveness of comeback actions of individual leaders. Next, in chapter 5, we move from the larger context of firm and industry cultures to the specific context of why someone was fired rather than where they were fired. Perhaps some forms of gross misconduct are so egregious that they transcend cultural tolerances.

CHAPTER **5**

Departure Causes as Barriers to Recovery

My dear dear lord,
The purest treasure mortal times afford
Is spotless reputation: that away,
Men are but gilded loam or painted clay.
A jewel in a ten-times-barr'd-up chest
Is a bold spirit in a loyal breast.
Mine honour is my life; both grow in one:
Take honour from me, and my life is done:
Then, dear my liege, mine honour let me try;
In that I live and for that will I die.

—Shakespeare, *Richard II*

AS SHAKESPEARE so accurately penned in his play *Richard II*, reputation is the purest treasure afforded to the noble leader. While departed CEOs and other leaders may be well positioned for rebound in terms of resources and experience, it is their reputation, and particularly their reputation among key gatekeepers, that is likely to make the difference between a successful career recovery and remaining mired in their troubled fall. Although in chapter 9, "Rebuilding Heroic Stature," we will look at how reputation is restored, in this chapter we will examine how the cause of exit impacts reputation and has a direct bearing on the likelihood of career recovery. Rather than speculate on whether or not reputation matters, we present the first systematic set of studies that demonstrates that a damaged reputation erects a substantial, and even insurmountable, barrier to career recovery.

Surely, the nature of the cause of one's downfall must matter. Consider the comebacks of such celebrity entertainers as actors William Shatner, John Travolta, and Hugh Grant, as well as sportscaster Marv Albert and NBA star Kobe Bryant, versus the career quicksand hit by the likes of pop icon and singer Michael Jackson, and silent screen star Fatty Arbuckle. Shatner is best known for his 1960s heroic role as Captain Kirk on TV's *Star Trek*, but his pop icon image fell with the death of the series—except for die-hard sci-fi fans. After a long period of less prominent roles in acting, singing, directing, and self-mocking reprises, he returned with resurgent popularity as the comical spokesman for Priceline, not to mention key roles in major films, such as *Miss Congeniality 2: Armed and Fabulous* with Sandra Bullock. At age seventy-six, he enjoys a hugely popular role on the hit TV series *Boston Legal* opposite Candice Bergen.

One of the biggest stars of the 1970s was John Travolta, who emerged as an arbiter of trendy taste in music and fashion following such period films as *Saturday Night Fever* and *Staying Alive*. Then his fame plummeted in the 1980s after a series of failed films panned by the critics. But, like William Shatner, he did not concede defeat. In 1994, he made one of the most breathtaking comebacks in entertainment history with his acclaimed role in Quentin Tarantino's *Pulp Fiction*. This launched several dozen blockbuster new roles in films such as *Get Shorty, Michael, Face/Off, She's So Lovely, Primary Colors*, and *The General's Daughter*.

Hugh Grant, best known for his roles as a blundering Englishman with an awkward, goofy politeness, seemed to have secured a breakthrough with his role in the 1994 film *Four Weddings and a Funeral*. Unfortunately, he blundered his way into a reputational disaster when, in 1995, he was caught with a prostitute just before a high-profile celebrity marriage to actress Elizabeth Hurley. Rather than retreat, he immediately signed up for the late-night talk show circuit; with self-ridicule he charmed his way back into the public's sympathy and secured starring roles in a long string of successful films such as *Notting Hill, Mickey Blue Eyes,* and *About a Boy.*

In 1997, the celebrated NBC sportscaster Marv Albert, who broadcast for the New York Knicks, the Rangers, and the Giants, also saw his notoriety soar and his career sink in the midst of an illicit sex scandal where lurid descriptions of kinky sex acts filled the news. He pled guilty to charges of misdemeanor assault on a mistress of ten years. As with Hugh Grant, the scandal was especially ill timed since he was engaged to marry an ESPN producer. Hours after his plea bargain, NBC fired Albert, and then he resigned from his job at MSG Network. A year later, he was rehired by the MSG and Turner networks, and in 1999 he returned to NBC.

Not all fallen celebrities find it so easy to rebuild their reputations. Silent film star Roscoe (Fatty) Arbuckle checked into San Francisco's St. Francis Hotel for Labor Day weekend in September 1921 as one of the most adored U.S. comedians, grouped with Charlie Chaplin, Harold Lloyd, and Buster Keaton. Soon afterward he was scorned because he was accused of the rape and murder of an actress who died after a party in his suite that weekend. Although he was cleared of all charges, he was banned from Hollywood work under his own name for over a decade. In June 1933, just when he was celebrating the lifting of that ban and a new major film contract, he died of a heart attack.[1]

Similarly, it has not been an easy career relaunch for singer Michael Jackson. After a series of allegations of child molestation and a trial revealing a bizarre personal lifestyle, followed by his spray of counteraccusations against media titans, he has largely retreated to sanctuary in the Middle East.

An extraordinary reputational rebound is that of Los Angeles Lakers guard Kobe Bryant, who fell from grace following a June 2003 charge of sexual assault. As his image disintegrated, so did ads featuring him that were produced for McDonald's, Russell Corporation's Spalding sporting goods division, Nutella, Coca-Cola's Sprite soda, as well as Nike's plan to create a line of signature sneakers and apparel.[2] Only three years later, after charges had been long dropped, Nike returned to its $40 million–plus apparel endorsement deal, following a 2006 game where

Bryant scored an astounding eighty-one points against the Toronto Raptors in forty-two minutes. The basketball game comeback may have taken only forty-two minutes, but it took a lot longer before Bryant made his first new TV commercial since the scandal broke. McDonald's, Coca-Cola, and the makers of Nutella terminated contracts worth $11.5 million.[3]

The Oxford Desk Dictionary defines *reputation* as "what is generally said or believed about a person's or thing's character."[4] We can derive from this definition two salient dimensions to reputation: the content of the reputation and the recipient or holder of that content. The scope of the content of a person's reputation can be summarized as "character," but, in the context of a person's reputation in respect to career prospects, can usefully be broken out into moral character, social character, and skill and ability. Moral character is concerned with adherence to a high moral code of conduct and primarily includes issues of honesty and integrity. Social character covers the realm of the person's interaction with others—how they relate to others, their ability to get along with people, and personality traits governing motivation and interaction with others. Skills and abilities relate directly to the person's past performance and their perceived ability to use their talents to translate that past performance into future performance in another context.

Each of these facets of reputation may have a different impact on the person's likelihood of recovery from career setback, be more or less salient in different circumstances (as discussed in the previous chapter), and be widely or narrowly known. Indeed, a person's downfall may be due to damage in reputation in one of these components, but others may see other components as being more salient, and so overlook damage in one area. For example, Bill Agee caused a scandal at Bendix, having rapidly promoted Mary Cunningham, under allegations of favoritism due to romantic involvement (the two later married), and then was ousted after a failed takeover of Martin Marietta Corporation. Despite this major career setback, the Morrison-Knudson Company hired Agee as CEO as a result of Agee's perceived ability to turn the company around. Morrison-Knudsen was not concerned by the events of Agee's personal life, hiring him with comments such as "He was a very capable fellow" and "He had a lot of the attributes we were looking for."[5] Indeed, reputational effects may not even be in the context of a "damaged" reputation, but merely fit in with the values or needs of the organization. For example, "Chainsaw Al" Dunlap had earned his hard-charging, abrasive reputation through his escapades at Scott Paper and previous employers, yet, despite this social reputation, which may have been perceived negatively by many, Sunbeam specifically sought Dunlap's reputation for turnarounds and hired Dunlap to address its troubles. Subsequently, however, since his ignominious exit from Sunbeam due to fraudulent accounting practices, this latter blemish on his moral character has overshadowed any positive reputation for his skills and abilities; and after an SEC ban on his being an officer or a director of any public company, he has retreated quietly into retirement.

The second dimension of reputation is the recipient or holder of the content of reputation. That is, how widely dispersed is the person's reputation and how firmly is it held? For example, a person may have been engaging in dishonest accounting for many years, yet this may be known to no one or to only one or two people, who keep it to themselves. In such a case, the flaw in moral character is not widely known, and, indeed, the person may have a wide reputation for good moral character or no reputation at all, good or bad, in this area. However, if that dishonest accounting is brought to light, splashed across the national newspapers, with ensuing investigations by the SEC or other authorities, then the reputation for dishonest moral character becomes very widely known and firmly held. While this shows the extremes of reputation dispersion and strength, most cases are less dramatic. When a person is fired from a CEO position, the reasons for dismissal may not be publicly known. Indeed, the true causes for the dismissal are often deliberately hidden because the board seeks to protect the reputation of the firm and itself and often engages in elaborate face-saving activities to disguise the true nature of the exit. Many euphemisms in press reports that the CEO resigned "for personal reasons" or "to spend more time with his family" hide more-damaging events or disagreements that could potentially harm the firm's reputation as well as that of the departing CEO, and both parties agree to present a picture of a more amicable departure than is really the case.

The Intertwined Nature of Reputations Between the Leader and the Enterprise

These attempts to hide the underlying reasons for the firing of CEOs point to the fact that the reputation of the CEO, who is the public face of the organization, is inevitably closely intertwined with that of the organization itself. A recent study by consulting group Burson-Marsteller underscored this interlinking of corporate and personal reputation, finding that the CEO's reputation represents 45 percent of the company's overall reputation among other CEOs, top executives, financial analysts, the media, and government officials.[6] The Burson-Marsteller study shows that the CEO's personal reputation can have a significant and positive impact on the company, with 95 percent of financial and industry analysts saying they would purchase stock based on the CEO's reputation, and 94 percent saying they would recommend a company's stock because of the CEO. On the other side of the coin, corporate reputations are also devastated when the CEO's personal reputation is destroyed through the CEO's misconduct. Witness the massive stock price declines of corporations whose CEOs have been the subject of scandal. ImClone's stock sank over 90 percent in the weeks following the revelations of CEO Sam Waksal's insider trading. Martha Stewart Living Omnimedia's stock dropped over 70 percent with allegations that Stewart herself profited from sales of ImClone stock with inside knowledge from her friend Sam Waksal. Tyco stock also plummeted more than 70 percent on the unraveling of CEO Dennis Kozlowski, which was initiated by allegations of avoidance of sales tax on his art purchases. All of these cases involve destroyed or damaged personal reputations that initially had little to do with the financial health or well-being of the organization, yet had substantial negative repercussions for the company.

This data would indicate that the CEO's personal reputation and the corporation's reputation are intertwined such that each is dependent on the other. The CEO is the public face of the corporation, and the performance of the corporation is attributed to the CEO by the public, and vice versa. Thus, when the organization is performing well and is seen by outsiders in a positive light, the reputations of both the organization and the CEO are enhanced; and when a mishap occurs, whether or not the CEO is personally the cause of the slipup, both the company's reputation and the CEO's personal reputation suffer. Indeed, Harvard Business School professor Rakesh Khurana has argued that this reflected glory of the intertwining of CEO and enterprise reputations has led to companies blindly pursuing charismatic CEOs who have high marketplace reputations as corporate saviors, without regard to the company's strategic situation or how appropriately the candidate's skill set matches the organization's actual needs.[7] Khurana argues that this irrational quest has distorted the CEO labor market, leading to stratospheric compensation of superstar CEOs and ultimately, perhaps, to the spectacular corporate failures we so often witness.

However, despite the strong interrelationship between the CEO's individual reputation and the corporate reputation, what happens when these interlinked reputations are torn asunder by the firing of the CEO? Even when the true nature of the exit is disguised, how does the departure from the organization affect the CEO's personal reputation, both widely among the public and narrowly among key gatekeepers, and what impact does any potential damage to the CEO's reputation have on the likelihood of career recovery?

Executive Search Recruiters as Gatekeepers to Career Recovery

Of course, there are many different scenarios for the career recovery of departed leaders and different avenues by which they may go on to lead another organization. Many CEOs choose to go the entrepreneurial route and start their own organizations—such as Bernie Marcus at The Home Depot—and often have sufficient resources of their own to do this. Others use an outside board membership and close personal contacts to enable them to bypass a formal search process in entering the organization. Some prefer instead to take only advisory roles as outside members on several boards. Many, such as former American Express CEO James Robinson or former Time Warner chief Nick Nicholas, continue to accumulate substantial wealth and maintain a hand in business by investing privately as advisory angel investors in small start-ups in areas of their interest, but never regain the prominence they once enjoyed.

Former CEOs without the advantage of strong networks or board connections or who choose not to take the entrepreneurial route must travel a road back to prominence that is guarded by the gatekeepers of the executive search industry.

In high-level executive searches, firms almost invariably retain an executive search firm to supply a short-list of candidates for the position. Thus, the executive search firms effectively act as gatekeepers, holding the keys to these upper-level positions for the fallen leader. In this market for executive talent, reputation is the coin of the realm. Actual skills and ability are often hard to evaluate, and while background checks and references are used, the ability to accurately gauge the candidate's skills and potential fit with the company's needs is at best an uncertain art. Given that, as previously mentioned, the CEO's reputation can have a substantial impact on the overall reputation of the firm, it is also likely to have the most *immediate* impact on the firm, at least as perceived by the outside world. Also, given that the directors making the ultimate selection and the executive search consultant (as gatekeeping intermediary) have reputations to protect, there is substantial incentive for them to select the candidate with the highest reputation regardless of the match between the candidate's abilities and the company's needs because of the uncertainty of the outcome and the limited ability to assess this fit. If the directors' selection turns out to be a bad choice as assessed by the CEO's actual performance on the job, the directors can point to their selection of the most noteworthy and reputable candidate available, thus protecting themselves from accusations of bad business judgment and consequent damage to their own reputations. Indeed, according to our interviews with prominent members of the executive search community, this very scenario transpires fairly frequently. Boards often perceive each individual on their short-list of candidates as bringing a different combination of skills, each set of which they perceive fairly equally to fit the needs of the firm. So they choose based on the candidate's broader reputation, which they expect will be judged the most positively by the market and will give them the greatest protection should the candidate not perform up to expectations. Therefore, the CEO's reputation becomes paramount in determining the likelihood of career recovery.

Executive Recovery from the Perspective of Executive Recruiters

Given its importance in the selection process, it is essential to know how reputation is transmitted in this marketplace for executive talent. In his book *The Headhunters*, John Byrne delved into the world of executive search and its reach, contending that executive search firms "have helped to change the nature of executive mobility and the way managers switch jobs," such that now almost all top-level executive searches that look outside the company involve a search firm.[8] If executive search consultants hold careers in the balance based on their judgment of a candidate's reputation, from what sources are they getting information in order to form the basis for such a judgment? In order to address this question and better understand the dynamics of reputation in the market for executive talent, we identified and surveyed the most commonly cited executive search consultants who are actively engaged in CEO and board-level searches (see table 5-1).[9] The executive search community, particularly those who deal primarily at the very top of the organization with CEO and board searches, is a fairly small group of people who are engaged in most major searches. So how information on reputation flows within this relatively small community plays an important role in determining the likelihood of career recovery for deposed CEOs.

Figure 5-1 shows the primary sources that executive search consultants rely on in getting information about a candidate's reputation, particularly the details surrounding their fall from grace. As can be seen from the figure, these consultants rely on primary data—their personal interaction with the candidate is the highest-rated item, followed by sources who have personal knowledge of the candidate: board members, senior managers, and other people who know the departed CEO. Relied on less are more general sources of information about the candidate's reputation: other CEOs, the media, and analysts. Finally, the small world of executive search is also very competitive, with our results showing that little information is passed from consultant to consultant since each protects their knowledge and relationships with these key constituents—their primary source of competitive advantage. From this pattern of relying on primary data to establish the candidate's reputation

TABLE 5-1

Survey respondents

Name	Firm
James M. Citrin	Spencer Stuart
Roger M. Kenny	Boardroom Consultants
Millington F. McCoy	Gould McCoy & Chadick
John Blaney	Blaney Executive Search
Chuck Brazik	Brazik Group
Dylan Davis	O'Brien and Company
Bill Dee	Hartsfield Advisors, Inc.
Richard A. Erlanger	Erlanger Associates
Gordon Grand III	Russell Reynolds Associates
Lawrence Griffin	Whitehead Mann
Ira J. Isaacson	Spencer Stuart
Kevin Jones	Crown Advisors, Inc.
Robert D. Kenzer	Kenzer Corp.
Charles H. King	Korn/Ferry International
Thomas L. McLane	The Directorship Search Group
Russell Reynolds Jr.	The Directorship Search Group
Rick Smith	Spencer Stuart
Rebecca Sohn	Lee Hecht Harrison
Charles D. Wright	Stanton Chase International
Bill Handler	Handler & Associates
Joel M. Kobletz	Boardroom Consultants
G. Roche	Heidrick & Struggles
Michael D. Kennedy	Korn/Ferry International
J. Veronica Biggins	Heidrick & Struggles
C. Clarke	Boyden Global Executive Search
Paul F. Crath	PricewaterhouseCoopers
Lois Dister	Cejica Executive Search
Becky Gates	The Link Partners
Joe Goodwin	The Goodwin Group
Deborah Harper	Harper Hewes Inc. Executive Search
William J. Kelly	Kelly & Company
Richard E. Kinser	Kinser & Baillou
Andrea Redmond	Russell Reynolds Associates
A. Daniel Meiland	Egon Zehnder International
William B. Reeves	Spencer Stuart
Pamela Rolfe	
Steven Schneider	Schneider, Hill & Spangler, LLP
Pamela Sedmak	O'Brien and Company
Billy Seitchik	Seitchik Corwin and Seitchik
Patrick H. Sugrue	Hendon & Sugrue Executive Search
Astrid von Baillou	
William H. Willis Jr.	William Willis Worldwide, Inc.
Andy Zaleta	Korn/Ferry International
Tom Neff	Spencer Stuart
Robert Hallagan	Heidrick & Struggles

FIGURE 5-1

Sources of information about exit

On a scale of 1 to 7, with 1 = don't use at all; 7 = rely on heavily.

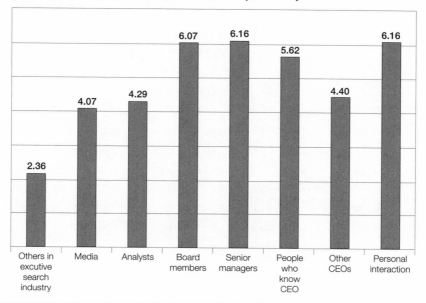

and gain information about the cause of departure, executive search consultants can develop a fairly detailed picture of the candidate's reputation in the marketplace and the context of their fall.

Causes of Forced CEO Exit

It is the context of the exit that has perhaps the greatest impact on the person's reputation and consequent likelihood of career recovery. In studying the exits of hundreds of CEOs, we examined the detailed reports of each exit and further discussed numerous exits and exit types with some prominent executive search consultants who had inside knowledge of many of the forced-exit cases we were studying. From this process, we categorized six basic underlying causes of exits that are a result of a forced, premature separation between the CEO and the organization, as opposed to a normal retirement exit or the voluntary departure of the CEO to move to another organization:

1. *Poor corporate performance*, where the organization has underperformed its peers, often consistently, for an extended period of time. In some cases, in order to avoid drawing attention to the poor performance of the organization, the board may try to disguise the underlying reason for the CEO's dismissal with euphemisms such as "The CEO has resigned for personal reasons." However, the perception from the outside world is that the company has been underperforming and a change has been forced as a result. In other cases, the organization is more up front about poor performance as the reason for the change, attempting to send a message to interested stakeholders that the board is conscious of the firm's underperformance and is taking concrete steps to change direction. Perhaps for potential liability reasons, the former approach is more common in corporations, while the latter is more common in professional sports organizations, for example, to appease fans.

2. *Personal misconduct* on the part of the CEO that either brings the individual into disrepute or, worse, is actual illegal behavior. Recent examples of this include Tyco's Dennis Kozlowski, who was indicted for avoiding sales tax on his art purchases, and ImClone's Sam Waksal, who was indicted for, and convicted of, insider trading. Other examples could include drug abuse, mismanagement of personal finances, or sexual harassment, the latter of which resulted in the ouster of J. P. Bolduc at W. R. Grace & Company.

3. *Illegal or improper behavior* on the part of the corporation for which the CEO has to take ultimate responsibility, regardless of whether or not the CEO participated in, knew about, or even condoned the actions taken by the organization. Many of the recent scandals, such as Enron, HealthSouth, and WorldCom, fall under this category. In each of these cases, the CEOs and members of their senior management have been indicted for accounting fraud, and the scandals have resulted in two of the largest bankruptcies in U.S. history. In these cases, it appears that the CEO was knowledgeable about, and participated in,

the illegal or improper behavior. But this is not necessary to force a CEO exit for such corporate malfeasance—for example, if the firm has been in violation of the Foreign Corrupt Practices Act, using bribes to obtain contracts even without the CEO's knowledge or consent, yet the CEO has ultimate responsibility for the culture and actions taken by the firm.

4. A *strategic disagreement* between the CEO and the board, where a strong board has a fundamental departure from the strategic direction in which the CEO is leading the organization or some other strong dissatisfaction with the CEO's running of the organization that results in the board ousting the CEO or forcing the CEO to resign from an untenable position. Such an exit reveals a strong board that is very involved in the strategic direction-setting of the company and has exerted its prerogative of power over the CEO. For example, Len Roberts and Frank Belatti, successive presidents at fast-food chain Arby's, clashed with chairman Victor Posner over corporate issues—Roberts over racial discrimination policy, and Belatti over moving the corporation from Atlanta to Miami—resulting in the exits of both men.

5. While performance and politics often collide in organizations, some exits are primarily driven by a *political or personality clash* between the CEO and a member or members of the board. Again, this type of exit reveals something of the dynamics of the board with board members who enjoy a strong power base within the boardroom and are prepared to exercise their power over a CEO who has lost power or the confidence of the board. John Mack, president of Morgan Stanley Dean Witter, clashed with chairman Philip Purcell, apparently over when Mack would take over the top spot. Mack had been CEO of Morgan Stanley and Purcell CEO of Dean Witter when they merged to form Morgan Stanley Dean Witter in 1997. It was widely believed both inside and outside the firm that while after the merger Purcell took the CEO role and Mack the presidency (although both drew the same compensation), there was an agreement that Mack would soon become CEO. Four years

later, it became apparent to Mack that Purcell would not turn over the reins, and the resultant clash resulted in Mack's exit, followed by the exits of many senior former Morgan Stanley employees.

6. While Mack's exit did follow a merger, it occurred some four years after a seemingly successful transaction and was portrayed as more of a later clash of personalities than a direct result of the merger. However, the *merger or takeover* of the firm by another firm often results in the CEO of the acquired firm leaving the organization either immediately or after a relatively short transition period, usually as part of the terms of the transaction, or if there is a culture clash between the entities and the CEO of the acquired firm, the CEO is seen as a hindrance to successfully blending the two organizations. The circumstances of the sale may have some implications for the performance of the CEO and the organization, but many mergers and acquisitions, particularly those of a friendly nature, have no negative performance implications for the CEO, even if he or she is forced out as a result.

While there are obviously unique circumstances surrounding each exit that will also have an impact on the individual's reputation, the reason for the CEO's exit is likely to have the largest systematic effect on reputation, particularly among the key gatekeepers to career recovery. While the board makes the ultimate decision about whom to hire into the CEO position, the key gatekeepers who determine which candidates are most likely considered in the pool of candidates are the executive search firms. As might be anticipated, the reason for the CEO's departure had a significant impact on the CEO's reputation among these prominent executive search consultants.

Figure 5-2 shows the perceived damage to a CEO's reputation for the various departure reasons discussed previously. As can be seen from the figure, these exit categories fall into two broad groups: those exit reasons that have a substantially negative impact on the departed CEO's reputation, and those where there is essentially no reputational damage due to the circumstances of exit. As might be suspected, particularly in light of recent scandals, engaging in illegal or improper behavior, whether by the individual or the corporation, has a devastating impact on the CEO's reputation. Dismissal due to personal misconduct and poor performance also has a "quite damaging" or worse impact on the CEO's reputation. But follow-on interviews with executive search consultants reveal that, particularly with performance-related exits, while failure is damaging to the CEO's reputation, the individual context surrounding the failure is vital. In the follow-up interviews, we asked executive search consultants about some specific cases of performance failure and the impact on that individual's reputation and future prospects, to get a better feel for how the individual context of the exit provided variance around the general impact of performance-related dismissal.

One such example we discussed was George Shaheen, who was a thirty-year veteran and the decade-long CEO of the global consulting firm Andersen Consulting (now Accenture). Shaheen left that position to become chairman and CEO of four-month-old Internet grocery delivery company Webvan in September 1999, in the midst of the dot-com bubble. Six weeks later, Webvan went public, making Shaheen's stock

FIGURE 5-2

Reputational damage caused by departure reason

Scale of 1 to 5 with 1 = very enhancing to reputation; 5 = devastating to reputation.

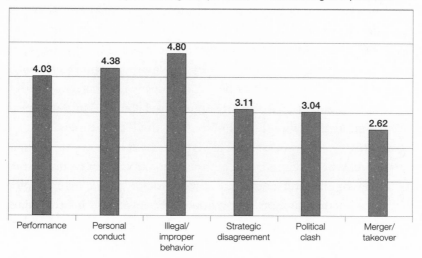

Type of exit

and options worth $285 million.[10] Nine months later, Webvan, unable to se-
cure further capital, went bankrupt and ceased operations, its stock worthless. While this was certainly a performance failure, the executive search
consultants we interviewed did not see this as a totally devastating blow to
Shaheen's reputation and career prospects. They acknowledged that Shaheen had made a bad judgment call in taking the position and in not seeing
the flaws inherent in Webvan's business model, albeit with the temptations
of potentially vast wealth in the Internet boom had things turned out well.
But the conclusion was that Shaheen was just not a good fit for the role, and
that Webvan was a doomed model from the start anyway. The executive
search consultants judged that Shaheen had obviously shown prowess in
leading a large, established, mature professional services firm, but wasn't
suited to a more entrepreneurial leadership role in a context where there was
a lack of current infrastructure and established track record. So while his
name would not likely appear on the executive search consultants' short-list
for an entrepreneurial operating role, should a vacancy arise to lead a large
professional services firm, Shaheen's name would certainly appear among a
very short list. Indeed, subsequently, Shaheen rebounded with his appointment as CEO of software company Siebel Systems.

Another example of a reputation surviving a performance failure is
that of Eric Schmidt, CEO of Web-search firm Google. Schmidt was a
key architect and evangelist of the Java programming language while chief
technologist at Sun Microsystems. He was tempted away from Sun in
April 1997 to become CEO of struggling software giant Novell. However, as a turnaround CEO, he was by his own admission "in over his
head," and four tough years later he left a company still struggling with financial difficulties and layoffs.[11] Despite this failure to fully transform
Novell, within two months Schmidt was hired as the new CEO of
Google, the hip and then profitable privately held leading search engine
on the Web, where Schmidt said cutbacks "so far amount to instituting a
$20 co-pay for an in-office massage."[12] For Google, Schmidt's technology
savvy, his reputation as a brilliant computer scientist, and his consequent
ability to understand the mind-set of the technologists at Google were the
overriding factors in hiring Schmidt. As board member and venture capi-
talist John Doerr explained, Google was more "like being at Sun Microsystems in the beginning again" than the turnaround situation Schmidt

faced at Novell, and consequently Google was a better fit with Schmidt's skills.[13] Under Schmidt's leadership Google has gone from being a fashionably cool search engine to an Internet juggernaut, lauded as the hottest technology company in the world, going head to head in different markets with Internet giants Microsoft, eBay, and Yahoo!, and, following one of the most successful IPOs in history, has thus far trounced these more established giants in their performance on the stock market. Schmidt has continued to lead Google to stratospheric heights as one of the most sought after advertising media sites and a choice employer.

These two examples demonstrate that while a performance-related exit can and does have negative consequences for the CEO's reputation, the impact of this may be selective if the context of the exit can be explained, and prior superior performance in another context can still pave the way for a positive reputation, even though the context of the future role will be more circumscribed than without the performance blemish. The George Shaheen example also brings to the fore the connection between reputation and future job prospects. While Shaheen suffered a performance-related exit, the context limited the damage to both his reputation and his perceived career prospects, such that he would still be a strong contender for a position in a context in which he had succeeded previously, despite the blemish of Webvan.

This experience, however, while not preventing his career rebound with Siebel Systems, may also have made him more sought after as a board member, even in an operating context similar to Webvan, where his experiences of the Webvan failure may place him in a good position to advise about the pitfalls in a similar context. Indeed, it is not uncommon for ousted CEOs to eschew new executive roles to instead focus on advisory roles as board members of high-profile companies. As examples: despite humiliating exits from the CEO position, F. Ross Johnson, former CEO of RJR Nabisco, who was made infamous by his portrayal in Bryan Burrough and John Helyar's *Barbarians at the Gate*, went on to serve as a director at American Express and Power Corporation of Canada;[14] John Akers, who was ousted as CEO of IBM, has since served as a director of W. R. Grace & Company, PepsiCo, Inc., The New York Times Company, and Lehman Brothers; and Arthur Martinez, who was CEO of Sears, Roebuck and Company, is now on the boards of the Federal Reserve Bank of

Chicago, Martha Stewart Living Omnimedia, PepsiCo, Inc., Liz Claiborne, Inc., International Flavors & Fragrances, and ABN AMRO. In order to address these career issues and the connection between reputation and career prospects, we asked executive search consultants specifically about the likelihood of future CEO roles and board memberships for ousted CEOs.

Figures 5-3 and 5-4 show that, in fact, the perception of likely future career roles parallels very closely to reputation, confirming the all-important role that personal reputation plays in this market for executive talent. Interestingly, and perhaps counterintuitively, with the exception of exit due to strategic disagreement with the board, the damage done to the individual's reputation due to the reason for departure provided a slightly greater barrier to obtaining a future board seat than a CEO position. While the difference in our findings is only slight and indicative, one might expect that given the prominence and influence of the role, damaged reputation might have a greater impact at the CEO level rather than a board position as one person among a group of directors. However, context and fit are more important considerations for the CEO

FIGURE 5-3

Likelihood of obtaining another CEO position

Scale of 1 to 5, with 1 = no chance of obtaining another position; 5 = almost certain to obtain another position.

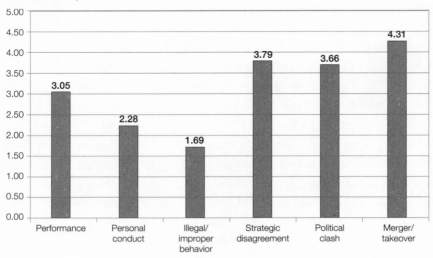

post; while reputation has a large effect, it is relied upon slightly more for board-level positions, where the exact fit of the executive's skill set with corporate needs may be less vital than for the CEO role itself.

It should not go overlooked that while reputation and career prospects were seriously jeopardized for three of the dismissal causes, for the other three causes, there was little or no reputational damage, and the likelihood of obtaining a future CEO position or board seat was perceived as being very good. This is perhaps counterintuitive to the general public, which might see any cause of a CEO being fired as having a negative implication for that individual's reputation and career prospects. But it demonstrates that this market for high-level executive talent values and judges reputation. This is also an important result for those going through these types of downfalls. The tendency is to feel that others think less of you when you have gone through an ouster; that if you don't hold the office of leadership in the organization, others will avoid you—in effect, that your reputation and social standing are irrevocably damaged regardless of the actual reason for the departure. As we will explore further in

FIGURE 5-4

Likelihood of obtaining a board seat

Scale of 1 to 5, with 1 = no chance of obtaining a board seat; 5 = almost certain to obtain a board seat.

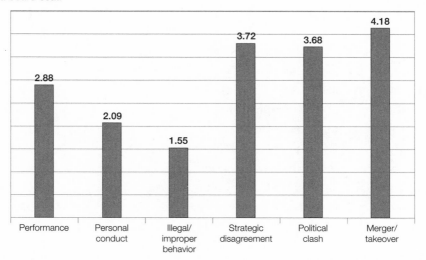

Type of exit

the next chapter, this may lead to people withdrawing from social and business interaction, which can stifle the recovery prospects for the individual. What these results show, however, is that despite the victim's often irrational fears, others—and particularly key gatekeepers, such as executive search consultants—do understand and take into account the circumstances surrounding the departure, and reputation may survive intact in many instances.

We have been talking so far in this chapter about reputation and the *perception* of the likelihood of career recovery, albeit it is the perception of the main gatekeepers to the executive suite. However, does this perception match actual outcomes for the increasing number of dismissed CEOs? A recent Booz Allen Hamilton study of the world's 2,500 largest publicly traded companies revealed that 253 CEOs left their position in 2002, nearly 100 of whom were fired for poor performance, a 70 percent increase over the number fired just the previous year.[15] In order to address this empirical question of CEO outcomes following dismissal, we studied all the CEO exits from the largest 1,000 U.S. firms over a five-year period to determine causes of exit and what happened to those CEOs who were dismissed. Of a total of 456 CEO exits over this five-year period, 60 were forced exits in the categories defined earlier; the vast majority of the remainder were retirement exits, and there were a few exits due to other reasons, such as the death or serious illness of the CEO or voluntarily leaving to take a position with another company. Given the relatively small number of firings and the results of the perceptual study with the executive search firms showing that we essentially have two broad reputational effects—exits that have a substantially negative impact on the departed CEO's reputation (those due to performance, personal misconduct, and illegal or improper behavior), and exits that have no negative repercussions for the CEO's reputation (those due to a strategic disagreement with the board, a political clash, or a merger or takeover)—we grouped the exits into these two distinct categories.

Table 5-2 shows the career outcomes, measured two years after the ouster, for deposed CEOs by type of exit. We categorized the career outcomes into one of three states. An active executive role means that the CEO has returned to a full-time position in another organization. This could be either being hired as a CEO or senior executive in another organization or founding another commercial enterprise and taking a full-time leadership role in that enterprise.

Alternatively, a deposed CEO could eschew a full-time executive role and instead engage in active advisory roles. This includes adding board memberships in other commercial organizations, effectively becoming a full-time professional director with multiple board memberships, or being involved as an angel investor with substantive hands-on involvement in the enterprise, as opposed to a passive investment.

It is not uncommon for these departed CEOs with substantial financial resources to focus on smaller, start-up firms in an area related to their expertise, taking a substantial equity stake in the business and devoting their time as an active adviser to the young entrepreneurial start-up—an approach taken by, for example, Nick Nicholas, former co-CEO of Time Warner, and James Robinson, former CEO of American Express. If a CEO failed to take either an active executive or advisory role within two years of exit, we categorized this as having retired from the corporate world. Of course, some of these executives may spend considerable time and energy following other passions, such as not-for-profit, charitable endeavors, preferring to donate their time in giving back to the wider community rather than trying to regain their former stature in the commercial world.

As can be seen from table 5-2, there is a substantially lower likelihood of regaining either an active executive or advisory role for those CEOs who departed due to exit reasons perceived by the executive search firms as reputation damaging—performance, personal misconduct, or illegal

TABLE 5-2

Career outcomes for deposed CEOs by type of exit

	Negative reputation exits	Neutral reputation exits
Regained active executive role	29.6%	39.4%
Regained active advisory roles	14.8%	27.3%
Retired	55.6%	33.3%
	100%	100%

or improper behavior. Indeed, fewer than half of such executives returned to an active role within two years of their departures. In contrast, two-thirds of those CEOs who were fired for reasons of strategic disagreement, political clashes, or merger and takeover—reasons that had no perceptual impact on their reputation—took active roles within the two-year period.

This evidence substantiates the fact that the perception of the executive search consultants matches the reality found by the departed executives. But more importantly, it shows that the damage to reputation, particularly among those key gatekeepers in the search industry, does substantially lower the prospects for career recovery for the departed CEO.

Reputation, then, is a powerful factor in the likelihood of career recovery for the departed leader. A damaged reputation can render a career worthless and make recovery extremely difficult. Just as for kings and noblemen in the chapter-opening quote from Shakespeare's *Richard II*, reputation is the most valuable possession the CEO has, and, as the quote concludes, is worth fighting to the end to protect and restore. And it becomes, as we shall see in chapter 9, one of the key factors in building a recovery. In the meantime, while we have focused in the last chapter on the corporate context of the exit, and in this chapter on the perception of others on the exit, we move now to examine the barriers to recovery built in the person's own mind and delve into the psychological effects of the exit on the individual.

6

Psychological Stresses as Barriers to Recovery

When Jill Barad was forced out of her position as CEO of toy maker Mattel, Inc., in February 2000, she was awarded a compensation package that included five years' salary and bonuses of $26.4 million, $708,989 a year for life in retirement benefits, forgiveness of a $4.2 million personal loan and $3 million home loan, $3.31 million to cover the taxes she would owe on the forgiveness of her loans, plus other perks, such as the payment of country club memberships and the option to purchase her office furniture for $1. Prominent shareholder activist Nell Minow commented on the stunning terms surrounding Barad's departure:

> *It [Barad's exit package] was worth between $45 and $50 million dollars. For someone who presided over the loss of over 70% of the share value as well as one of the most disastrous acquisitions in American history, she got a lot of wonderful parting gifts, including over $20 million in cash. This was very telling—the company knew that she needed some assistance in managing her money, so the company provided financial advice for her, which clearly she needed. It would have been nice if she'd had that advice beforehand. If you're on a board, one of the primary obligations is to deploy the corporation's assets to ensure the best return to shareholders. Somehow this board thought they would get an outstanding rate of return*

to shareholders by giving her a mortgage on her $3 million house. In light
of her departure, they not only forgave the mortgage, they also paid the
taxes on the forgiveness of the mortgage on the ultimate Barbie Dream-
house. They do this because it's not their money.[1]

With such lavish packages doled out to departing CEOs adding to
statistics that show that U.S. CEOs make more in a day than the average
worker earns in well over a year, it is not surprising that most people see
a vast disconnect between the world these leaders live in and their own,
and fail to see a CEO's downfall as inducing much suffering, let alone
constituting a catastrophic setback.[2] Indeed, for the majority of people
who suffer career setback, the financial hardship induced as a result of
job loss can be the primary cause of stress to them and their family, and
may result in their being forced into less-than-optimal employment in
order to sustain basic financial needs. Add to this the all-too-frequent an-
nouncements of thousands of layoffs at major companies, and the relative handful of fired CEOs seems to merit little concern. Consequently,
little thought is given to the fate of departed CEOs and other prominent
leaders on their own falls from grace.

However, while financial concerns are certainly often reduced, that
doesn't imply that the stress caused by exit is reduced in turn. It just
means that the form of stress is different. Indeed, the psychological damage to an ousted leader can be substantial and can erect a sometimes-
insurmountable barrier to recovery. A director of a major media company,
who had kept in touch with the CEO that his board had ousted,
poignantly captured the anguish felt by the CEO, the sources of some of
that stress, and the general sentiment of the larger society's indifference:

He's gotten through this in some sense—in another he'll never get fully
through it—you never survive something like this. I think it'll follow him
till the day that he dies. He was devastated. But, he put his life together
again, he's got his health, and his family. He'll be OK. It was an awful ex-
perience. I know him well. I know his wife, I know his kids. I have an enor-
mous sympathy for what he had gone through, even though he may have
brought it on himself. That doesn't make much difference. No one should
have gone through what he went through. It was brutal. Even the stories in
the press were unbelievable. Still, life goes on. It's not a tragedy of life and

death. I mean, basically, who cares . . . other than him? It's not the end of the world. Again, he comes out of it with enormous wealth. Not that that replaces his ego, which was probably permanently damaged.[3]

The personal tragedy may mark the end of a stellar career, or at least a major milestone in the life of an individual. As Andy Warhol remarked back in 1968, "In the future, everybody will be world famous for fifteen minutes." These CEOs have enjoyed far more than Warhol's fifteen minutes in the sun—at least in the world of their own organization—yet the final infamous fifteen minutes as they come crashing down from their lofty position may be the most revealing of their character. Some use the downfall as a springboard for bigger and better things in the future. Some never really get beyond the crushing blow dealt by the ouster, being caught in self doubt and depression or in a constantly raging feud with their past adversaries. The psychological damage caused by the separation from their organization, and some of the circumstances that surround the ouster, can erect barriers to recovery. The psychological resilience that is within the character of the individual can determine whether they can surmount these barriers.

The Burden of Separation

While reputation, discussed in the last chapter, represents the identity of the person to the wider world, people also have their own personal identity—who they see themselves as being. A substantial body of research shows that professionals and people at higher levels in the organization obtain a larger amount of their personal identity from their career; for these individuals, who they are is much more closely tied to what they do than it is for other groups.[4] This is probably more true for leaders of organizations than perhaps for any other group. The CEO, besides being privately identified with the organization, is also the public face of the organization and so is identified as the personification of the organization by outsiders and insiders alike. Often, a heroic myth develops around the leader, internally to the organization by stories and legends of the CEO's exploits and behaviors, and externally by the media, a demanding social and business calendar, and numerous symbolic and ritual functions that the CEO has to perform. In *The Frenzy of Renown*, literary scholar Leo Braudy argues that society always generates people who are eager to live their lives in the public eye.[5] This same group is studied by psychologist David Giles in *Illusions of Immortality: A Psychology of Fame and Celebrity*, where he explores both the addictive nature of celebrity and the tensions within the celebrity psyche since the public spotlight that creates fame is also the same glare that torments the celebrity in downfall.[6] Braudy contends that while fame seekers make up a small part of the population, their presence is both inevitable and welcomed by society because it allows the majority to see their own distinctiveness and possibilities:

> *In a society committed to progress, the seeking of fame, the climbing of the ladder of renown, expresses something essential in that society's nature. Even the more grotesque forms of ostentation are connected to normal desires to be known for one's talents or for oneself. Entertainers and politicians, who court public appreciation (and possible disapproval) on a grand scale, cannot be considered normal members of their society. But they are certainly extensions of everyone's culturally fostered desire to be given his or her due. . . Fame allows the aspirant to stand out of the crowd, but with the crowd's approval; in its turn, the audience picks out its own dear individuality in the qualities of its heroes.[7]*

Even within this group of fame seekers there are two distinct underlying motivations driving this quest for renown. There are those whose primary gratification comes from the wide recognition of themselves and the trappings that come with contemporary fame. As Katharine Hepburn put it, "When I started out I didn't have any desire to be an actress or to learn how to act. I just wanted to be famous."[8]

We refer to this quest for prominence in the leader's context within an organization as *heroic stature*: the temporal celebrity status conferred on the person due to their position in the organization. Alternatively, there are those whose primary drive is a deep-seated need for immortality, to make, and be recognized for, a lasting contribution or difference to the world through their presence in it, and who only seek contemporary recognition as an indicator of the lasting recognition that comes from their contribution. Isaac Newton fought long and costly battles in the scientific and wider community against other prominent, rival contemporary scientists to be recognized as the originator of scientific discoveries in optics, celestial mechanics and differential calculus, knowing and seeking the immortal reputation that these discoveries would confer.[9]

We refer to this drive for a lasting legacy as the leader's sense of *heroic mission*: the immortal fame conferred on the person through their lasting accomplishments. The burden of separation felt by the deposed leader is composed of a sense of loss of both heroic stature and heroic mission, but just as these two constructs represent different motivations, so is their loss felt through different manifestations.

The Leader's Identity with the Organization: The Loss of Heroic Stature

For business organizations, the CEO's role is unique. In today's world of a thriving business press, the CEO has become the personification of the firm. Moreover, with the current media frenzy for gossip and intrigue, and a personification of business, highly compensated CEOs have taken on a persona in the media that is sometimes almost as big as the companies they represent. CEOs become instantly recognizable and indeed synonymous with their organizations. Some of this celebrity has been brought on by the CEOs themselves, creating a heroic image to go along with their superstar compensation levels. Indeed, it is not unknown for CEOs to compare themselves to sports and entertainment celebrities, particularly when justifying their similar compensation levels. However, some of this is also the result of society's demands and, in particular, the business press. The personification of a large organization through building a legend of its leadership sells more magazines than a faceless corporate entity.

Tales of Lee Iacocca's storied career in the auto industry; legends of Bill Hewlett and Dave Packard tinkering in their garage; Steve Jobs's heroics at Apple, NeXT, and Pixar; Bill Gates's battles with the Justice Department—all contribute to thousands of column inches of newspaper and magazine coverage, not to mention best-selling books, which would be a harder sell without these colorful portrayals. In Shakespearean terminology, CEOs have greatness thrust upon them, becoming the stuff of celebrity, whether they like it or not. This celebrity status can become blown out of proportion to the achievements that merited the acclaim, and thus the status itself puts increased stress on the CEO. Psychiatrist Steven Berglas argues in his book *The Success Syndrome* that the consequence of the celebrity is to put psychological pressure on the individual to escalate performance to warrant the elevated status and live up to the continually escalating expectations of followers.[10] Even if they don't find themselves on the cover of *Fortune* magazine or on the front page of the *Wall Street Journal* on a daily basis, the CEOs are celebrities within their domain: the company and the community in which they live. Indeed, one CEO interviewed for this study commented that he had to be very careful about what he said, since fifty thousand people were ready to jump into action at his whim. If he merely expressed a passing preference for some state of affairs, it was likely to transpire.

Along with celebrity comes sycophantic behavior from those who surround the CEO and those who want to gain favor with or from the officeholder. Ceremonial duties, from giving speeches to Rotary clubs or alma maters to chairing fundraising activities for the local museum, put demands on the CEO, but at the same time put them in the center of their community's social circle. This elevated sense of celebrity engenders a strong intertwining of the CEO's personal identity and that of the organization. It becomes difficult for the CEO to disentangle their celebrity status from its source, the holding of the CEO position. While the CEO is in office, the fawning sycophants and the evidence of numerous non-business social invitations assure the CEO that they are wanted as a person. However, with their exit from office, the invitations rapidly dry up, and the fall in social status can be dramatic, causing immense psychological damage to the CEO who has believed in this celebrity.

The sudden downfall not only takes away the trappings of power, and does it in a painfully public way, but also cuts the leader off from the social stature in the organization and the larger community, which slashes deep into the fallen leader's ego. Leaders go from being the center of attention—constantly sought out by others and instantly recognizable and respected by a large group of people both within the organization and in the community at large—to at best, dropping from sight, and at worst, being vilified and outcast by the very company and community that once lauded them. Numerous ousted CEOs we interviewed commented on the seemingly overnight switch from being "who's who" to "who's he?"—a telling picture of the hurt felt by the result of the loss of status conferred by the CEO position. Tom Barrett, former CEO of Goodyear Tire & Rubber, related that he used to be constantly in demand to speak at his alma mater, the Massachusetts Institute of Technology (MIT), until he was no longer CEO:

> *I used to go to seminars, and one thing or another, and all of a sudden once you don't have that job, you don't even get a phone call. So figure that out . . . All of a sudden you're not in demand . . . You really make a personal sacrifice to do a lot of those things. To go to MIT, I'd fly up there, work until 2 in the afternoon, take the plane, fly in and spend all this time with them, and I just think they're not very appreciative, because really I have a better story to tell now than I had then. But they're dumb, they don't know that.*[11]

The ouster thus represents a loss of the leader's heroic stature. The celebrity nature of the leader's position, both inside and outside the organization, reinforces their identity with the organization. For these leaders, the identity of the individual becomes so intertwined with the identity of the organization that, at least in the mind of the leader, they become one. The forced separation of the organization's identity from that of the individual leaders can result in the feeling that they have lost the larger part of themselves; the leader sees the organization as an integral part of their being. Ralph Waldo Emerson's maxim that "an institution is the lengthened shadow of one man" is certainly the perspective of these leaders.[12]

Besides the often sought-after heroic stature that accompanies the leader's position, CEOs frequently find the role of CEO inherently satisfying and mentally challenging. The rewards of being the top person in the organization—although often substantial in tangible, material terms—are often outweighed by the enormous psychological rewards the person reaps from being in the CEO position. These rewards come from both the trappings of power and deference shown by others and the intrinsic reward of running an organization and achieving organizational goals. As the most senior executive officer of the company who reports only to the board of directors, and thus has no direct supervisor on a daily basis and often only nominal supervision in total, the CEO has a great amount of freedom to make decisions on behalf of the company and the opportunity to set the direction of the organization in an unfettered way. This freedom of direction is found by most CEOs to be very inherently satisfying. Tom Barrett lamented, "What you do miss in retrospect is that, as CEO, you can take a total entity, whatever it is, and you can really shape it, where all the employees are better off and the shareholders consequently will be better off, and you can absolutely shape something totally. I really miss that."[13]

Many CEOs also find the ultimate responsibility for the organization and the great number of employees in its ranks to be a source of immense satisfaction. Knowing that they are directly responsible for the fate of the working lives of a great number of people adds to the satisfaction of achieving the CEO position and becomes a source of frustration upon their ouster. One CEO expressed his concern for those he left behind and the internal frustration that it generated:

I feel that because of my disagreement with the board here, there's going to be a lot of people's lives impacted. You've got a lot of guys who have uprooted their families and have moved across the country [to be my senior managers]. Who knows now what happens to them? So, I guess I've got a lot of internal conflict that has generated tremendous amounts of frustration and I can't do anything about it. I can't—I in essence got into a power struggle with the board and I lost. And now a lot of people's lives are going to be impacted by it. So I've got a lot of frustrations. I'm not real happy.

The Leader's Drive for Immortality: The Loss of Heroic Mission

Along with loss of heroic stature, the tearing apart of the person's and the organization's identity, and the loss of the inherent satisfaction of the role itself, comes the enormous setback to the leader's heroic mission— the leader's desire to make a lasting contribution that ensures an immortal legacy. Great leaders are usually driven by a quest for immortality—a deep-seated psychological need to validate their existence for themselves and to provide meaning to that existence by seeking to make a contribution that will outlast their mortal body and not be readily eroded by the sands of time. This heroic sense of personal mission is the internal feeling that the leader, or hero, has a unique role to fill in the world and that only the hero is capable of fulfilling this quest. This concept is captured by the nineteenth-century social reformer John Ruskin in his statement "Really great men have the curious feeling that the greatness is not in them but through them." These leaders have a sense of destiny about their contribution and see the organization as an extension of themselves, with the organization's sole purpose being to fulfill their heroic mission. Thus their downfall and separation from the organization can cause intense frustration due to the sense of their mission going unfulfilled. They feel that the very purpose of their existence has been taken from them, that their life's work has all been in vain, and thus they see themselves as an empty shell with no purpose.

This frustration and its subsequent barrier to recovery can be mitigated, or at least come to terms with, if leaders are confident that they will continue the journey on the path they began with the organization and that ultimately the mission will be accomplished. Leaders can still believe that their heroic legacy will be established and the organization will continue in the direction they have set; then leaders can often reconcile their separation from the organization, maintaining their identity with the organization even when separated from it, realizing that their heroic mission will be fulfilled and their place among the immortal ensured. This fear is certainly eased if the successor is a trusted protégé. A timeless example, and indeed a metaphor for leaders' quest for their own "promised land," is the biblical narrative of the prophet Moses. Moses, having led the Israelites through the wilderness for forty years, came to the brink of fulfilling his heroic mission of leading his people into the promised land; he was given the opportunity to see the land from a distance but knew he was not destined to enter it. In his penultimate recorded words to his successor, Joshua, and his people, Moses commands them to: "Take to heart all the words I have solemnly declared to you this day, so that you may command your children to obey carefully all the words of this law. They are not just idle words for you—they are your life. By them you will live long in the land you are crossing the Jordan to possess."[14] In this concluding statement to his successor, Moses establishes the solemn importance of the heroic mission his leadership has set and lays out the means to ensure the fulfillment of that mission through following his directions, and in so doing, he makes peace with the fact that he will not be the one to see it fulfilled.

Even without this luxury of confidence in the successor, this barrier of the fear of unfulfilled heroic mission can still be overcome if the leader has confidence in the overall organization's tight hold on the leader's vision. When forcibly separated from Apple Computer, the company he had cofounded, Steve Jobs held his successor, John Sculley, in contempt but had confidence that the organization as a whole still reflected the values he had imbued it with. He laid out the conditions under which he would feel that his heroic mission had been fulfilled:

> To me, Apple exists in the spirit of the people that work there, and the sort of philosophies and purpose by which they go about their business. So if Apple just becomes a place where computers are a commodity item and where the romance is gone, and where people forget that computers are the most incredible invention that man has ever invented, then I'll feel I have lost Apple. But if I'm a million miles away and all those people still feel those things and they're still working to create the next great personal computer, then I'll feel that my genes are still here.[15]

However, if deposed leaders fear that without their presence and guidance, the organization will not be able to achieve the leaders' heroic mission or, worse, that the organization's progress toward the mission will be dismantled by their successors, this can cause great frustration because they believe that their life's work will be invalidated and their mission left unaccomplished. One CEO we interviewed clearly expressed this latter fear: "I feel like there's lots of unfinished things. I'm fearful that these things are going to get sidelined. I'm fearful that a lot of what I have put in place here is going to be undone. And it bothers me a great deal . . . I've got a lot of internal conflict."

In this circumstance, the leader is left with a sense of great loss because they see their life's work to this point as being wasted, the heroic quest they have been on as going unfulfilled. This can be a devastating blow to the psyche of the fallen leader because they are confronted with the stark reality of their own mortality and the limits of their ambitions to make a lasting contribution. For most people, this reality has been struggled with in what is documented as the midlife crisis, but such realities are often ignored by leaders with a strong drive for immortality and a mission in life of heroic proportions.[16] In their book, *Decision Making at the Top*, Gordon Donaldson and Jay Lorsch examine the psychological factors that influence the motivation of top managers, and note the top managers' adjustment to the limitations of the impact of their career as they recognize that they have in all likelihood reached the pinnacle of their career:

> *Thus they begin to feel that company success equals personal success. Second, they have reached the narrowest part of the company's hierarchical pyramid. There is only one CEO, and those who work directly with him must somehow accept the fact that, at their age, the internal competitive game has ended. They have reached the pinnacle of their career without climbing the last rung on the ladder. They must reconcile their earlier dreams with the reality of what can be accomplished, a reconciliation all adults must make.[17]*

All adults, that is, except the CEO.

The Double-edged Sword of Greatness

The CEO, just as leaders in other fields, has previously not had to face such realities; he has climbed that last rung on the ladder, and his career has usually known no limits or incurred no major setbacks. Leaders' careers have generally gone from strength to strength, climbing constantly and rapidly up the career ladder to reach the very top of the organization. No significant or prolonged setbacks have occurred during their career, no obstacle has been too great to overcome, and no final ceiling erected to block their way to the highest office.

Every step up the career ladder is a combination of skill and luck—the talent of the individual combined with such factors as being in the right place at the right time, knowing or being associated with the right mentors, and taking advantage of the opportunities that arise. The leader has, through constantly beating the odds at every career juncture, gained a sense of the hero in the ascent to the top, and yet now, like the mythological Icarus, is suddenly faced with a new reality of falling from the heights by being forced to prematurely fall from the position they have worked so long and hard to achieve.

In Greek mythology, Daedalus was imprisoned with his son Icarus by King Minos and sought to escape by building wings of feathers secured by wax. Having crafted wings for himself and his son, he instructed his young offspring to keep at a moderate height, so that his wings would not get clogged by the dampness of low altitude or melted by the heat from rising to close to the sun. But once they set off and successfully made their escape, the young Icarus became exulted by his new ability and soared high in the sky, where the sun began to melt his wings. Soon, with the feathers dispersed, no amount of flapping his wings would keep him aloft, and he came crashing down into the sea.[18]

As with Icarus's plunge from soaring in the heavens to a crushing death in the sea, one is compelled to wonder what the impact is on the ousted leader. Is the fall from grace in fact that much harder given the lofty heights from which the fall occurs? Or does the experience of a stellar career and the mechanisms built into high position provide a (sometimes golden) parachute to ease the fall? In particular, do these spectacular falls provide lessons and insights for stumbles at all levels? We contend that the old adage "The bigger they are, the harder they fall" rings true for the departed leader. There are unique characteristics of leaders' positions and celebrity that elevate them to lofty heights, and unique circumstances of the downfall that make the fall from grace even harder to bear. However, despite the dramatic descent borne by the displaced leader, the event is one from which some make a spectacular recovery. Indeed, the intensity with which leaders' need for immortality is felt and is fulfilled by their pursuit of a heroic mission, while causing a devastating blow when the quest suffers catastrophic setback, can also be the factor that sparks recovery as leaders redefine their heroic mission and begin another journey toward immortality.

The Consequences of Separation Circumstances

The burden of separation from the organization is exacerbated for the leader by the additional baggage of the unique circumstances surrounding the leader's ouster. When someone suffers a significant setback, the ability to shift the blame onto some external cause or person reduces the damage to the individual's psyche since their downfall could not be due to some inadequacy in their ability or effort. For example, if a company eliminates a division or closes a plant, thereby eliminating thousands of jobs, the experience of any one of the laid-off workers is very different from that of the dismissed CEO on whom the failing performance of the organization is blamed. The shop-floor worker among the thousands laid off when the plant closes can hardly blame himself for his state of unemployment or consider it due to his individual lack of ability or effort, whereas the CEO is left to continually second-guess his past decision making.

In many instances, particularly in business and political settings, several factors make it harder to shift the blame for the ouster to an external factor. First, the ousting of leaders from their positions is a decision made by a group, be it a board of directors or an electorate. Thus, leaders' ousters are a collective decision and not an individual one, lessening the possibility of attributing the dismissal to a personality or philosophical conflict between the victim and a single person who had power to dismiss them. A second factor that impacts attribution is the fact that unless the organization is subsumed into another organization, the leader's position is never eliminated, as can happen with other positions in an organizational downsizing or restructuring.

These factors reduce the ability of the leader to rationalize his ouster as an isolated, random occurrence with little to do with their own ability as leader, being either at the whim of an individual or under the fate of economic circumstances. Instead, leaders are less able to completely externalize the blame for their downfall and can be left questioning not just "Why did this happen to me?" but also their shortcomings and role in their own downfall. Add to this the glare of publicity that surrounds the leader's public exit, and the realities of the leader's situation become inescapable.

Public Nature of Exit and the Fear of Failure

The toppling of a leader, be it a CEO, a politician, or some other public figure, brings the spotlight of publicity glaring down on the individual and the circumstances surrounding the downfall. This glare of publicity and media attention takes away the leader's ability to deny or hide the occurrence of the setback. When this spotlight is not present, as is generally the case for most career setbacks, there is a tendency for the victim to live in denial of the event. Psychologist Katherine Newman, in her study of downward mobility in the American middle class caused by career setback, found that some executives attempted to put on a façade of getting up and going "to work" every morning to hide the fact that they had lost their jobs.[19] Some do this as a form of psychological denial, some to keep them in the routine of a regular job, some to save face with their neighbors, and some even to hide the fact from their families that they are unemployed. Even with departing CEOs, in a substantial portion of cases their forced departure is disguised by an elaborate collusion with the organization. Attempts are made to save face or cover up an exit forced by the company, such as keeping the CEO on as a "consultant" or even on the board for a short period following their ouster from office. It is generally perceived by both CEOs and the board to be in no one's best interest for the true reasons for departures to become public, and so there is frequently a concerted effort to deny the true circumstances of the exit and pass the exit off as an amicable split and a smooth transition for the benefit of the organization. These face-saving charades supposedly help minimize the damage to the CEO's reputation, to increase the likelihood of finding another position. However, this public denial of the true nature of the event can itself erect barriers to recovery.

The ousted CEOs have, of course, a primary concern about their reputation and the impact the dismissal will have on that most precious of possessions. This may lead CEOs to also view a public denial of the event as being in their best interest initially, even if the CEO feels that his departure is unjust and later wishes their side of the story had been aired in public. However, the initial shock is strong enough to prompt the reaction of not wanting this event to be more public than necessary. This is especially true for CEOs who have a substantial portion of their net worth in the company's stock at the time of exit. In such cases, they usually want to divest themselves of a large portion of the stock and do not want the market to react negatively to the departure. This also brings up the overlooked fact that the financial contracts and arrangements that the CEO has with the firm, while often providing generous financial settlement, have the potential to be an additional source of stress, albeit of a very different nature from the stress caused by a lack of financial resources felt by so many who suffer career setback. In this case, the stress arises from the restrictions imposed on the funds. While CEOs are often provided with generous financial incentives to leave the organization, the severance agreement usually contains clauses preventing them from working in the industry or going public with their side of the ouster story, eliminating the opportunity to repair the reputation dented by the ouster and to reprove their abilities. This forces CEOs to essentially put a value on their reputation and therefore their future opportunities, which can result in increased stress. One CEO we interviewed, formerly of a large industrial company in the Midwest, articulated his frustration:

> *Of course, I was immediately offered jobs by our competitors, but I can't take those jobs and still keep my stock options and stuff like that. So you have to find a whole new life because they tie you up so you can't do anything unless you want to give up a hell of a lot of money. If you're forty, hell, you can do that, but when you're sixty-five you can't do that . . . We all have egos. That is hurt. I guess what bothers you as much as anything is that you know people really don't know the true story of what you accomplished in life, in the outside world. I got [a letter] last week from a guy who said, "Hey, we know what the hell we're doing today because of the things you put in place." . . . I got credit, and I really mean this, from the people at [my company], but they're still working there, at one thing or another, and I've got whole drawers of letters and stuff. I got credit from them, but not from the board or the outside world because [the board] had to defend what they did.*

In this lamentation, we see how financial concerns exacerbate the burden of separation due to loss of heroic stature and heroic mission in three specific ways: a wide recognition of what has already been accomplished, a frustration in not being able to complete this mission, and a restriction on being able to fulfill the mission in a related area. Thus while there is undeniably a more significant disconnect between the experience and stress undergone by departed leaders, and particularly CEOs, than by most people, departed leaders have to contend with a deeper psychological setback and frustration that tends to dominate their minds and poses a significant barrier to recovery.

The CEO as Scapegoat

The darker side of public denial is in cases where the CEO is scapegoated as a sacrifice for the sins of the corporation—for example, when the company is involved in some improper behavior, such as collusion or market manipulation. Even if such CEOs have no direct involvement, they are removed as a scapegoat, taking the responsibility and blame for the actions. Even when they are generously compensated financially for taking such a fall, the negative impact on their reputation, social standing, and ego is substantial, if not devastating. A member of a board that had ousted its CEO in just such a case commented:

> We had a little ethics problem. But you see, we didn't paint it to the outside world that way. We didn't want to do that. So we made a deal, and he [the ousted CEO] wasn't allowed to talk even though he's convinced it wasn't handled properly—you don't want to start debating these things publicly. We put him in a position where he couldn't debate it, and he didn't, did he? He started to a time or two, but [our lawyers] reminded him of how his contract was written. Which I'm not saying is bad for the company, but for the individual, it's pretty brutal.

These contractual prohibitions from telling their side of the story can seriously impede disgraced leaders' ability to restore their image and reputation, which are key to successfully redefining and rebuilding their career, and so represent yet another substantial barrier to recovery.

Scapegoating can also occur for performance-related firings. While the CEO is directly responsible for the performance of the organization, there is obviously some disconnect between the CEO's decisions and the performance outcome for the organization due to changing environmental circumstances and the organization's ability to execute its strategy. Not infrequently, under conditions of poor performance, a CEO may be fired as a signal by the board to internal and external constituencies that change is needed even if they don't believe that anyone else would have performed better in the circumstances. This symbolic scapegoating happens frequently in professional sports, for example, as coaches of losing teams are routinely fired as a signal to the players and the fans that the owners are not content with the current performance of the team.[20]

Private Denial

The other side of denial for fallen leaders is private denial. By this we mean that the CEOs deny to others, but more importantly to themselves, that they were forced to leave, preferring to insist that it was their decision to leave the organization. They can often support this with the "evidence" that they resigned and were not fired directly, since in most cases of forced exit the CEO is "given the opportunity to resign" by the board, with the implication that in reality the CEO has no choice but to do so. However, the "evidence" of resignation, together with the public reports that also deny a forced exit, allows the departed CEO to deny the true nature of their exit.

These duplicitous techniques of impression management, engaging in elaborate face-saving charades at whatever level, reflect the pervasive fear of failure in our society and reflect the defense systems that individuals use to cope with failure.[21] While there is an underlying fascination with failure in our society—as the media gleefully chronicles the downfall of celebrities and well-known public figures just as they laud their success on the way up—there is little empathy in the fascination. While our society has a greater tolerance of entrepreneurial failure than most, even lauding the pioneering spirit, failure can still have negative repercussions resulting in social isolation. Indeed, there is considerable evidence that people become increasingly isolated the longer they remain unemployed.[22] For CEOs, part of this isolation may derive from their own behavior while in office. Often, they isolate themselves, suspecting that subordinates and others who try to befriend them have ulterior motives and are merely using them for their position. This oft-lamented loneliness at the top may lead to loneliness after the fall, as the departed leaders, because of this isolation while in office, find that they have developed few deep relationships. Add to this the victims' increasing embarrassment about their circumstances and the inability of those in supporting roles to know how to cope with the experience of their friend or loved one, and isolation can become a substantial barrier to overcome. In a study of white-collar unemployment, Stephen Fineman found in his interviews with those who suffered from such career setback that often their friends and other potential sources of support simply didn't know how to react to their situation and ended up offering platitudes or clichés as encouragement. Fineman writes, "Few had the knowledge or experience to [offer appropriate support]. Few had ever seen their spouse or friend in such circumstances. The pre-employment role relationship had not been formed around such issues: they were strange and confusing to the potential supportee (hence the retreat to benign clichés or truisms)."[23]

Worse still than using clichés is the pity and sympathy that those in the support network naturally offer. These supposedly encouraging statements often revolve around how bad things are in the economy and how others are going through the same thing. Although meant with the kindest of intentions to offer encouragement to the victims that they are not alone, these comments are often interpreted to reinforce the victim's feelings of hopelessness, rejection, and the stigma of their current position in society. Fineman again notes:

> The process of stigmatization was a particularly vicious circle for those already feeling they had failed and been rejected. For them the world was bleak, so they were more sensitive to possible discrimination. They, like everyone else, felt different, and usually uncomfortably so. They sensed others' embarrassment at their predicament, which could compound their own. Conversations and social interaction became strained because of the lack of a central anchor in their lives. This missing stabilizer created an uncomfortable vacuum. Family and friends were confused as the familiar reference points were missing. The job had patterned the features of life which formed the social links; now the job had gone, ambiguity prevailed. What was there to talk about? As time passed without a job, conversation about this area became progressively more taboo or difficult, like the effect of a malignant illness that is clearly not responding to treatment.[24]

However, while failure and career setback are socially taboo subjects, this aversion to addressing the topic, on the part of both the victim and their support networks, is counterproductive to recovery for three reasons. First, it allows the victim to continue to act in denial of the downfall since the topic of their setback is avoided. Second, the avoiding of the subject by others acts to hinder help that may be given effectively if those supporters knew how to act in this situation. Third, the increasing isolation brought about by the victim's withdrawal from social interaction and the lessening of offered interaction by others reduces the victim's potential network, which, as we shall see in chapter 8, is a key factor in recovery and in aiding the practicalities of beginning the rebound.

While the public nature of the leader's downfall certainly causes public embarrassment to the leader and can exacerbate the damage sustained to the leaders' reputations, one side effect of the publicity is that it reduces the possibility for denial of the event and forces the leaders and their support network to face the reality of this situation. This can have a positive or a negative effect, however. On the positive side, it can reduce the awkwardness of the initial interactions with supporters since the downfall is already known and public. It can also curtail the denial behavior of the victim and set them earlier on a path to look at other options and seek practical help from their support network before fair-weather friends drop away. On the negative side, the embarrassment of the public exit can cause victims to attempt to hide, becoming reclusive, completely cutting themselves off from their support network, and even rebuffing the offers of assistance that pour in from supporters. Additionally, even knowing about the victims' downfalls often does not help the supporters in knowing how to deal with the situation, and so even if the victim is ready for encouragement and support, often those in the support network flounder in providing that needed assistance.

Getting Trapped in Mutually Ensured Destruction

Even though, as elaborated earlier, there are factors that reduce the ability of departed leaders to externalize blame for their exit, pinning the blame on an external factor is still prevalent. While an invaluable step in helping to restore credibility, as we shall see later in chapter 7, it also has the potential to sap scarce energy and resources if the battles are not carefully chosen. As we saw earlier, Bernie Marcus, founder of The Home Depot, clearly blamed Sandy Sigoloff for his dethronement at Handy Dan Home Improvement Centers and had two potential battles to fight from that exit—one against Sigoloff for unfair dismissal and to claim compensation owed to him, and the other to defend his reputation against a frivolous accusation brought by Sigoloff. Marcus chose to focus his resources on the second of these, which he considered the most vital because it attacked his reputation. His limited resources of time, opportunity, and money led him to walk away from the first battle, to expend those resources in the founding of The Home Depot rather than engaging in expensive and consuming litigation.

In externally assigning blame to other people or circumstances, if CEOs cannot pinpoint an individual or group to hold responsible for their ouster, they may cite circumstances beyond their control, such as the general economic climate, cyclicality in the industry, or competitor unfair advantages. However, more frequently, blame is targeted toward specific individuals whom the CEOs hold responsible for the situation, whether it be particular members of the board who turned against them, or excessively ambitious potential successors who sought the ouster, or predecessors who could not let go of the reins, or management team members who failed to perform adequately. In such cases, CEOs perceive the ouster as a coup d'etat, and the protagonists as villainous assassins who have turned against their leader in a contemptuous display of disloyalty. This brings a strong parallel to the observation of Elisabeth Kübler-Ross when talking about a catastrophic diagnosis and impending death:

> *In our unconscious, death is never possible in regards to ourselves. It is inconceivable for our unconscious to imagine an actual ending of our own life here on earth, and if this life of ours has to end, the ending is always attributed to a malicious intervention from the outside by someone else. In simple terms, in our unconscious mind we can only be killed; it is inconceivable to die of a natural cause or of old age. Therefore death in itself is associated with a bad act, a frightening happening, something that in itself calls for retribution and punishment.*[25]

Similarly for CEOs, this "bad act" of their overthrow is attributed to individuals who have instigated their departure, which can only be rectified by "retribution and punishment." The strong identity that the CEOs had with the organization and the inability to separate their identity from the organization lead them to see the organization not as something greater than themselves, but as a part of themselves. Thus, whereas people at other levels of the organization see the corporation as bigger (and more powerful) than themselves, CEOs are not frightened of the organization and its power, seeing it as an extension of themselves, and so will be unafraid of attacking those who enforced the separation from their shadows. However, rarely do they attack the organization as a whole, but rather target an individual member or a small contingent of the board that they felt was responsible for their ouster. In most cases, the organization is retained in high regard, and the offending individuals are isolated in CEOs' minds from the rest of the organization. If, subsequent to the ouster, CEOs file a lawsuit against the company and certain named individuals, it is often only the named individuals on which CEOs place the true blame. CEOs focus on the behaviors of these board members whom they regarded as having gone beyond the gentlemanly rules of the boardroom and the boardroom norm of supporting the CEO. The decisiveness of a coup requires behind-the-scenes machinations that CEOs regard as sly, backstabbing behavior designed to seal their fate without the chance to defend themselves. The terms *kangaroo court* and *coup* are frequently used by ousted CEOs in describing the ouster process.

The internal bitterness felt by CEOs against the individuals they feel are responsible is manifested behaviorally in actions against the individual or organization, beginning (at least in CEOs minds) a feud between the two parties. In one illustrative example of this feuding behavior, one CEO described his situation when he sat down with his successor, who he regarded as the instigator of a coup against him:

> *He called me and said that we've got to talk. So we went to a restaurant and got a private room, and he said to me, "Why are you fighting this? Where do you get the money to fight this?" And I replied, "You know, I've got $6 million of the company stock, where do you think I get the money to fight you? I've put aside a million dollars for this and I'm going to beat your ass, and in fact my lawyers want you in court because they want to hear some explanations from you and the other board members about what you did to me. They're all going to be put on the stand." He said that there's no way they'll negotiate, and I said, "I don't give a damn. I want to see you in court unless you come up with a reasonable settlement that my advisors tell me is good." So they did, and I took it. It cost them a lot of money. I didn't need the money, but I sure took it. Why not? I don't appreciate the things they did. I don't appreciate what they tried to*

do to me. They tried to screw me out of money and medical coverage, but they had to make good on it. I don't like this new man, I think he's a cheat. I think his record is terrible. I don't like the way the company has been going since I left. I think it's headed for the tubes.

While the exacting of revenge in this manner can aid in the recovery process for departed CEOs, there is a great risk that this feuding behavior will not come to a quick or favorable conclusion. If revenge is not accomplished, the CEOs are likely to get stuck in a loop of feuding behavior and anger with those at their past organization whom they blame for their ouster, and become unable to close that chapter of their life and career. This feuding behavior can become the all-consuming passion that takes all of the energies of the CEOs. This has the effect of at once distracting the CEOs from opportunities to rebuild their career (and thus represents another barrier to recovery) while intensifying feelings of anger caused by the ouster.

The Nature of Resilience

The theoretical construct that uniformly underlies the accumulation of knowledge on the psychological impact of job loss is stress.[26] While losing one's job is undoubtedly stressful, whatever the circumstances, as we have explored earlier, some circumstances surrounding the leader's downfall can greatly exacerbate the stress experienced.[27] Due to these extreme levels of stress, we observe, as we would expect, that not all leaders are able to rebound from their catastrophic career setback. Indeed, our research indicates that only a minority are able to stage a successful career comeback, and only a very few exceed the heights from which they fell. As we reported in the last chapter, when we examined in depth the CEOs who were fired from the largest one thousand public companies in the United States over a five-year period, we found, combining all ousters, that only 35 percent resumed an active executive role within two years of departure, 22 percent stepped back and took only advisory roles, generally investing in and advising smaller organizations than those they left, and 43 percent effectively ended their career and went into retirement.[28] While the barriers to recovery that we have examined all play a role in hindering recovery, what we are interested in is what makes some people resilient to catastrophic setback and able to overcome these formidable barriers.

The countervailing force to stress is resilience and personal hardiness. There has been a great deal of academic research into resilience and related concepts. Much of this research coalesces around a few essential characteristics that distinguish those who are resilient to setback from those who fail to rebound. The first of these characteristics is what Diane Coutu called the ability to face down reality.[29] This is the ability to soberly assess, understand, and accept the reality of the setback, and to avoid the behaviors we discussed earlier that lead to attempts to deny or cover up the setback. In our terms, this is the decision of *fight, not flight*— to stand up to the reality of the situation and not flee from it or shirk the battles that lie ahead in restoring the reputation and career of the leader. For fallen leaders, the notion of "fight, not flight" certainly extends to being able to accurately understand the reputational damage caused by the downfall, and consequently being able to assess which battles are worth fighting to protect and restore that reputation, and which will result in the futile feuding behavior previously described.

Dr. Salvatore Maddi, the founder of the Hardiness Institute, conducted one of the pioneering studies on hardiness and resilience, tracking over four hundred employees at Illinois Bell Telephone before, during, and after the breakup of the Bell System in the early 1980s. Maddi and his colleagues found that almost two-thirds of the employees suffered significant mental or physical trauma due to the stress of this transition. Examining the one-third minority who, in contrast, maintained health and performance and actually thrived during this stressful period, he found that their resilience was due to a combination of attitudes they held, actual behaviors they engaged in, and specific patterns of giving and receiving social support and encouragement. While much of the focus for departed leaders on their recovery may be on what they themselves can do through their behaviors and attitudes on their own, it is critical not to overlook the power of *recruiting others into the battle* for recovery or to ignore the collateral damage that is felt by these loyal supporters in their network.

These support networks are invaluable in providing both the encouragement to overcome the psychological effects of the downfall and the practical assistance to help restore fallen leaders' reputation and facilitate avenues and entry into new career possibilities. But as Maddi pointed out, even though leaders have been ousted from their organizational position and are at the point of greatest need of the support of those in their network, both a giving and a receiving aspect to these relationships are still important even in these toughest of times. In their time of distress, people who have suffered setback often forget that those to whom they look for support have themselves often been negatively impacted by the stress caused by the downfall since they suffer through the empathetic distress caused by the damage done to someone they care about, as well as the increased care and attention that that person needs. Consequently, in order to support those in the support network, leaders need to respond empathetically to those from whom they are receiving support, and encourage and engage them in the process of recovery. At this point of extreme stress on relationships, fallen leaders discover who their foul-weather friends really are—those relationships are often strengthened due to going through a period of distress, while many fair-weather friends desert the fallen leader or disassociate themselves for fear of being associated with failure and the potential damage that may have on their own reputations.

Answering the "Why Me?" Question

One of the psychological traps that can ensnare a person and diminish the likelihood of speedy recovery from setbacks of any kind is the haunting question of "Why did this happen to me?" Instead of letting this question lead to destructive second-guessing and self-pity, the thing that distinguishes resilient people is that they have an answer to this question. They are able to rationalize a story of why this event occurred and why it is not a reflection of their overall abilities, competence, or character, and fit it into the larger picture of their overall career and life goals. The psychological research on stress conveys that people who are able to best cope with high-stress events hold three attributes: *decisional control*—the perception of having choices of actions to determine future outcomes; *cognitive control*—the ability to fit stress-inducing events into an overall life picture and by so doing diminish their negative importance; and *cop-*

ing skill—an arsenal of developed responses to stressful situations that the person can draw upon to minimize the effects of stressful events.[30] For people to answer the "Why me?" question, the dimension of cognitive control is all important in being able to put the event into a larger context of the person's overall career and life goals, giving the event a meaning that can then be portrayed as a positive platform from which to rebound. The feeling of decisional control then enables fallen leaders to feel in control of their rebound and the future options they may pursue to recapture and exceed their past accomplishments. Having a rationalization of the downfall is an essential first step not only for the person's psychological well-being and recovery, but also for the process of restoring the person's reputation in the wider community. Being able to construct a rationalization of the events, decisions, circumstances, and personalities that surround the ouster—such that even if it reflects some poor decisions on the part of the individual, it is not reflective of an overall lack of competence but is due to a collusion of circumstance—is essential in being able to *rebuild the heroic stature* of the individual and restore their image and reputation in the marketplace, first among those with whom the leader has direct contact and then to the wider audience.

Part of the coping skill that is essential for rebound is what Diane Coutu refers to as *ritualizing ingenuity*.[31] This is the ability to improvise solutions to the situation or problem the person is facing, without the obvious resources that one might normally require to obtain the solution. People who are adept at this skill have become known in the psychological and organizational literature as *bricoleurs*.[32] As organizational psychologist Karl Weick explains, when people are put under pressure, they typically revert to what they are most familiar with, and thus creativity is typically stifled under great pressure; however, "bricoleurs remain creative under pressure, precisely because they routinely act in chaotic conditions and pull order out of them. Thus, when situations unravel, this is simply normal natural trouble for bricoleurs, and they proceed with whatever materials are at hand. Knowing these materials intimately, they then are able, usually in the company of other similarly skilled people, to form the materials or insights into novel combinations."[33]

Leaders typically work in uncertain environments and constantly have to make decisions without vital information. They have to make sense of multiple events and forces that can have adverse impact on their organization, and position the organization for any eventuality. Thus, they often have this ability to be able to make sense of their own newfound circumstances and utilize the resources available to reconstruct their careers. It is important to note, however, that the creativity of a bricoleur is not the randomly inspired idea that most think of when they contemplate creativity, but is in fact more often a rational process or routine of addressing problems. Information and materials are sought in a comprehensive and systematic way, and where they are missing, they are compensated for by improvising based around a defined approach to solving the problem. This process may make the creative process appear uncreative, but in fact the very logic of the process allows creative solutions to arise without having to reinvent the process itself. By going through this process and taking the first steps toward recovering the career trajectory, leaders are able to *prove their mettle* and begin to regain trust and credibility with those who hold the keys to reentering the upper echelons.

Perhaps the most common theme, though, in the research on resilience is the necessity of a core sense of meaning in the person's life. While this sense of meaning can take many forms, from a deep-seated religious conviction to a determination to simply live life to its fullest, psychologist Suzanne Kobasa notes that at the most basic level, it is above all commitment to the person's life's activities. She states that "committed persons have a belief system that minimizes the perceived threat of any given stressful life event. The encounter with a stressful environment is mitigated by a sense of purpose that prevents giving up on one's social context and oneself in times of great pressure."[34] Research into this subject by Austrian psychiatrist and Holocaust survivor Viktor E. Frankl stemmed from firsthand experience in the Auschwitz concentration camp where he realized that in order to survive he had to find some purpose in his continued existence. In his book *Man's Search for Meaning*, Frankl recounts the horrors of life and death in the concentration camps and the necessity of a prisoner to have a sense of meaning in his life in order to survive the horrific ordeal of everyday life in the camps.[35] Once someone lost his sense of meaning and purpose, decline, decay, and death often followed in rapid succession. Frankl writes, "Man's search for meaning is a primary force in his life and not a 'secondary rationalization' of instinctual drives. This meaning is unique and specific in that it must and can be fulfilled by him alone; only then does it achieve a significance which will satisfy his own will to meaning."[36]

We have found that in the context of leaders ousted from their organization, their sense of heroic mission is often the driving meaning behind their career and, as in Frankl's description, is a mission that they feel can only be fulfilled by themselves; subsequently, this drive can enhance their ability to recover from catastrophic setback. Given that in their prior position they viewed the organization as the means to fulfill their need for immortality and sense of heroic mission, this sense of accomplishment obviously takes a devastating blow upon the separation of the person from the organization, as we have described. However, this same sense of a larger-than-life heroic mission can come to be the saving grace of fallen leaders if the means to achieving it can be redefined from the prior organization and reconceptualized into a new path. Charting this course toward *rediscovering heroic mission* enables leaders to put the separation from their former organization behind them and begin the new heroic quest.

We have seen how the downfall of the leader stands apart from the career setbacks affecting other members of an organization, whether due to cutbacks, downsizing, or other causes. This is not to denigrate the gravity or impact of career setbacks at other levels, but rather to note that despite the popular notion that well-compensated leaders do not suffer unduly from career setback, in fact psychologically the setback can be dramatically more catastrophic. Everyone suffering career setback encounters psychological barriers to be overcome that are often not helped by the social norms of avoiding failure. But given the psychologically more severe nature of the leader's downfall, it is particularly instructive and provides lessons for all who suffer setback to examine how leaders overcome such catastrophic downfalls and regain their drive to strive for still-increasing accomplishments. We have conceptualized the nature of resilience and what sets resilient leaders apart. This essentially boils down to five fundamental components of resilience:

1. Fight, not flight—the ability to face up to the reality of the situation and distinguish those battles that need to be fought to restore reputation from those that drain energy and purpose.

2. Recruiting others into battle, effectively using the support networks available while recognizing the collateral damage felt by these key others as a result of the downfall.

3. Rebuilding heroic stature through rationalizing the events that led up to the downfall, providing an answer to the question "Why did this happen to me?" that enables the leader to put the event into context and provide a rational explanation to others, thus allowing the rebuilding of reputation.

4. Proving your mettle. Regaining trust and credibility utilizing the creative skills of the bricoleur to improvise based around a defined approach to solving the problem to start on career rebuilding.

5. Rediscovering your heroic mission by reconceptualizing the deep-seated purpose of past endeavors to chart a new course.

We turn now in the remaining chapters to these five key steps to turning tragedy into triumph that resilient leaders use to rebuild their careers.

CHAPTER 7

Fight, Not Flight— Facing Up to the Issue

Which office do I go to to get my reputation back?

—Ray Donovan, the secretary of labor under President Ronald Reagan[1]

THE FIRST DECISION that a person faces in responding to a significant career setback is the question of whether to fight or take flight—to fight against allegations or to retreat and weather the storm. The main principle we will demonstrate in this chapter is that the key determinant in the fight-or-flight question is the damage incurred or potential damage to the leader's reputation. While allegations, or the fallout from a public downfall, can be damaging in and of themselves, fighting them can exacerbate the damage by extending and making more public the accusations in order to disprove them. Particularly if the battles extend to the court of law as well as the court of public opinion, the collateral damage of the fight may itself prove insurmountable. Therefore, it is only when the allegations themselves are sufficient to cause—or have already caused—a catastrophic career setback, and would block a career comeback, that they certainly need to be fought. In fact, revenge itself as a motivator can energize a victim's campaign for recovery and bring some cathartic relief over an injustice suffered. At the same time, vengeance can become pathologically distracting and even

escalate to destruction. Consider, for example, Hewlett-Packard's prominent public meltdown in September 2006—escalating rounds of public
and private exchanges surfaced information that triggered unwelcome investigations by the SEC, the California Attorney General's Office, the FBI,
and Congress. Following multiple leaks from the boardroom of highly
confidential and sensitive strategic information, Mark Hurd, the recently
hired CEO, was concerned. He and the board agreed that an investigation
of the leaks was needed since no one would confess to being the wrong-
doer. The chairman, Patricia Dunn, executed the board's wishes by having the company's general counsel hire an outside private investigator.

Spiraling finger-pointing began in March 2006 when the investigation identified a director, George Keyworth, as the source of the leaks.
When the chairman named him and the board asked him to resign, he
refused. Another director, Thomas Perkins, furious that a friend had
been humiliated, resigned in anger; he was especially upset about the
highly questionable investigation techniques, in which fraudulent iden-
tities had been used to obtain personal phone records. Although the
board had not been aware that these methods had been used, Perkins felt
that it should have prevented this kind of investigation. In September
2006 he began a media campaign directed at Dunn, which in the course
of a week led to the resignation of his friend Keyworth, the early departure of Dunn by January 2007 as chairman, and a fusillade of investigations by legal authorities concerned about the espionage, which included
files on the media, the original leaks, and the completeness of reports to
the SEC concerning the event. It is hard to identify the winners of this
escalated acrimony.

Where Do I Go to Get My Reputation Back?

The fraught choice between fight or flight and the potential damage to
one's reputation, even when successfully fighting unsubstantiated accusations, could not be better illustrated than through recounting the cau-
tionary travails of Ray Donovan, the secretary of labor under President
Ronald Reagan.

Donovan was one of twelve children from a working-class Catholic
family in Bayonne, New Jersey. His parents died when he was young,

and he helped raise his siblings, working as a union electrician and an insurance salesman. In 1959, he joined the Schiavone Construction Company, a small firm with assets of less than $20,000, as vice president in charge of labor relations and financing. By the time Donovan left the company in 1981 to become secretary of labor, he was part owner of the firm, which had contracts totaling more than $600 million.[2]

Donovan had become a big Reagan supporter, serving as chairman of the Reagan-Bush Committee in New Jersey and raising over $600,000 for Reagan during the 1980 presidential campaign, including a fundraiser where he persuaded Frank Sinatra to sing.

Following his election to the presidency, Reagan nominated Donovan to be secretary of labor, despite opposition from many of the major unions. During protracted hearings in the Senate over his nomination, allegations were made of illegal labor practices by the Schiavone Construction Company and of potential ties to the Mob. Donovan denied these allegations, putting them down to what he termed "the New Jersey Syndrome," saying, "If you are in the contracting business in New Jersey, you're indicted, and if you're Italian, you're convicted."[3] Despite the controversy, Donovan was confirmed by the Senate and became secretary of labor.

However, shortly after his confirmation, Donovan's name appeared in connection with a grand jury investigation of Teamsters Union extortion rackets, and his name was mentioned in wiretapped conversations of a Schiavone subcontractor believed to be linked to the Mafia. Soon after, allegations resurfaced about illegal relations between Schiavone and a New York laborers union, and after an investigation by the FBI, a special prosecutor was appointed to investigate the case in December 1981. Additionally, in January 1982, a federal grand jury in Brooklyn was assigned to investigate Donovan. In the meantime, it emerged that the FBI knew of some of these allegations before Donovan's confirmation hearings, but had failed to disclose that fact to the Senate committee, determining it to be "not pertinent."[4]

By seeking and accepting a highly visible leadership position, Donovan had put himself under intense public scrutiny, whether he liked it or not. Leaders often find themselves held to a higher standard, and while the leadership position serves to enhance their reputation, it also puts that reputation constantly under the microscope.

Despite calls for his resignation, even from unnamed sources inside the White House who felt that the allegations themselves were politically damaging to the Reagan administration, President Reagan supported Donovan in his intention to stay in his job during the investigation, stating to the press that the appointment of a special prosecutor carries no connotation of guilt. Donovan himself criticized those who were calling for his resignation, saying, "Quite obviously, some of our elected officials are not content to allow facts to be determined in an orderly manner. They seem more interested in a wonderland school of justice that stands for judgment now, trial later."[5] In June 1982, both the federal grand jury and the special prosecutor, Leon Silverman, dismissed the allegations, with the special prosecutor reporting that there was "insufficient credible evidence" to warrant prosecution of Donovan on any charge. However, when asked by a reporter whether his investigation had cleared Donovan, Silverman repeated his statement of "insufficient credible evidence," specifically declining to state that his investigation had "exonerated" Donovan, and adding that a "disturbing number" of allegations linked Donovan "in one form or another to reputed organized crime figures," but that "extensive investigation produced insufficient credible evidence upon which to base a prosecution that the secretary was untruthful in his denials, either before the Senate Labor Committee or the grand jury, of any and all such associations."[6]

This lukewarm clearance from the special prosecutor, while freeing Donovan from the prospect of defense in a court of law, certainly didn't clear his name in the court of public opinion, and despite Donovan claiming to be "extremely pleased, but not surprised" by the special prosecutor's assessment, it didn't assuage the flow of allegations. Indeed, before the special prosecutor even closed his investigations, he got new evidence for another fourteen allegations, and in August, one of the main witnesses who had testified in the Donovan case was murdered in a Mob-style killing. However, in late September 1982, the special prosecutor closed the second phase of his investigation, still without evidence to prosecute Donovan. At a reception to celebrate his victory, Donovan quipped, "I always believed and I still believe that there has only been one resurrection in the past 2,000 years—but some people tell me I've had four."[7]

Despite this second clearance and the continued support of President Reagan, there was still ongoing pressure on Donovan to resign, particularly from senior members of the Reagan administration, who still considered Donovan a political liability. In what became known as the "turkey-blind interview," White House chief of staff James Baker III told a reporter in an interview conducted during a turkey shoot on his Texas ranch, "Ray Donovan shouldn't be in here. What's he thinking about? He's got his good name now. He's vindicated. Now he ought to do what's right for the President."[8] Donovan, however, refused to back down and indicated he intended to stay through a second Reagan term, saying, "I paid such a high entrance fee, I'm gonna stay for the double feature."[9]

However, a month before Reagan's reelection in 1984, Donovan was indicted on fraud and larceny charges and took a leave of absence. The following March, a New York State Supreme Court judge ruled that Donovan had to stand trial on 137 counts of grand larceny and fraud, and Donovan, despite insisting that the charges were baseless, was forced to resign to defend himself. Reagan, ever the loyalist to his key supporters, accepted his resignation "with deep personal regret," telling Donovan, "I want you to know that you leave the Cabinet with my friendship and gratitude for the years of service you have given this administration—and for the tireless efforts you have made in my campaigns."[10] Despite being embattled since his confirmation, Donovan had survived longer in the job than any Republican appointee since the Eisenhower administration.

More than two years later, on May 25, 1987, after a marathon trial that itself lasted almost nine months, a jury acquitted Donovan and his fellow defendants of all charges. As soon as the jury foreman finished recounting the not-guilty verdicts, Donovan turned to the chief prosecutor and asked the now famous question, "Which office do I go to to get my reputation back?"[11]

In asking this question, Donovan was angrily pointing to the fundamental issue that leaders face in engaging in battles to protect their reputation: that the accusations and battle themselves can irreparably damage the leader's reputation regardless of the outcome—that even winning such a suit is merely a Pyrrhic victory. Indeed, this is unfortunately a feature of most cases where leaders are forced to protect their reputation through the courts. The reality is that the media portrays, and the public remembers, bad news more prominently than good news, and consequently reputation sustains damage that can take a long time to repair. Ray Donovan won the legal battle but lost his public reputation. Clearly, picking which fights are important to the protection and restoration of public reputation is a key factor in career recovery.

What we learn from the Donovan case is that allegations themselves can be extremely damaging to reputation. As a leader, you have to not only do the right thing, but be perceived to be doing the right thing. A consequence of seeking a leadership position is being put under intense public scrutiny, being held to high standards, and enhancing a reputation that is constantly under threat. As legendary investor Warren Buffett puts it, "It takes 20 years to build a reputation and five minutes to lose it." [12] Even successfully defending against allegations does not entirely mitigate the damage done in those five minutes. However, sometimes you are compelled to fight.

Regaining Control to Cope with Stress

While it seems that such public instances of defamation or humiliation are hard to hide from and thus force the victim to fight back, in fact the dominant emotion is often to seek shelter from the storm of negative publicity rather than to go out and battle seemingly overwhelming forces against the victim. However, the task of acknowledging and redirecting the stress caused by the career setback, particularly one that is potentially devastating to the individual's reputation, is a necessary precursor to career recovery.

Career distress can be one of the greatest sources of life stress. Leaders who have achieved prominence and public reputation are identified with their career and organization and also identify themselves closely with their organizational role. The loss of this role can be particularly devastating and stressful for leaders in this position. The hackneyed expression, "The bigger they are, the harder they fall," certainly rings true for those suffering public downfall and displacement from a prominent leadership role.

While the psychological and physiological symptoms of chronic stress caused by such events can have a profoundly corrosive effect, many of the prescriptions of our therapeutic society are not appropriate stress responses for many creative individuals and leaders. Stress is the perception of helplessness in dealing with serious demands. Overcoming stress means regaining control of the situation, not avoiding it by escaping on a faraway vacation or retreating from the media spotlight. There is no such thing as objective stress existing on its own. We only stressfully respond to people, places, and events; our response is dependent upon our perceptions of the adequacy of resources to deal with the stressor(s).

Therefore, since stress is an interpretation of events according to one's feeling of competence and strength, it is unlikely that the vacations, retreats, and other avoidance techniques so often prescribed will yield creative individuals the sense of potency and connectedness they require to feel back in control. Research on psychological hardiness, the foundation of resilience, in responding to stress suggests that victims must regain control, make commitments to external events, respond to challenges, be willing to take a radical approach, and essentially become blind to their fears.[13] Coping with stress does not mean avoiding, accommodating, or accepting the stress. It is not about reducing the *importance* of stress through denial, avoidance, projection, and withdrawal. Nor is it merely about reducing the *effects* of stress through exercise, diet, meditation, and support groups. Coping effectively and productively requires reducing the *source* of the stress, perhaps through direct confrontation.[14] Despite the short-term pressure of confrontation, the ability to fight the source of stress is the most likely long-term resolution to the problem.

The highly public battles between Jeffrey Katzenberg and The Walt Disney Company, and specifically his former mentor and boss, Michael Eisner, serve to illustrate the challenges and difficulties, but also sometimes the necessity and benefits, of engaging in battles to restore reputation and perceptions of justice following a forced exit, as well as the often personal nature of these encounters.

Jeffrey Katzenberg grew up on Park Avenue in New York, the son of a well-to-do stockbroker. As a teenager, having been kicked out of summer camp for disciplinary reasons, he volunteered for John Lindsay's mayoral campaign and, through his energy, loyalty, and enthusiasm, became a fixture on the campaign team and later at the mayor's office. After a succession of short-term jobs (some more salubrious than others), including six months as a professional gambler, through connections Katzenberg ended up as an executive assistant to Barry Diller at Paramount. After a brief stint working directly for Diller, Katzenberg was placed by Diller in the marketing department of Paramount, where he met Michael Eisner, the new head of Paramount Studios. Katzenberg proved his worth as a reliable, energetic, loyal, and increasingly indispensable fixer who quickly rose in his responsibilities until he became president of production, Eisner's number two in the organization, at age thirty-one.

This appointment under Eisner began a turbulent mentor-protégé relationship between the two that would span sixteen years. Both had strong personalities, which at times clashed, yet each recognized the value of the other in advancing his own career. But, as often happens in long-term mentor-protégé relationships, over time the protégé desires increasing recognition as a peer rather than being a subordinate in the relationship, while the mentor continues to view the relationship as having a distinct hierarchy.

In 1984, when Eisner was lured to the ailing Walt Disney Company as CEO, Katzenberg went with him as head of Walt Disney Studios, where he focused on the languishing animation division, historically Disney's core competence, which had been in the doldrums since Walt Disney died some eighteen years earlier. Katzenberg successfully turned around this fundamental part of the business, leading to several animated hits, most notably the record-breaking *The Lion King*. As part of Katzenberg's compensation deal on joining Disney, Frank Wells, the president of Disney and number two behind Eisner, promised Katzenberg an incentive that included 2 percent of the profit from "all forms of exploitation" of the projects that Katzenberg put into production, meaning not only the films themselves but all the related merchandising and other spin-offs that the films created.

Following his success at Walt Disney Studios, Katzenberg began expanding his horizons, getting involved in the consumer products and theme parks sides of the business. However, Katzenberg's increasing prominence within the company, and the industry at large, also served to increase the acrimony developing between himself and Eisner. One illustrative contributing incident occurred when Katzenberg wrote a twenty-eight-page memo on restoring the fortunes of Disney, essentially laying out his manifesto for the strategy of the business. Eisner was livid about the memo, both because he saw corporate strategy as his role and because he considered much of the content plagiarized from a memo he himself had written years earlier while at Paramount. Eisner warned Katzenberg to keep the memo to himself, but it was circulated within the company, further angering Eisner.

Despite the deteriorating relationship between the two, during contract renewal negotiations, Wells told Katzenberg that if either Wells or Eisner left the company for whatever reason, Katzenberg would become number two. A later conversation between Eisner and Katzenberg, which included Katzenberg's future in the company in response to Katzenberg's desire for more responsibility, also gave Katzenberg the impression that if for any reason Wells were to leave, Katzenberg would move into the number-two slot behind Eisner.

On Easter Sunday 1994 these hypothetical scenarios were put to the test when Frank Wells was tragically killed in a helicopter crash. Given the prior conversations, Katzenberg assumed that he would be named president of Disney, succeeding Wells. However, Eisner issued a press release proclaiming that he would assume Well's responsibilities in addition to his own and that no successor would be named. Katzenberg tried to discuss this issue with Eisner several times but could not get a satisfactory answer. He gave signals of leaving unless Eisner followed his word. Eisner believed that Katzenberg was taking his case public, with articles in the *New York Times*, the *Wall Street Journal*, and the *Los Angeles Times* that proclaimed his importance to Disney.

Shortly after this, Eisner was forced to enter the hospital to have heart bypass surgery. Despite the vacuum of leadership that this potentially left at the top of the organization, Katzenberg was not included on the list of people Eisner's office called to tell of his condition. Soon after Eisner came back to work, the two had another meeting. Katzenberg said that he realized that Eisner was never going to follow through on his earlier promise, and he was determined to resign. Eisner asked for a few days to work things out. On Eisner's first full day back at the office, he called Katzenberg and handed him a four-page press release announcing a restructuring of the company and the departure of Katzenberg. The announcement had already been sent to the press before the discussion with Katzenberg.

The ensuing showdown between these two Hollywood titans following this acrimonious split so soon after Wells's untimely death was worthy of any soap opera. The battles commenced playing out in the media, as newspapers and magazines from Los Angeles to New York eagerly covered the struggle. Despite Eisner trying to play down the story, telling the *Los Angeles Times*, "This is not a Shakespearean tragedy—this is people moving on with their lives, and doing new and interesting things," the media couldn't get enough.[15] With Eisner refusing to let Katzenberg attend premieres of movies that he had produced and not allowing farewell parties for him to go ahead, the drama continued to unfold. The media war soon turned nasty, with Katzenberg encouraging his friends to take snipes at Eisner, and Eisner tapping company insiders and board members to take retaliatory swipes at Katzenberg. Katzenberg's friend music mogul David Geffen proclaimed that "Eisner's lack of kindness, lack of generosity, and inability to give credit were simply shameful,"[16] while Steven Spielberg predicted that "Jeffrey Katzenberg's exit will be Michael Eisner's Machiavellian loss—and Corporation X's El Dorado."[17] Meanwhile, Disney board member Stanley Gold told *Vanity Fair* magazine, "I thought Jeffrey was an extremely talented, hard-working, efficient executive for most of the 10 years he was [at Disney]. But there came a point in time where Jeffrey's ego and his almost pathological need to be important overtook his good judgment."[18]

Although he was taking his own share of barbs, the media battle waged by Katzenberg was stinging enough for Eisner to seek to curtail it, and he met twice with Katzenberg to see how he could stop the flow of articles. Katzenberg responded, "You know how to stop it. You have not fulfilled one single promise that you made to me in terms of how you were going to deal with this. You've done an assassination job on me. I've yet to be paid a nickel. Deal honestly with me."[19]

When Eisner continually delayed a settlement, Katzenberg finally engaged litigator Bert Fields and sued Disney in April 1996, demanding a lump-sum payment equating to 2 percent of the estimated future income from all the projects he had put into production, as was in his deal with Frank Wells.

While the media battle had been nasty, the prospect of a battle in the courtroom, which potentially could reveal much more of Eisner's and Disney's dirty laundry, was one that they desperately wanted to avoid. Katzenberg and Disney had agreed that the trial would be divided into two parts. The first part would establish whether Katzenberg's claim was valid—that is, whether Disney owed Katzenberg any money at all. Only if Katzenberg were successful in this part would there be arbitration about how much. However, settlement talks continued as the trial date approached, and ten days before the trial covering the first issue, Disney caved in, agreeing to pay Katzenberg an initial $117 million—$77 million as a down payment against the finally arbitrated figure and $40 million to settle claims related to merchandise based on Katzenberg's film and television productions.

There is often a conscious decision to be made as to whether to fight or walk away. Sometimes there is a need to fight for what is in your contract—often at these high levels organizations try to renege when contracts signed in the good times seem too generous when things turn sour.

There is a tough balance to be drawn here between the potential financial gain to be achieved from pursing what is owed in a contract, and both the potential reputational damage that can occur in commencing this battle and the opportunity cost in pursuing the battle. In Katzenberg's case, he considered it worth the cost despite the potential risk to his reputation and the opportunity cost in taking his time and energy away from his future venture as cofounder of DreamWorks.

When the final arbitration came, some of the dirty laundry did get out. Eisner was forced to take the stand, and the acrimony that had developed between Eisner and Katzenberg became fully apparent. Behind the scenes, Disney director Stanley Gold was trying to bring the two sides closer to a settlement even as the arbitration went on, in an attempt to avoid further airing of Disney's inside accounts. Indeed, the trial would potentially force Disney to play down its future prospects in order to reduce the settlement and at the same time have an adverse impact on its stock as this pessimistic view was aired. In the end, before this scenario developed, Gold managed to broker a deal, and on July 5, 1999, Disney and Katzenberg settled, for a sum reported to be close to $270 million.

Despite this victory, however, Katzenberg was cognizant of the ordeal of fighting against his former employer: "It's a little like being in a car accident and the insurance company paid you off. Unfortunately, it doesn't take away from the trauma."[20]

Katzenberg's battle with Eisner and Disney also provides several lessons for those seeking to achieve justice after a malicious dismissal. While some—such as Bernie Marcus on his dismissal from Handy Dan, on advice he had received from others who had been through such an experience—chose not to fight their former employer for contractual settlements but opted instead to focus their energies on new ventures, Katzenberg viewed this calculation differently. Ultimately, for Katzenberg, the opportunity provided by the settlement with Disney was the springboard for his rebound, giving him the means to found Dream-Works. But perhaps more importantly, Katzenberg considered the reputational risk of engaging in the battle as worth taking given that Disney and Eisner faced potentially greater damage to their reputation.

Although it is rare for such fights to have a positive impact, the public nature of Katzenberg's fight actually helped build his reputation. Katzenberg was already known in the industry for his tenaciousness. His refusing to back down from a confrontation with Disney and his former mentor, Eisner, added to that reputation, and his achievements at Disney became better known rather than being hidden behind the corporate façade. Consequently, his stature in the industry rose through engaging in battle—from being an almost unseen number two behind Eisner to a principal and driving force behind DreamWorks. Also, threatening to turn the tables—exposing Eisner's and Disney's dirty laundry in public—ended up providing him with leverage to settle the suit. It is a worthwhile lesson that the threat of the behemoth may not be as great as you think—it may also have a lot to lose in terms of reputation.

The fight also shows who your friends are—David Geffen, Steven Spielberg (both of whom would join with Katzenberg to form Dream-Works following Katzenberg's departure from Disney), and other friends spoke out to the press on Katzenberg's behalf. Engaging in battle forces people to choose sides and show their support (or lack of it). This winnowing clearly shows whom the person can depend on and engage for support and help toward career recovery, a subject we will explore further in the next chapter.

Picking Your Battles

Despite Katzenberg's success in his battle with Disney and the frequent necessity for leaders to fight to protect their reputation, it is also essential to pick your battles carefully. Just as Sol Price advised Bernie Marcus to walk away from suing Sandy Sigoloff and Handy Dan for compensation he was owed, it is often better to deliberately avoid costly battles when your reputation is not at stake. Pursuing such actions, while they may be considered justifiable battles of principle, often results in at best Pyrrhic victories, since the costs in time, energy, and lost opportunity often outweigh the benefits of winning the battle, as Price had himself discovered. Indeed, for public figures, the potential destructiveness of the media on reputation needs to be carefully considered before waging battle.

This is particularly important when the choice to engage in battle is made before the allegation has resulted in actual damage, as Katzenberg experienced by being fired from Disney. Some, however, may perceive a rising threat and seek to quash a potentially damaging allegation before it leads to actual downfall. In this case, you need to carefully consider the seriousness of the allegation, its potential consequences, and the consequences of engaging in battle before you commence. While an accusatory report in the media can seemingly force a response, remaining silent may lead to a short-term bruising of the reputation and ego but allow the short attention span of the media and the public to wander to the next story, whereas a fighting response could lead to further disaster. Public figures, particularly politicians, are particularly vulnerable to this provocation, being constantly bombarded with media accusations, many of which fade away in days if there is no response. While their reputation and ego may be wounded, their position itself may not be in danger. It is only when the accusation itself could cause a downfall that the need to fight the battle is actually forced. Too many public figures make the mistake of responding to the provocation of media accusations and ultimately lose the battle, or at best gain a Pyrrhic victory at a high cost to themselves.

In the early 1990s, British prime minister John Major's Conservative government was under a seemingly constant flow of allegations of sleaze, ranging from sex scandals to unreported lavish gifts from people attempting to gain influence, which led to successive resignations of government ministers.

It was against this background that in October 1993 the *Guardian* newspaper, a major daily broadsheet antagonistic toward the Conservative government, received a tip from Mohamed Al-Fayed, owner and chairman of the famed Harrods department store and the equally reputed Ritz hotel in Paris, among other business interests. The bitter takeover battle for Harrods that Al-Fayed had waged in the mid-1980s against Lonrho had stirred considerable controversy in and out of government. Added to this, Al-Fayed had for years been seeking British citizenship and had done his best to ingratiate himself with the British establishment toward this end, but his applications for citizenship for himself and his brother had been repeatedly denied. Al-Fayed told the *Guardian* that some Conservative members of Parliament (MPs) had accepted cash and other gifts for asking questions on his behalf to Parliament during his battle with Lonrho, through his lobbyist, Ian Greer. The *Guardian*, on October 5, 1993, published a profile of Ian Greer and his lobbying tactics, naming two Conservative MPs, Tim Smith and Neil Hamilton, as accepting gifts from an unnamed British company, including (for Hamilton) a week's holiday at an, as of then, unnamed five-star European hotel. Despite these potentially serious allegations, neither Smith nor Hamilton responded, perhaps due to the anonymity of the source, and nothing adverse transpired.

Then, almost a year later, in September 1994, Al-Fayed, through an intermediary, attempted to get an appointment with the prime minister to seek the withdrawal or revision of a pending government report that was critical of his company and his actions in the takeover battle for Harrods. The intermediary told the prime minister that Al-Fayed was in possession of allegations of wrongdoing by members of Major's government and was "contemplating passing them on to others."[21] When Major refused, Al-Fayed contacted Peter Preston, the editor of the *Guardian*, and told him that he was now willing to go public with, and substantiate, his allegations. Through the *Guardian*, Al-Fayed named Tim Smith, then a junior minister for Northern Ireland, and Neil Hamilton, a junior minister in the Department for Trade and Industry, as having accepted cash for asking questions to Parliament on his behalf during the Harrods takeover. Sir Robin Butler, the cabinet secretary, and later Lord Nolan, were asked to investigate Al-Fayed's allegations, during which two other ministers, rising star Jonathan Aitken, a junior minister in the Ministry of Defense, and home secretary Michael Howard, were also named by Al-Fayed and came under media attack.

Here were four ministers all named in the press, all facing allegations of corruption from the same source. Were these accusations serious enough to warrant a fight, or would ignoring them and resorting to flight, in the hope that the heat would die down, be the astute approach in protecting their careers? The different reactions from the four are instructive as we consider the circumstances under which it is better to fight public accusations and when it is better to wait for the storm to pass.

Taking Flight Yields a Fatal Setback

The day the allegations were made public by the *Guardian*, naming Al-Fayed as the source (October 20, 1994), Tim Smith immediately resigned his post as a Northern Ireland junior minister. At the next election, he stood down from his seat and, as a former accountant, sought to rebuild a career in business, though he also faced disciplinary action by the Institute of Chartered Accountants. His career remained in tatters, and he never regained the stature he held before these allegations surfaced. By his actions, Smith in effect was admitting to the wrongdoing and then taking flight without telling his side of the story. By so doing, he was allowing only one side of the story—and the most damaging and sensationalized side—to dictate the outcome. As Smith discovered, this approach most often proves to be a fatal setback, erecting an insurmountable barrier to career recovery.

An Avoidable Fight

Neil Hamilton took a different approach. He denied the allegations, calling his visit to the Ritz a visit to what was effectively for Al-Fayed a "private residence" and thus not relevant to be reported to the parliamentary Register of Interests as a gift. Two days later, "a line was drawn under the matter" as Sir Geoffrey Johnson, chairman of the Select Committee on (parliamentary) Members' Interests, and cabinet secretary Sir Robin Butler declared themselves satisfied with Hamilton's disclosure of relevant interests. However, the *Guardian* did not relent, publishing sequentially more damaging allegations daily against Hamilton, until five days later, on October 25, 1994, John Major asked for, and received, his resignation. In his letter of resignation to the prime minister, Hamilton stated, "I shall clear my name," having been "forced to leave office because of foully-motivated rumour and a media witchhunt," and immediately sued the *Guardian* for libel to the tune of £10 million. For almost two years, Hamilton pursued his action against the *Guardian*, even attaining a change in the 1689 Bill of Rights concerning parliamentary privilege to allow the libel suit to occur. Then suddenly, on September 28, 1996, the day before the trial was to begin, Hamilton abandoned the case when the government produced documents to his lawyers that undermined his assertions and corroborated the *Guardian*'s case. In what was called at the time "one of the most astonishing cave-ins in the history of the law of libel"[22] by the *Guardian*'s editor, Hamilton's career was left in ruins, and, despite the support of his local constituency association to fight the next election, he lost his seat to an independent candidate by a large majority. Still determined to restore his name, Hamilton subsequently sued Al-Fayed himself for libel in 1999, and, although this action went to trial, further damning evidence of Hamilton's taking cash for political influence resulted in his losing that suit and left Hamilton in financial ruin.

The lesson for leaders whose reputations are put in danger is that reputations, long built, can be destroyed by relatively trivial misdeeds. While the "cash for questions" allegations were serious breaches of parliamentary ethics, Smith and Hamilton allowed themselves to be bribed for relatively small amounts, perhaps because they thought the questions themselves were worthy of being asked. However, in accepting payment, they put their careers in jeopardy. By simply declaring commercial interests through consultancy arrangements with the companies involved, they could easily have absolved themselves in the eyes of Parliament. While their questions would perhaps have been tainted by known bias, they could still have been asked with equal effect.

Fighting Without the Facts on Your Side

Jonathan Aitken took a path similar to Hamilton's, but with even more disastrous results. Aitken was a blue-blooded Conservative, son of Conservative MP Sir William Aitken and Lady Penelope Aitken, grandson of the first Baron of Rugby, and nephew of media baron Lord Beaverbrook. He was educated at the elite institutions of Eton and Oxford, spent his summers writing speeches for the chancellor of the exchequer, and made a fortune in his twenties from investment deals in Australia and Canada. Aitken was a fast-rising star in the Conservative party, tagged as a future party leader and potential prime minister, and was known to be one of the most well-connected people in Parliament, with friends around the world. When the allegations broke in October 1994, Aitken was prepared. For months previously, he had corresponded with *Guardian* editor Peter Preston, who had contacted Aitken to try to uncover the details of the allegations from Al-Fayed that Aitken, at the time the minister for defense, had stayed at the Ritz in Paris while secretly meeting with Middle Eastern businessmen who had paid for his hotel bill. In order to try to substantiate this, Preston even went so far as to impersonate Aitken to obtain a copy of the hotel bill from the Ritz but gathered no more substantive evidence with which to pursue the story in his newspaper. In the days that followed the accusations, Aitken denied the allegations and, despite the increasing controversy, held back from announcing a libel suit (unlike Hamilton); he retained the support of the prime minister in keeping his position. He also fought back with the release from "government sources" of the details of Preston's methods of obtaining his hotel bill, arousing substantial criticism directed toward the source of the allegations against him. This diminished the *Guardian*'s credibility in making the accusations and reduced the pressure on him.

However, the controversy surrounding Aitken would not recede. As the *Financial Times* commented the next April, "the skeletons in Aitken's cupboard will not stop rattling."[23] Indeed, days after the *Financial Times* article appeared, Aitken was finally provoked into action by the broadcasting of a BBC television program entitled *Jonathan of Arabia*, which investigated Aitken's links with the Middle East, followed by a *Guardian* article making similar allegations, including that Aitken tried to arrange prostitutes for a Saudi prince. These new allegations prompted Aitken to issue a writ for defamation against the *Guardian* and Granada Television, the producers of the television program. In launching his suit, Aitken declared, "If it falls to me to start a fight to cut out the cancer of bent and twisted journalism in our country with the simple sword of truth and the trusty shield of British fair play, so be it. I am ready for the fight. The fight against falsehood and those who peddle it."[24] Despite Aitken's launching the suit, the prime minister, having had so many forced resignations from the government, took a different path from the one he had followed with Hamilton and allowed Aitken to retain his job of chief secretary to the treasury. However, less than three months later, as the allegations against Aitken continued, he was removed from his post in a cabinet reshuffle, and, despite support from his local constituency party, subsequently lost his parliamentary seat at the next election, in May 1997, when Tony Blair's Labour party swept the beleaguered Conservatives from power.

In June 1997, a month after the election, Aitken's libel action against the *Guardian* and Granada Television reached the courtroom. Because Aitken's political significance had evaporated, and thus the media's interest had diminished, on the eve of the trial, the *Guardian* and Granada offered to let Aitken drop the case, with each side paying its own costs. Aitken refused, and the action went to trial.

In its defense that the stories were justified, the *Guardian* and Granada brought up all the prior allegations that had dogged Aitken, including his stay at the Paris Ritz in 1993. Aitken claimed in court that the billing for his hotel room had been the result of an error on the hotel's part and that his wife had paid the bill in cash; and later, when he realized that she had inadvertently paid only half the bill and the other half had been billed to a Saudi Arabian friend, Abdul Rachman, Aitken sent a check to Rachman to cover the difference. After twelve days of trial, before she was to testify, Aitken's wife announced that she had separated from Aitken. The next day, Aitken's case spectacularly collapsed as the defense produced evidence that Mrs. Aitken had been in Switzerland at the time Aitken claimed she paid the hotel bill in Paris. The *Guardian*'s editor emerged triumphantly from the courtroom pronouncing that Aitken had "impaled himself on 'the simple sword of truth'," and that he had now "made his fatal mistake by lying on oath to the High Court."[25]

The *Guardian* then publicly pressed for perjury charges to be brought against Aitken, which they subsequently were, and in January 1999 he was convicted of perjury and sentenced to eighteen months in prison; he was left bankrupt with outstanding legal bills extending to several millions of pounds.

The mere appearance of impropriety can destroy reputation. Even when nothing untoward actually occurs, the appearance of it can lead to speculation, which can grow to rumor with unstoppable momentum. For Aitken, a multimillionaire, paying a trivial hotel bill, rather than letting it get paid by someone else, would have erased any allegations, and the story would no longer be newsworthy. Even though the paying of a small hotel bill would likely not have influenced his ministerial decision making, the appearance of being susceptible to influence was enough to make it damaging.

If you fight, be sure of your ground. The most obvious lesson from the Hamilton and Aitken sagas is that, in the end, neither had the facts on their side. They fought based on the poker player's strategy of bluffing and continually raising the stakes in the hopes that their opponent would back down. This strategy may work some of the time, but in the face of an opponent who won't back down, it can lead to disaster. The interesting corollary of this is the importance of allowing, and sometimes taking, the graceful exit. It is true that many animals will not attack unless they are backed into a corner that they cannot retreat from. Allowing the opponent to gracefully retreat can prevent a bloody escalation in a war that ultimately no one wants to engage in. Similarly, allowing for your own retreat by not backing yourself into a corner or predestined course of action is important. Even at the last moment, the night before the trial was set to begin, Aitken was offered such a retreat but failed to take it.

Standing Your Ground While Refusing to Be Drawn into a Fight

The fourth, and most senior, minister accused by Al-Fayed, Michael Howard, was perhaps his main target. Indeed, the whole "cash for questions" disclosure by Al-Fayed was reported to have been prompted by Al-Fayed's disappointment over his failure to obtain British citizenship, for which, as home secretary, Michael Howard was ultimately responsible. Adding fuel to the fire, Howard was also a minister at the Department of Trade and Industry (DTI) at the time that department launched its investigation into Al-Fayed's takeover of Harrods—an investigation that produced a highly critical report that began, "The Fayeds dishonestly misrepresented their origins, their wealth, their business interests and their resources to the Secretary of State, the Office of Fair Trading, the House of Fraser [parent company of Harrods] board and shareholders, and their own advisors." [26]

As the stories broke about Smith and Hamilton, Howard took out a court injunction against the *Financial Times*, preventing it from running a story with allegations directed toward Howard. The injunction itself, however, served to raise questions in Parliament, forcing Howard to answer his actions. By now, other papers had brought up the potential role that Howard may have had in initiating the DTI investigation of Al-Fayed, and the fact that Howard's second cousin had been a director of one of Lonrho's subsidiaries (the rival bidder for Harrods), fueling the speculation of potential bias against Al-Fayed. Thus, while the full extent of the allegations against Howard were not public due to his injunction, rumor of the allegations were rapidly spreading. Against normal Home Office policy of refusing to comment on individual citizenship applications, Howard made a statement explaining that the proper procedure had been followed in Al-Fayed's case, outlining in detail all the steps taken. The procedure included that the final decision be made by a junior minister and not by him, although the application had reached his office three times, and each time he had directed the junior minister to fully investigate and make the final decision. Without referring to any further allegations, a day later Howard also issued a statement that Sir Robin Butler's inquiry had also cleared him of any improprieties.

Unlike Hamilton and Aitken, Howard refused to be drawn further into a battle to defend himself against Al-Fayed's allegations. He simply issued a brief statement recounting the facts of his actions, denying responsibility for the actions he was being accused of, and let the matter drop. As with the others, though, pressure and the accompanying temptation to fight back did continue to pursue Howard, but he remained aloof from the allegations.

In the ensuing government investigations, it emerged that Al-Fayed had accused Howard of accepting a bribe of at least £1 million to instigate the investigation of Al-Fayed's takeover of Harrods. When the government committee report cleared Howard of wrongdoing, Al-Fayed went to the High Court a week before the general election, seeking judicial review of the parliamentary inquiry.

In the wake of the Conservatives' election defeat and the subsequent resignation of John Major as leader of the party, Howard stood for the party leadership. However, the continuing questions in Parliament about his handling of the Al-Fayed citizenship application—including, ironically, the revelation that Howard had tried to get his junior minister to ignore the results of the DTI inquiry and grant the application—essentially ruined his chances of winning the leadership.

Some six months later, with the leadership election lost, Lonrho's Tiny Rowland issued a writ against Al-Fayed, accusing him of offering Rowland ownership of the upscale shirtmaker Turnbull & Asser, as well as $10 million in cash, to lie to the parliamentary committee and back his claims that Howard had taken the million-pound bribe. Al-Fayed was arrested but in the end never charged, with the charges officially dropped less than a week before Rowland's death.

Despite the continuing allegations, Howard refused to follow Hamilton and Aitken's path of suing for libel, even in the face of a direct challenge from Al-Fayed. In the High Court trial of Neil Hamilton's libel action against Al-Fayed, Al-Fayed responded to Hamilton's lawyer's assessment that Al-Fayed's allegation against Howard was "utterly baseless" by saying, "Why are you so sure it was baseless? I am the person who knows exactly how it happened—a million pounds and a half a million. He was paid through his uncle Harry Landy, who is a crook. I have challenged Mr. Howard to sue me, I have called him a crook. If he had any dignity or honor and knows he hasn't committed a crime, he would sue me."[27]

Howard never sued, and in the fall of 2003 emerged as the leader of the Conservative party after Iain Duncan Smith's leadership was challenged by his party.

Two major principles emerge out of the choices made by these four politicians, which summarize the lessons of this chapter. First, preemptive actions are often more effective than reactive actions. Howard took a preemptive injunction against the *Financial Times* to prevent the initial allegations from surfacing against him. In doing so, he succeeded in being more in control of how information was disseminated and was able to put his case forward to an official, closed enquiry before the allegations were made public. By that time, the official investigation had cleared him, and thus he was able to stay above the fray, pointing to his exoneration by the official investigation.

Second, it is important to be able to have an objective, dispassionate perspective on the severity of the accusation and then to pick your battles accordingly. In the aftermath of it all, even the *Guardian* editor who instigated the stories that led to the downfalls of Smith, Hamilton, and Aitken was surprised by the result, admitting that if they had not been provoked by the articles, none would have succumbed to the downfalls that they experienced. In an article trying to understand the Aitken perjury, Preston wrote, "Why on earth did he do it? Why begin to weave such a tapestry of mendacity? It seems, when you go back over the correspondence, another enigma. He could have locked the door and done nothing. We had no means of breaking it open."[28] Once again, the most essential lesson for leaders from these downfalls is that some attacks to reputation are inevitable due to the position leaders place themselves in, but unless the attack is serious enough to directly result in a downfall, or can be simply quashed without engaging in a bloody battle, the battle is often more costly than the allegation itself. Thus, it can at best only result in a hollow, Pyrrhic victory, and at worst result in downfall, and is a risk not worth taking. As the ancient war strategist Sun Tzu reputedly said in his classic *The Art of War*, "Ultimate excellence lies not in winning every battle, but in defeating the enemy without ever fighting."

While we have focused in this chapter on the question of when to fight accusations and when to weather the storm and take flight, we have also seen, particularly in the example of Jeffrey Katzenberg, the instrumental role that friends and other acquaintances play in providing support and advice in the process of recovery. We turn in the next chapter to look in more depth at the vital role played by others as the source of support networks and practical connections to rebound from setback.

CHAPTER **8**

Recruiting Others into Battle—Social Networks and Collateral Damage

THE OLD ADAGE "It's not what you know, it's who you know" rings especially true at the very top of the organization. A recent investigation into how CEOs are selected, by Harvard Business School's Rakesh Khurana, revealed that almost all the names thrown into the hat for the top job were candidates known to the directors of the board, either personally, through their own friends, or by reputation.[1] This revelation of the inner workings of the boardroom demonstrates that friends, acquaintances, and reputation are the keys to career recovery for CEOs. While we delved into reputation in the last chapter, and will again in the next, we turn now to how friends and acquaintances—social networks—play a vital role in career recovery. In doing so, we also must not forget that these people, especially close friends and family, go through much of the roller coaster of emotions faced by the individual as they share the triumphs and tragedies encountered in making this forced career transition.

The Vital Role of Acquaintances

While it is easy to imagine the strong, supportive role played by friends in going through this trauma, it is often acquaintances who play the pivotal role in finding the next career step. Indeed, prior research has shown that acquaintance ties and friendship ties play very different roles in enhancing career mobility, with many opportunities for new careers in other organizations stemming not from close friendship ties, but from weaker acquaintance ties.[2] Part of the reason that acquaintance ties are so valuable is their much greater volume and reach. Most people tend to have far fewer close friends than they do acquaintances, and close friends all tend to know one another—thus limiting both the size and the scope of the friendship network. However, people tend to have many acquaintances, all of whom have their own, often very different networks of close friends and acquaintances.

The extended reach of acquaintance networks was first examined in a study conducted in the 1960s in a Michigan junior high school, which asked students to list and rank order their eight best friends.[3] The researchers then traced out the total number of people reached by following along a network of the top two choices. That is, the first and second choices of each person were counted, and then the first and second choices of these people, and so on, counting only those names not previously chosen. They then repeated the procedure for third and fourth choices, and so on through the seventh and eighth choices. What they found was that the smallest number of people was generated through the first and second choices—the closest friendships—and the largest number from the seventh and eighth choices—the acquaintances.

By now, most people are familiar with the game of the Six Degrees of Kevin Bacon, the idea that you can connect almost anyone in any Hollywood film to a film with Kevin Bacon within six steps of separation. For example, if you wanted to link Al Pacino with Kevin Bacon, the link would be that Al Pacino was in *The Godfather: Part III* with Eli Wallach, and Eli Wallach was in *Mystic River* with Kevin Bacon, thus giving a total of two steps. This small number of steps is far from unique. In fact, members of the computer science department at the University of Virginia put together an algorithm to calculate the number of steps from any actor who has appeared in a Hollywood film to Kevin Bacon, and found that they could link any one of the 622,920 actors in their database to Kevin Bacon in an average of 2.944 steps.[4] While this at first seems amazing, that you can link one person to basically anybody in

Hollywood within a few steps, the concept first came to light in another experiment in the 1960s with even more remarkable results—that in fact, by the power of acquaintance networks, you can link almost anyone with almost anyone else within a few steps.

How many times have you met someone for the first time only to discover within a few minutes that you know someone in common? The experimenter Stanley Milgram called this the "small world" phenomenon and set out to see how this acquaintance network effect worked.[5] With a colleague, Milgram selected a person in Boston and then selected people at random from the state of Nebraska. Milgram gave the people in Nebraska a document and asked them to send it to someone they knew personally who would be more likely to advance the progress of the document toward the recipient in Boston. As each recipient passed on the document, they also mailed a postcard to Milgram so that he could trace the number of steps between these two randomly selected individuals, some thirteen hundred miles apart. Milgram found that, on average, it took only 5.2 steps to reach the recipient in Boston!

The combination of these examples demonstrates the reach and scope of acquaintance networks, and in this lies the power of these networks for aiding in career recovery. This occurs at all levels of employment. Labor economists have known for a long time that American blue-collar workers find out about jobs more through personal contacts than by any other means.[6] The same process is even truer for professional and managerial jobs. But what is also true is that, particularly for the professional and managerial roles, people find these positions more often by weak acquaintance ties than by strong friendship ties. In the famous study that revealed this finding, Mark Granovetter discovered that of those finding their job through a contact, only 16.7 percent were found through close friends—people they saw twice a week or more; 55.6 percent were found through acquaintances whom they saw on occasion, but at least once a year; and 27.8 percent were found through distant acquaintances whom they saw less than once a year, such as old college friends, former coworkers, or people they knew through professional associations.[7]

It is probably surprising to you that Granovetter found not only that did the bulk of job contacts come through acquaintances rather than through friends, but also that more came from people seen less than once a year than close friends seen twice or more per week. It is not, as we shall see later in the chapter, that these close friends don't want to or are not motivated to help. Rather, they tend to have the same overlapping social circle as the person trying to find a job, so they bring little new information about available jobs. On the contrary, distant acquaintances have much different social circles and are likely to bring fresh information that would otherwise be impossible for the person to find. As Granovetter concluded, "Usually such ties [that resulted in a new job] had not even been very strong when first forged. For work-related ties, respondents almost invariably said they never saw the person in a nonwork context. Chance meetings or mutual friends operated to reactivate such ties. It is remarkable that people receive crucial information from individuals whose very existence they have forgotten."[8]

In moving from general managerial and professional job markets to the CEO and boardroom levels, the importance of networks and, particularly, loose ties becomes even more pronounced. Just as Hollywood is a relatively defined community, such that it is often easy to link anyone to Kevin Bacon in far fewer than six steps, so in the corporate world the community of CEOs and directors is such a highly interlocked network that Wharton's Michael Useem dubbed it "the inner circle."[9] University of Michigan professor Gerry Davis and colleagues found that, just as in Hollywood, any two of the 4,538 individual directors from the largest 516 firms in the United States included in their study could be connected by just 4.3 links or degrees of separation.[10] Useem found that the network of directors who served on two or more companies' boards links together nearly all the important companies in both the United States and the United Kingdom, cutting across industries, and was highly influential in intercorporate resource exchanges, including directorships and executive positions for members of the inner circle. Indeed, Useem found that it was deemed an essential prerequisite for top managers to be an outside director of at least one organization and that invitations to join boards "tend to move along the networks of ancient friendships and personal contacts," thus maintaining the interconnected nature of the inner circle.[11]

The value of these acquaintance networks is that the search process goes both ways. That is, companies that are looking for new CEOs, and indeed for people at all levels of the organization, use their broad acquaintance networks to search for suitable candidates. As Rakesh Khurana unveiled in his treatise on how companies search externally for a new CEO, almost all the candidates are already board members of other companies and are known through this corporate elite network to the directors of the firm searching for the CEO. Khurana notes that almost all candidates are suggested by the directors of the firm, and even when, as in most cases, an outside executive search firm is employed, its contribution to the generation of potential candidates is negligible.[12]

Even if one is not looking for a position in an established organization but wants to create a new organization, the use of these acquaintance networks can prove vital to doing this successfully. The perfect example of this is Bernie Marcus and the founding of The Home Depot. Marcus was the CEO of Los Angeles–based Handy Dan Home Improvement Centers, a subsidiary of Daylin Corporation, when he was abruptly fired in April 1978 by Daylin's chairman, Sandy Sigoloff, despite, and perhaps because of, being the rising star at Daylin. Marcus—along with two of his colleagues, Arthur Blank and Ron Brill, who were fired by Sigoloff right after he ousted Marcus—went on to start Home Depot, the most successful home improvement retailer ever. But how Marcus got the funding to enable him to open his first Home Depot is a story of building and using networks, a skill of which Marcus is a master.

Years before, while CEO of Handy Dan, Marcus had considered acquiring a small chain of home improvement stores on the East Coast, Philadelphia-based Panelrama. Although he never went through with the acquisition, through the due diligence he came to know the CEO, Gary Erlbaum, and they struck up a friendship. In 1976, Erlbaum was having a conversation with his investment banker, Ken Langone, about the home improvement industry and who were the best operators in the business. Erlbaum mentioned Handy Dan and that he and Marcus knew each other through this previous unconsummated deal. Langone was skeptical of Handy Dan because its parent company, Daylin, was in bankruptcy at the time, but Erlbaum assured him that Handy Dan itself was profitable and that Marcus was an excellent manager. Langone asked Erlbaum if he would call Marcus and introduce them, which he did. Langone flew out to Los Angeles to meet Marcus and was impressed by Marcus and the operation he was running, and on his return to New

York he started buying up the publicly traded stock of Handy Dan (Handy Dan was 85 percent owned by Daylin, while 15 percent was traded publicly). Over a short period of time, Langone bought up nearly all the publicly available stock and kept in regular contact with Marcus.

Shortly after his dismissal from Handy Dan, Marcus received a call from Langone. But instead of sympathizing with Marcus's predicament, Langone enthusiastically encouraged Marcus to look at the opportunity that this event provided: to create his own vision for a much larger warehouse-style home improvement store. Langone advised Marcus that instead of lamenting the disaster of being fired by the whim of Sigoloff or attacking Sigoloff directly through a lawsuit for unfair dismissal, he should strike out on his own and build a better store than Handy Dan. Moreover, Langone gave Marcus more than verbal encouragement by becoming a timely partner who believed in him and provided enthusiasm and credibility from Langone's own reputation and relationships. Through the help of Langone, Marcus was able to raise $2 million in seed capital from Langone's investors as a result of the money he had made for those same investors through gains in Handy Dan stock—Langone convinced them to "roll over" some of their profits and back the person who had enabled those prior gains. In so doing, Langone was putting his reputation on the line with his investors to enable Marcus to prove his ability to continue to perform.

A lesson on the value of building relationships, even in trying circumstances, is that even distant relationships that don't appear to be of any long-term consequence may be key to recovery when careers derail. Consequently, the lesson here is to never burn bridges and to treat people well even in inconsequential business transactions. It wasn't an accident that Marcus had treated Erlbaum with honesty, respect, and courtesy in his dealings with him, even when the potential takeover of Erlbaum's business had fallen by the wayside. This is part of Marcus's character. So while he didn't know or expect that Erlbaum would be a key connection in his future recovery from setback by recommending him to Langone, it is unsurprising that it happened. If it wasn't Erlbaum, it may well have been someone else who had been treated well by Marcus somewhere along the course of his career. While it may appear rare for someone to build a positive relationship with the target of a failed takeover, this building of positive acquaintance networks was one of Marcus's skills. His skill at building and maintaining relationships, even relationships that others would perhaps let drop, was key in aiding his recovery.

A further example is Marcus's relationship with Hoyne Greenberg, a former vendor to Marcus at Handy Dan. Shortly after Marcus was fired from Handy Dan, Greenberg called Marcus and told him that he was going to take him to a new home improvement store that had just opened. When Greenberg told Marcus that it had been opened by Pat Farrah, Marcus, having in a previous encounter been unimpressed with Farrah, said that he wasn't interested in going to see it, but Greenberg insisted, coming to Marcus's home the next morning to pick him up. When Marcus walked into the store, it was just as he had imagined his own store to be. Greenberg reintroduced Marcus to Farrah, and this time Marcus saw him in a different light—as enthusiastic and irrepressible rather than obnoxious and cocky. While Farrah's enterprise soon failed because his financial skills were not up to his merchandising prowess, Marcus persuaded Farrah to join Marcus and Blank as the third partner, and Farrah proved critical in making The Home Depot a merchandising success.

What is interesting about the relationship with both Erlbaum and Greenberg is that Marcus didn't reach out to either one—both of them initiated the contact back to Marcus, presumably out of the respect they had for him, and the way Marcus had treated them in the past was sufficient for them to want to go out of their way to help Marcus even when there was no immediate or obvious potential benefit to themselves. In Greenberg's case especially, Marcus was already dismissed from Handy Dan and thus no longer had the positional stature of being a CEO who could provide business to Greenberg.

Acquaintance ties are most valuable for the connections they provide. Both Erlbaum and Greenberg acted as bridges to other people who became vital in Marcus's success. Erlbaum introduced Langone to Marcus, and Greenberg convinced Marcus to give Farrah a second look. Even though Erlbaum and Greenberg did not themselves have the resources to help Marcus's predicament, because they had such different networks than Marcus, they were able to provide vital links to people who could provide those resources—links that Marcus could not have made himself.

Even with people with whom he had a stronger business relationship, Marcus operated in the same manner. Although Langone had helped raise $2 million in seed money, this was not enough to get Marcus's venture off the ground, so further financing was essential. Marcus applied to numerous banks for a line of credit to enable him and his partners to purchase stock and sign store leases but was turned down by bank after bank. Another acquaintance, however, provided the much-needed financing. Despite launching their new venture in Atlanta, Marcus turned to the banker in Los Angeles whom he had used at Handy Dan, Rip Fleming at Security Pacific National Bank. Rip had become a trusted adviser to Marcus at Handy Dan, with both Marcus and Fleming believing in a strong relationship between banker and client rather than simply a transaction-based relationship. Thus, Marcus kept Fleming fully informed of the state of Handy Dan, and Fleming trusted that Marcus would tell him the bad as well as the good news.

Despite this prior relationship, Fleming was reluctant to issue Marcus a line of credit. Marcus, however, would not take no for an answer and flew out to Los Angeles to meet with Fleming and sold him on the idea. In the end, Security Pacific National Bank provided a $3.5 million line of credit, which enabled Home Depot to get off the ground. But unbeknownst to Marcus, the proposal was repeatedly turned down by the bank's loan committee and was only approved when Fleming marched into the president of the bank's office with his resignation letter in hand threatening to quit unless the bank granted Marcus the loan.

This remarkable set of circumstances (and many more untold here) that led to the founding of The Home Depot demonstrate the value and effect of even distant relationships in facilitating comeback. Among the primary lessons from Marcus's story is that the way you build relationships impacts your prospects for career recovery. Marcus had a modus operandi of building relatively strong relationships even in those circumstances that for most people would be at best weak acquaintanceships. His relationship with Rip Fleming is a prime example. Whereas most people would have a more transaction-based relationship with their banker, Marcus was concerned with building a more open and trusting relationship with Fleming. This wasn't a one-off with Marcus but was the way he operated in general with employees and others connected or unconnected to his business interests. Characters like Marcus who build these types of relationships are much more likely to engender the types of behaviors that we see in response from people like Rip Fleming, who put his own career on the line for Marcus. They know that he would do the same for them and that there is an implicit trust right from the beginning of the relationship. Marcus didn't know about Fleming's actions on his behalf until he was invited to Fleming's retirement dinner years later and the president of the bank told Marcus the story. Fleming didn't need to tell Marcus—knowing that he had helped out was enough. But when Marcus found out, he wanted to return the favor and hired Fleming as a consultant for life to Home Depot.

Relationships are the precursor to successful business dealings. When searching for seed money, Marcus walked away from an investment by Ross Perot because he wasn't comfortable with the relationship and how it was developing, and how he foresaw it would develop in the future. In a similar fashion to his tumultuous relationship with Sandy Sigoloff, Marcus knew that if there wasn't the basis for trust and a workable relationship, then it wasn't worth going into business, however great the need for the resource.

While these acquaintance ties were vital in facilitating Marcus's career recovery, he also had the benefit of support from stronger friendship ties. Particularly important were his strong relationships with Arthur Blank, his cofounder, and Ken Langone. Langone had started off as an acquaintance introduced by another acquaintance, Erlbaum, but had developed into a strong friend, particularly after Marcus's dismissal from Handy Dan. Both of these key friendships had developed out of business relationships—Blank as his CFO at Handy Dan and Langone as an active investor in the company.

Marcus, then, was a master at relationships. It didn't matter whether these were distant acquaintances, people he dealt with on a more regular basis professionally, or close friends—Marcus treated others with respect, honesty, and trust. These traits were then reciprocated by people in his network when he needed help, allowing Marcus to bounce back in his career and sow the seeds for what has become the world's second-largest retailer.

As in Marcus's case, while acquaintance ties are extremely valuable, mostly in providing connections to extended networks that would otherwise be unavailable, you also need the help of stronger ties that provide a different function of support through the recovery process. This leads us into a greater examination of the importance of strong relationships in facilitating career recovery.

The Support Role of Strong Relationships

The role of the person's network is important in terms of both the connections and the support the network offers. The primary function of weaker acquaintance ties, as we have seen, is in providing those vital connections to future opportunities, and, indeed, acquaintance ties are often better than strong friendship ties at fulfilling this function. However, strong friendship ties are where support is drawn from, particularly in overcoming the psychological barriers to recovery discussed in chapter 6.

Social support from family, friends, and former colleagues can be very influential in reducing the levels of stress felt by the individual suffering from career setback and in encouraging coping behaviors. The continued, and even enhanced, contact with family and friends helps promote social interaction that is often drastically cut after job loss, since a large share of the person's interactions with others usually occurs during the workday. The fallen leader is particularly in need of social support from family and friends because the fall from grace in terms of social position in the community at large cuts deep into the person's ego. The fact that numerous ousted CEOs whom we talked to commented on the seemingly overnight switch from being "who's who" to "who's he?" is a poignant reflection of the distress caused by the loss of the status that came with their prior position. As an indication of the intensity of the stress caused by catastrophic career setback, and the vital importance of strong support systems, one CEO we interviewed commented, "My family and children supported everything I did. I enjoy every single birthday, and I'll take all of them I can get because I remember the day [during the turmoil of the ouster] when I thought I'd never have another one."

Research has shown that professionals who are unemployed have a tendency to isolate themselves from potential sources of support due to the shame and stigma they perceive attached to their downfall.[13] Top leaders are especially prone to such behavior due to the public nature of their downfalls and the subsequent feeling of being outcast, further exaggerated in cases when the portrayal of their reason for exit has potentially damaging implications for their personal or professional reputation. In consequence, the feeling of being outcast may be a self-fulfilling prophesy since the ousted leader avoids contact with others, even close friends and family, for fear of rejection after losing their status gained through the leadership position. This feeling is exacerbated if the person perceives that their downfall has uncovered the disloyalty of many of those they previously considered friends. The old adage "A friend in need is a friend indeed" becomes particularly salient as previous friends and acquaintances seemingly fall by the wayside once the leader has lost the status conferred by their prior position. One CEO who characterized his ouster as a political coup by a faction of the board saw the polarization in his mind between those who remained loyal friends and those who proved to be only fair-weather friends, saying of the former, "There were a number who supported me, and, by the way, I know they were threatened," and of the latter group, "They just went along [with the ouster]— some of them were unhappy about it, but that's the way it goes. I don't consider them friends either, if you can't stay and fight to the end."

This self-imposed isolation is also in many cases partly attributable to self-doubt that arises in the leader's mind about their ability to effectively lead an organization. Until now, the leader's career has gone from strength to strength, and, as social scientists have long established, there is a strong tendency for people to attribute desirable outcomes to their own skills and strengths.[14] This induces a strong sense of self-confidence in the leader in their abilities, which is shaken to the core by the career setback. As the former CEO of a diversified consumer products company told us, "I've always been, until probably now, relatively cocky about my ability to find someplace where I can do something and be happy. I can look at businesses, the working parts of businesses, and figure out where to leverage myself. I always had a great confidence that in a variety of different kinds of businesses I would be able to add value."

The addition of the caveat "until probably now" indicates that whereas previously there was a strong sense of confidence, that confidence has been undermined by the setback. Even in cases where the setback has not

deterred the leader from venturing forth once again into a new enterprise, the confidence in the ability to be as successful as in the past may
be diminished.

It is in alleviating this isolation and self-doubt, and even depression,
that friends and family can play a vital role. Henry Silverman, the CEO
of Cendant, was once regarded by Wall Street as a top deal maker, building by acquisition a company called Hospitality Franchising. He brought
together such brands as real estate brokerage Century 21, Ramada Hotels, Howard Johnson Hotels, Days Inn, and Avis Rent A Car, to yield
20 percent–plus growth rates and soaring stock prices. The stock
jumped from $4 per share in 1992 to over $77 per share before the scandal hit. Following a merger with a direct marketer called CUC that
looked like the perfect complement to his own company (with the
merged entity renamed Cendant in late 1997), his empire and reputation
unraveled. A series of investigations revealed massive accounting improprieties in the former CUC that led to inflated earnings of $700 million
over three years. The subsequent stock meltdown cost roughly $13 bil-
lion in market capitalization.

Silverman, whose father was CEO of a commercial finance company, had been driven to emerge from the shadow of his father's success:
"You want to be recognized for what you achieved rather than what
your parents achieved."[15] After honing his skills with notorious corporate raiders and gilded investment bankers, Silverman had become a legend through his own empire building as well. In the wake of the CUC
scandal, his diligence and management style came under attack. The
anger and humiliation ate away at him. While he hadn't been ousted
from his company, his reputation had been destroyed and his prospects as
a deal maker were severely diminished. But the personal angst was, for
Silverman, as bad as the professional humiliation. "My own sense of self-
worth was diminished," he recalls.[16]

Despite the pressures on him to address the effects of the scandal, and
thus the unavoidable work schedule he maintained, socially he and his
wife withdrew into isolation. Silverman's wife, Nancy, explained that
they couldn't face having to address the scandal at every social event:
"We didn't have the heart to sit and talk about it."[17] So they spent as
much time as they could away from New York in a house they rented

from friends. Over time, though, it was primarily his wife and close friends who helped him through his consuming anger.

With the help of his wife and friends such as financiers Leon Black and Darla Moore, as well as some professional counseling, Silverman found ways to direct his rage. As he told us later, "I was too emotional, especially at the outset. I felt like I had been mugged: personally, professionally, and financially. I went (for one hour) to a stress therapist who was very helpful. His advice: exercise, exercise, and more exercise. In hindsight, I should have been more professional and detached."[18] As a result, he became a workout enthusiast, but exercise alone did not fill the void created by his need to regain his credibility. He told us, "It never occurred to me not to stay and fix the problem. Whether or not it was my fault was irrelevant; I was the CEO and I was responsible."[19] Amidst a government investigation, he replaced all of CUC's leadership and sued its accountants, Ernst & Young. Perhaps more importantly, though, Silverman enlisted his closest network, his board of directors, as the front line in turning the business around. He told us directly:

> *I was brutally frank with the board—no sugarcoating. I told them we were "screwed," that we/they were blameless but might have personal liability anyway, and that it was my job to make certain that Cendant survived and ultimately prospered. I overcommunicated during a very difficult period, and kept my board involved in every decision we made. Believe it or not, I learned crisis management when I was a Navy JAG officer in the 1960s. Imagine, the U.S. government teaching me to "tell the truth, tell it all, and tell it now." That was our mantra (and continues to this day).*[20]

We also talked to all the members of the board, who confirmed that Silverman came to them immediately, communicated constantly, told them everything, and made his battle and the shareholders' battle their battle for justice.

Silverman sold noncore businesses to repurchase 20 percent of the outstanding shares to boost the stock price. He began rebuilding through smaller acquisitions and making alliances with firms like John Malone's Liberty Media, rebuilding credibility and driving e-commerce traffic for his service businesses. Evidence of Silverman's recovery came when another friend, Michael Leven, who used to run Days Inn for Silverman before going on to found hotel group U.S. Franchise Systems, went to visit Silverman, and Silverman asked him, "Are you here to buy or are you here to sell?" Leven replied, "Well, Henry, I guess you're back."[21]

Henry Silverman could easily have given up when things were at their darkest. Indeed, his instincts were pushing him to hide away from society and his own problems. However, his close friends and family were friends indeed, coming to his aid in his darkest hour and helping him regroup and put his problems into perspective. Having a family and friends such as these is a priceless resource when things are at their worst. Many, however, find that they did not pay attention to these relationships when things were going well—other demands on their time cut into the time required to build these strong bonds—and only realize this lack of depth in their relationships when things turn sour. Paying attention to these relationships is therefore vital in good times if they are to remain strong in tough times.

There are obviously degrees of relationships, from the close bonds of family to the distant, little-seen acquaintances. While bonds with family and the closest friends may be tight, it is also important to generate a wider set of reasonably strong bonds with people who will stand behind you in times of crisis. When Jeffrey Katzenberg split acrimoniously from The Walt Disney Company, as we described in the last chapter, he had the strong and vocal support from a number of his friends in the industry. Indeed, Katzenberg was able to draw support from people in all aspects of the industry: actors, film directors and producers, talent agents, and even competitors and those who were still at Disney. Actor Warren Beatty, who had clashed in the past with Katzenberg over criticism of the movie *Dick Tracy*, now came out in his defense, saying, "I've never worked with a studio executive more energetic, more generous with his time, more fun. There's no corporate piece of manpower in the business more valuable than Jeffrey."[22] This sentiment was echoed by film director Steven Spielberg, contending, "He's the most valuable free agent around."[23] Top talent agents also had strong support for Katzenberg. Jerry Katzman, president of the powerful William Morris Agency, said, "When Jeffrey gets on the phone and calls talent, they love it. He's absolutely seductive."[24] Creative Artists Agency (CAA) founder and later Disney president Michael Ovitz agreed that "Jeffrey is a pleasure to do business with. He is responsive, accessible, and someone who will give you a quick answer. I would rather do business with Jeffrey Katzenberg, even if he doesn't agree with my point of view, than someone with less knowledge who is slower in getting you an answer—that is death for an agent."[25] Even Robert Daly, cochairman of Warner Brothers, Disney's biggest competitor, conceded, "Jeffrey is one of the best executives in the movie business."[26]

Remarkably, even those closely connected with Disney talked to the press about Katzenberg's loss as it impacted Disney and them personally. Film producer Robert Cort, president of Interscope Communications, whose films were primarily distributed by Disney, commented to the *Los Angeles Times*, "In the film industry, we live on a perpetual fault line. There are always shocks—and this was a big one. Jeffrey was a fixture. The company reflected a lot of his personality. It will take some time to re-establish the balance of our lives."[27] Even Katzenberg's successor as head of Walt Disney Studios, Joe Roth, commented on the impact that Katzenberg had on Disney: "The intensity of [everyone at the studio's] bond to Jeffrey is a great testament to him—and daunting to me. I didn't anticipate it. For the umpteenth time in my life, I miscalculated."[28]

All of these public testimonies from friends across all aspects of the industry serve several functions for Katzenberg. First, they help reassure him of his stature in the industry and the value of his accomplishments, thus reducing the likely onset of self-doubt in one's own abilities that often sets in following such a career setback. Second, the public support from credible figures lends legitimacy to him and enhances his value in the marketplace. We will talk in the next chapter about rebuilding heroic stature following a downfall. These public comments help retain and limit damage to the heroic stature, or perception of key others in the industry. Ultimately, retaining or rebuilding this public perception is a key to regaining the same or greater position later. Third, public comments such as those in support of Katzenberg give the articulators of such comments a vested interest in his career recovery. These people have publicly stated their support and their impression of the value of Katzenberg, so it is in their interest to see their predictions fulfilled.

Beyond these supportive public testimonies, Katzenberg also garnered the practical support of his two closest friends in launching his rebound.

Katzenberg's recovery and the formation of DreamWorks began imme-diately after he was fired. As Katzenberg returned to his office from his meeting with Michael Eisner in which he was told that the press release of his departure had already been released, his secretary told him that Steven Spielberg was on the phone waiting for him—the news had al-ready reached Spielberg, who was vacationing in Jamaica at the home of fellow film director Robert Zemeckis. As Spielberg offered condolences to Katzenberg, Zemeckis shouted in the background, "Why don't you guys do something together?" Spielberg, still trying to console Katzen-berg, quoted from the movie *Back to the Future*, saying, "Where you're going, you don't need roads." Katzenberg, having heard Zemeckis's re-mark, replied, "What do you mean, 'you'? I'm thinking 'we.' "[29]

A few days later, Katzenberg was at Spielberg's home, and Spielberg related that he too had had long-standing mentor-protégé relationships, similar to the relationship between Eisner and Katzenberg, and that he too might be ready to branch out on his own. With the seed sown, Katzenberg also wanted his other good friend, David Geffen, involved. Geffen and Spielberg knew each other well from the time they worked together with Warner Brothers, but neither particularly liked the other, and they were more rivals than friends. As Geffen characterized the re-lationship, "I was jealous of him, but I respected him and wanted his ap-proval, and we were thrown together a lot."[30]

Geffen had recently sold his company, Geffen Records, to MCA, and his contract to remain chairman of the record business following the merger was about to expire. He was, though, a billionaire as a result of selling his company, and was pursuing other interests, such as art collect-ing, and had become friends with President Clinton. He was not sure about throwing in his lot with Katzenberg, much less Spielberg. Katzen-berg, however, was still eager to have Geffen on board, and Geffen was eager to help his friend, particularly since he felt somewhat responsible for Katzenberg's exit from Disney, because Geffen had encouraged Katzenberg to campaign for advancement at Disney.

The three finally agreed to begin their new studio late in September 1994, a few hours after the three had attended a White House dinner for Russian president Boris Yeltsin. Katzenberg and Spielberg returned to their hotel and after further discussion called Geffen, who, as Clinton's guest, was staying in the Lincoln Bedroom of the White House; they persuaded Geffen to meet them at the hotel, where the three of them agreed to pursue their new venture. Geffen recalled his motivation for joining this historic venture: "The reason [DreamWorks exists] is because Michael Eisner wouldn't give Jeffrey the job. Jeffrey is the catalyst for all this. I mean . . . he said to me, 'Do you want to do this?' and I said, 'No. This is a lot of work and I'm a very, very, very rich man' . . . But I got caught up in it and I did not want to hand him a 'no' as he had gotten from Michael Eisner. I did not want to be another person who didn't want to give it to Jeffrey." [31]

On October 12, 1994, the three of them gathered at the Peninsula Hotel in Beverly Hills to announce the first new movie studio in more than sixty years—what the *New York Times* called "the biggest merger of talent since Charlie Chaplin, Mary Pickford, Douglas Fairbanks and D. W. Griffith founded the United Artists movie empire in 1919." [32]

In Katzenberg's case, his close friends clearly not only played a vital role in supporting him publicly and through their one-on-one involvement with him in thinking through his options, but also were instrumental in forming his new career role. While this is obviously not the typical scenario, as we discussed in chapter 4 on corporate cultures, some industries are more closely bound than others and have a culture where people can move freely from firm to firm within an industry. In what we termed the baseball team cultures, strong connections within the industry can be particularly helpful. Unlike in many other industries, the "small" nature and close interconnectedness of Hollywood meant that it didn't matter that Spielberg and Geffen had overlapping networks with Katzenberg, because it was in this small world that he was reemerging, and they all knew the right players. It is the nature of the search, and understanding how dispersed are factors such as industry or geographic reach, that determines the salience of acquaintance versus strong friendship ties in finding the next position. If one is changing industries or looking within a much more dispersed industry or geographic region, acquaintance ties become much more likely to aid in finding the next position. But in tightly connected industries, where it is common for people to move from one firm to another, friendship ties often prove valuable in connecting to the next career position as well as more personal emotional support.

The Collateral Damage

While the person is going through the transition forced upon them through catastrophic career setback, others, particularly close family and friends, also undergo trauma as a result of the setback. Although they are looked upon for support, they are also going through similar emotional experiences as they try to give the assistance that they can. There has been a good deal of research into the collateral damage felt by spouses, in particular, and other close friends and family when a person has a career setback. Spouses are likely to suffer from psychological problems such as anxiety, depression, or psychosomatic illnesses, though not with the same intensity as the person dealing with job loss.[33] The stresses of setback can also lead to strain in the marriage and family, with research showing that job loss can lead to a three- or fourfold increase in the likelihood of separation and divorce.[34] There is also a correlation with an increased risk of child abuse.[35]

Friends and coworkers also are affected by the setback of their friend and colleague. While the research shows that the more time people facing career setback spend with friends, the less psychological distress they endure, it is also true that the longer the person is without a job, the more stress this places on those friends and the more the person tends to reduce the frequency of social contact. Carrie Leana and Daniel Feldman, in a study of large layoffs within two communities, found that many who were laid off described themselves as suffering from a "social disease" in which friends increasingly avoid them due to their own inability to cope with the stress caused by the setback to their friend.[36]

When the individual coping with setback is a prominent leader, that adds another dimension to the stress imposed on family and friends. In this case, the intense media frenzy can result in friends and acquaintances being pestered for statements or inside information about the person or events involved in the setback. This happened in the Katzenberg case, when friends such as Spielberg and Geffen were repeatedly questioned by reporters about Katzenberg's character and reaction. In the extreme, when legal action is pursued following the leader's dismissal, friends may also be asked, or indeed forced, to testify in court, undergoing depositions and even in-court cross-examinations, which may be used against the friend they wish to support. In the trial of Martha Stewart, her close friend Mariana Pasternak, who was vacationing with her when Martha made the trade of ImClone stock that subsequently came under investigation, was called as a witness by the prosecution to testify against her friend.

Conclusion

Even when family members and friends want to pull away from the stress of a setback, it is important to remember that the loyalty of close friends and the wider connections of acquaintances are vital to the recovery process and an essential foundation on which to build a career rebound. However, much of a leader's ability to once again build an organization or gain the faith of another organization in a leadership role lies in the wider perception of those beyond close friends and even more distant acquaintances. We turn, therefore, to what a leader must do to regain the support of a wider audience in launching their comeback. In essence, this is rebuilding the heroic stature, or public reputation, with which the leader was previously perceived.

CHAPTER **9**

Rebuilding Heroic Stature

IN THE SOCIAL SCIENCES, there is a growing literature on what is termed *image restoration theory*. In this theory, two conditions are necessary for an attack on a person's reputation to pose a substantial risk to it: the act is undesirable and has serious repercussions, and the person can be held accountable or responsible for the action that led to the attack—that is, that the accusation is valid. As we discussed in chapter 7, sometimes accusations are not important enough to warrant combating and may be best defended by ignoring them and not adding further fuel to the fire, which prevents the accusations from turning into a conflagration. Essentially, this confounds the first condition. While any attack is undesirable, some are not directly threatening to the person's position and thus do not have the repercussions that could seriously damage the person's reputation. Certainly, a reputation can be damaged through an accumulation of small hits, to the point that a further seemingly insignificant attack can be the last straw. But most of the reputational attacks that result in downfall are of a serious nature and can be distinguished as such.

Given a major attack on the person's reputation, and particularly one that leads to downfall, the accountability question comes into play. The occurrence of the downfall itself indicates that the person has been held accountable by the organization, but that is not necessarily the end of the story, particularly in terms of the person's ability to rebound from the setback. By virtue of being in a leadership position, leaders are often held to account for the misdeeds or performance of the organization even if they were not directly responsible. Additionally, the story portrayed publicly through the media may not tell the whole story, but may serve to cover up the true reason for dismissal for the benefit of the organization or the board, in the case of businesses. Thus, it is vital for the leader to be able to make their side of the story known to those wider audiences beyond their friends and acquaintances who may play gatekeeper roles in providing access to future opportunities—communities such as executive search firms or sources of funding for a new venture. The leader must be able to spread the word about the true nature of the adversity, maintaining the confidence held by others in the leader's ability to perform.

Great leaders acquire a heroic persona that gives them a larger-than-life presence. When that is removed, and the trappings, status, and positional power of office are taken away, leaders risk the loss of their identity, which, in their minds and the minds of others, has become intertwined with the organization they led. Such personalities are not comfortable merely being one of the crowd, but have a need to lead others and stand out from the masses. Great leaders achieve this by developing a personal dream that they offer as a public possession. If it is accepted, they become renowned, but if it is ultimately discarded, they suffer the loss of both a private dream and a public identity.

Telling Your Side of the Story

When Bernie Marcus was fired from Handy Dan and sought support for his new venture with The Home Depot, he went on the road, taking his story to numerous potential investors and bankers, many of whom closed the door on him despite his compelling vision and rational explanation for his downfall at Handy Dan. But as he continued knocking on doors and gained the support of vital backers, the momentum shifted and people began to rally around him, enabling him to regain a position of leadership. They rallied because, despite his setback, they still believed in him, his heroic identity, and his heroic mission for his new venture. Marcus was effective at getting across his side of the Handy Dan story and gave them something to believe in. They were further encouraged by the solid support for Marcus from key backers like Ken Langone. When a hero stumbles, the constituents have to reconcile two images of the person—the larger-than-life presence and the new fallen state. It is essential for the leader to maintain the faith in their prior heroic status and eliminate the confusion of images by ensuring that others know what really happened, externalizing or isolating the reason for the downfall, providing a rationale for others to believe in the leader's new mission, and building on the support of those loyal backers to reach a wider audience.

In our interviews of fired CEOs, we found the greatest frustration derived from not being able to rebuild their heroic stature by telling their side of the story. Both noncompete and nondisparagement agreements can undermine departing CEOs' ability to prove that they are not leaving due to failures in competence or character. The noncompete clause makes it hard to return to industries where the CEOs have proven themselves and where their skills are best known. A noncompete agreement initially held back Tom Stemberg, the founder of Staples. In January 1985, Stemberg was fired from a New England supermarket chain as CEO of its primary division after challenging the integrity and realism of bosses who were promising the board undeliverable results.

Launching his career, Stemberg had sterling credentials as a Baker Scholar honors graduate from the Harvard Business School. He began as vice president of sales and merchandising for First National Supermarkets, based in Connecticut. He later became a division president of its Finast unit, but then things unraveled. The chairman was shot in a gangland-style slaying, and his predecessor was found guilty of price-fixing and taking kickbacks. When Stemberg challenged the deliverability of stated plans, he was fired and given a year's severance pay if he upheld a noncompete clause on his severance agreement.

Stemberg was distressed by this firing—a sudden tarnish on his once glistening career in the industry—but he felt trapped in a corner. Even though a former supermarket chain owner, Leo Kohn, who had recently sold his own chain for $100 million, had offered to back Stemberg in a new business, they could not tell the world what had really gone on with Stemberg's previous employer, in order to rebuild his stature by taking on a new or existing supermarket chain, due to his contractual legal constraints. Such agreements, while initially financially attractive, can prove to be significant liabilities in moving forward and force you to switch careers into unfamiliar arenas. While Stemberg's agreement prohibited him from the grocery business, it allowed him to stay within the world of retail, so he ultimately switched to another retail environment.

After six months of searching for opportunities, he was inspired by chance to look into discount retail stores with long hours—he was unable to get a replacement ribbon for his printer on the Fourth of July due to limited stock and closed stores. By 1986, he launched his office supply chain, Staples, in a large former supermarket building in Brighton, Massachusetts. Now, two decades later, the chain is the world's largest office supply retailer, with 1,780 stores in 21 countries generating $16 billion in revenues and employing roughly 20,000 associates. Stemberg himself has recently moved from Staples to become a venture capitalist at the highly respected firm of Highland Capital Partners.

Similarly, the exiting CEOs may also have their hands tied and be unable to get out their side of the story when they are constrained by financial inducements tied to nondisparagement clauses in separation agreements. Often, the deposed CEO is attracted to inducements on departure, especially if they are mutually binding between the exiting CEO and the firm. Later, however, they come to rue the fact that rebuilding their career is constrained by the inability to set the record straight and regain people's belief in their leadership. Furthermore, rumormongering from the firm can still harm them through false stories with sources that cannot be traced, and the former CEO can have trouble enforcing the reciprocal nondisparagement guaranty from the firm.

We have interviewed several people who had seven-figure separation agreements that were contingent on their toeing the party line on their exit. One fired CEO told us, "The agreement that we reached was that basically I'm going to get what works out to a million dollars to put on a public face that [this is a smooth transition for the company]. You know, don't go public with the true reasons as to why I'm leaving. And since I've still got a half-million shares in the company myself, I don't want to see the stock drop, so I've got no interest in going public with the true reasons as to why I'm leaving."

In this instance, the organization placed the blame for the exit on the CEO and restricted the CEO from coming out with their side of the story to rebuild their reputation. While in many instances these public relations cover-ups can harm the reputation of the departing CEO, especially when the CEO takes the blame for things beyond their control or responsibility, they may not always be detrimental to the departing leader. Indeed, the fact that the organization is trying to minimize the damage to itself can potentially have positive benefits for the CEO if it portrays the succession as a smooth, voluntary one, such that the CEO's reputation is not damaged despite the turmoil that ensued behind the scenes. The damage comes, however, when the CEO is publicly sacrificed regardless of the CEO's culpability in the accusations leading to the ouster. In such cases, the CEO's lack of ability to challenge false accusations and set the record straight can lead to damaging speculation in the press that can spread the reputational damage, making it all but impossible for the CEO to recover. The perception portrayed by the media can be a far stronger force than the reality behind the story. As noted lawyer Alan Dershowitz wrote in his introduction to Fenton Bailey's book *Fall from Grace: The Untold Story of Michael Milken*: "The sad truth is that today, the media has more power than ever before to create, out of whole cloth, ersatz individuals to replace the real people whose names they bear, and who make far less 'interesting' copy. This unprecedented power to malign can destroy innocent people so quickly, so thoroughly and so pervasively, that it may take an individual the better part of a lifetime to restore a savaged reputation—if at all."[1]

Managing Perceptions to Restore Confidence

Even in circumstances where leaders are guilty of a misstep that results in their downfall, their ability to rebuild is dependent on restoring the confidence of a wider public in them by isolating the misjudgment from their overall capability. In this instance, the task is more than getting out your side of the story to the widest audience possible; it's being able to put the incident or misjudgment behind you in the minds of key constituents to enable them to place trust once again in you and your vision, when that trust may have been damaged or even shattered. This takes time, but also careful management of perceptions.

One example is George Shaheen, who left as CEO of Andersen Consulting (now Accenture) to head up Webvan, an Internet-based grocery home delivery service, at the height of the dot-com boom. Despite the short-lived existence of Webvan and its spectacular failure, Shaheen's misjudgment in taking the position did not destroy his reputation among the all-important executive search community. The damage was limited due to the ability to interpret the move as one that, although very risky, had a potentially huge payoff that justified the risk. The after-the-fact explanation that the enterprise was doomed before Shaheen arrived—but that this was not knowable beforehand, or at least that anyone would have been blind to this conclusion given the euphoria of the Internet bubble—allowed others to excuse this misjudgment. Additionally, the recognition that the greater risk was offset by an even greater potential reward, given the fantastic compensation package offered, added to the excusableness of the career change. Consequently, key gatekeepers in the executive search community (we spoke to several who conduct CEO and board-level searches) were able to look past the failure at Webvan, allowing Shaheen to regain the stature he had when at Andersen Consulting.

Shaheen thus embodied the elements for successful image restoration. There was a clear denial of culpability or shifting responsibility for the mishap, which occurred through the explanation that the situation was doomed before he arrived. The offensiveness of the act was reduced by the understanding of the temptations of the Internet bubble and the concurrent irrational investments and judgments that this provoked among a large number of normally more rational people. This gave the appearance that the decision to jump from the established relative safety of Andersen Consulting to the risky world of Webvan was reasonable given the booming Internet economy of the time. Finally, the lure of such enormous prospective wealth offered an explanation of the motive behind the move that appeared rational. Thus, even though the move did not play out as planned, Shaheen was still able to overcome the mistake by providing a reasonable explanation for why it occurred to people who understood the context of the time in which the move was made. Consequently, although this rationalization was done in hindsight, few faulted Shaheen for leaving a premiere consulting firm for an uncertain start-up, and he was able to regain his stature among key constituents, positioning himself for a return to a leadership position in another organization. Subsequently, in April 2005, Shaheen was named CEO of the software company Siebel Systems.

Martha Stewart's Rebuilding Strategies

Perhaps the most public downfall in recent times was that of Martha Stewart. The day after Stewart was indicted by the Department of Justice (DOJ) for obstruction of justice in its investigation of potential insider trading of ImClone stock, Stewart took out a full-page advertisement in *USA Today* and the *New York Times*—and launched a new Web site, marthatalks.com—with the following message to her public:

An Open Letter from Martha Stewart

To My Friends and Loyal Supporters,

After more than a year, the government has decided to bring charges against me for matters that are personal and entirely unrelated to the business of Martha Stewart Living Omnimedia. I want you to know that I am innocent—and that I will fight to clear my name.

I simply returned a call from my stockbroker. Based in large part on prior discussions with my broker about price, I authorized a sale of my remaining shares in a biotech company called ImClone. I later denied any wrongdoing in public statements and in voluntary interviews with prosecutors. The government's attempts to criminalize these actions make no sense to me.

I am confident I will be exonerated of these baseless charges, but a trial unfortunately won't take place for months. I want to thank you for your extraordinary support during the past year— I appreciate it more than you will ever know.

For more information, please visit the special website I have established for you at www.marthatalks.com. I will do my best to post current information about the case, and you will be able to contact me there at Martha@marthatalks.com. I look forward to hearing from you.

Sincerely,

Martha Stewart[2]

Right away, in the opening sentence, Stewart is disconnecting the action upon which the allegation is based from her business and, by implication, her business judgment. This clear separation at the outset is an important precursor to allowing people to maintain or rebuild trust in her business judgment. She also portrays her actions as perfectly reasonable, again allowing people to believe in the soundness of her judgment and behavior. The personal tone of the open letter was also accompanied on her Web site by a statement on her behalf from her attorneys, Robert G. Morvillo and John J. Tigue:

Martha Stewart has done nothing wrong. The government is making her the subject of a criminal test case designed to further expand the already unrecognizable boundaries of the federal securities laws.

The indictment reveals that the predicate for the entire investigation— the accusation that Martha Stewart sold her ImClone shares based on inside information—has proven to be false. It is most ironic that Ms. Stewart faces criminal charges for obstructing an investigation which established her innocence. This turn of events can only be characterized as bizarre and raises questions about the motivation for such peculiar charges.

Though the government has not charged her with insider trading, it alleges that public statements drafted by her distinguished attorneys in June 2002 about the reasons she sold ImClone stock constitute a fraud. These unprecedented charges are baseless. The press releases were issued in response to Congressional leaks that Ms. Stewart sold her ImClone shares because she was tipped that its cancer drug application was going to be denied—another allegation that has proven to be absolutely false. In this country, those who have been falsely accused of a crime have always been free to proclaim their innocence without fear of being punished by the government for their resistance. These press releases did little more than truthfully deny that she had been tipped on Erbitux [ImClone's new cancer drug]. *To attempt to criminalize such statements and use the federal securities laws to deprive those under investigation of the ability to speak out in their own defense violates basic principles of American democracy and is most disturbing.*

As to the remainder of the allegations, we are also unaware of any case in which a witness has voluntarily submitted to an unsworn interview by a federal prosecutor—and then been prosecuted for allegedly false statements that have nothing to do with the stated purpose of the interview. In this case, the focus of the interview was Erbitux and Martha truthfully denied being tipped as to its status.

Why then has the government, after nearly a year and a half, chosen to file these charges? Is it for publicity purposes because Martha Stewart is a celebrity? Is it because she is a woman who has successfully competed in a man's business world by virtue of her talent, hard work and demanding standards? Is it because the government would like to be able to define securities fraud as whatever it wants it to be? Or is it because the Department of Justice is attempting to divert the public's attention from its failure to charge the politically connected managers of Enron and WorldCom who may have fleeced the public out of billions of dollars?

We urge the media to ask these questions—and to consult with legal experts on the validity and broader implications of these extraordinary charges. We believe such an inquiry will verify that this indictment is unique and goes well beyond any other criminal securities law case. We ask the public to withhold judgment until the government's unfounded charges are publicly aired and refuted. When this happens, we are convinced that justice will follow and Martha Stewart will be fully exonerated.[3]

In taking this action and defending herself in this manner, Stewart was recognizing that while the judgment of the courts of law were important in restoring her name and career, the fight was more urgent, and at least as important, in the court of public opinion. Stewart realized that hiding is not a strategy. Trying to hide and avoid publicity until either the glare of media attention turns to the next story or the full facts can be disclosed through a courtroom or other forum is not a viable option if one seeks to protect a reputation from sustained damage. Rather, it is vital to take a proactive stance in getting your side of the story out.

Often, silence in the face of bad news, especially when the opportunity to defend oneself has been presented, is taken as admission of guilt. Therefore, getting an alternative view of transpired events out to the public is of highest importance.

In taking this two-pronged attack of an open letter to supporters and a statement from her attorneys, Stewart was addressing distinct constituencies within the wider public. Stewart is a public figure who has to some extent polarized the public—many people love her, while many others love to hate her. She has very high name recognition and is loved by many in a way that not many public figures are. Her fans feel that she is a part of their everyday lives as they consult her shows and magazines for advice on their home and homemaking, which itself forms a core part of their own identity. In emulating Stewart, they identify with her, and she becomes almost an intimate friend, indispensable for advice on all things to do with their home. Mostly because of this strong identity and closeness that many people have with Stewart's public persona, there are equally others who react against this influence and vilify her, mocking people who have become too "Martha-esque." Stewart recognizes this polarization and addresses her first open letter to the former group; she writes in a very personal tone, cementing her strong identity ties to these people by addressing the letter intimately to her "friends and loyal supporters."

It is imperative to recognize the constituencies involved. Rarely do leaders and public figures have a single constituency whose concerns demand attention. More often there are multiple constituencies whose concerns need to be addressed. In Stewart's case, there is not just the DOJ but the media and the public, which itself is divided between those favorably disposed toward her and those predisposed against her. Only briefly referenced in her public statements but still of major concern is her organization itself, Martha Stewart Living Omnimedia. This constituency consists of not only its employees and others directly connected to the organization, but also external groups such as analysts, shareholders, and advertisers. Even beyond these are more directly personal constituencies such as family, friends, and acquaintances, who also need reassurance of their confidence in the person; these close parties tend to be dragged into the maelstrom as they are constantly questioned by their own acquaintances, people they meet, and even the media.

In the letter, Stewart clearly proclaims her innocence and her intention to fight to clear her name. However, beyond this she also does several other interesting things. First, in the opening paragraph, she separates Martha Stewart the person from Martha Stewart the organization. This is an attempt to separate and protect her business interests from what she claims to be a personal matter. More importantly, though, with this audience, it personalizes the issue, tying it to her and making it central to restoring her personal reputation, which, again particularly with this audience, is likely to garner more sympathy and support than if it were portrayed as a business-related problem.

Second, she thanks the readers for their support. This does several things: it makes the implicit assumption that the readers are, and will continue to be, "friends of Martha" who support her through thick and thin; as an open letter obviously destined to be read by millions of people, it intimates that the readers are not alone in their support for Stewart—indeed, everyone in her circle of "friends and supporters" is going to be behind her. Therefore, for the readers to drop support would be both disloyal, if not outright betrayal of a friend, and going against the norm of expected behavior.

Third, she lets her friends know both how she will keep them informed and how they can be in personal touch with her during this trial. This keeps the personal connection between herself and her audience and indeed makes the reader feel even more identified with her since they now perceive that they have a specific invitation to be in contact with her.

It is vital to be aware of the concerns of these constituencies and the role they may play in recovery from the setback. In cases such as Stewart's, while trying to avoid a guilty verdict in the courtroom was certainly an imperative and would have greatly facilitated her career recovery, ultimately the real battle was in retaining the adulation of her large body of supporters in the general public, who would be the final arbiters of whether she remained a beloved figure and authority on homemaking despite a subsequent guilty verdict in the courtroom. Separating the issue from having anything to do with her area of expertise, such that no one questioned that there was any diminution in her abilities to be a role model for homemakers, was an essential first step in maintaining her heroic stature. In setting up her Web site marthatalks.com and in writing her personal letter, Stewart demonstrates a clear understanding that she recognizes the importance of keeping her fan base informed and on her side. Without actively connecting to and retaining the loyalty of this group from which she derives her success, even a victory in the courtroom would have been a hollow victory in a still-ruined career. Instead, despite what would turn out to be a defeat in the courtroom, the public acts as the essential gatekeeper to renewed success and enables her to return to her former stature. The lesson here for other contexts, depending on the circumstances of the fall and the likely path to recovery, is that other constituents, such as executive search firms, may act as the key gatekeeper to entering the recovery path, and so the concerns of these constituents must not be overlooked even though it may appear that the main battle lies elsewhere.

In contrast to this personal correspondence, the statement from Stewart's attorneys has a different tone and is directed toward a different audience. The target audience is revealed in the last paragraph, where the attorneys "urge the media" to take note of their points and ask questions on the motives behind Stewart's prosecution. This recognizes the hugely important role the media will play in influencing the extent to which Stewart's reputation will be damaged in the minds of the wider public due to this lawsuit. Indeed, it is recognition that, given her stated innocence, it is only how she and the actions she has allegedly taken are portrayed by the media that will have a lasting impact on her reputation among the wider public beyond her core fan base, which Stewart addressed with her own letter.

It is a truism that the media loves to build people up and fawn over the famous, but loves even more to tear those same people down when they begin to topple from grace. Even prior to the allegations of insider trading, Stewart had had plenty of experience with both faces of the media as someone who drew attention both as one they loved to love and as one they loved to hate. Stewart and her attorneys are well aware of this double-edged sword of the media and indeed suggest that her celebrity is one of the primary causes of the pursuit of this case since the DOJ could be sure of a great deal of publicity surrounding it, perhaps, as the attorneys' question indicates, deflecting attention from the DOJ's "failure to charge the politically connected managers of Enron and WorldCom who may have fleeced the public out of billions of dollars."

In taking this tack, Stewart's attorneys, while knowing that publicity of the lawsuit is inevitable, are trying to deflect media criticism from her and onto another favorite media villain, the government. In the statement, Stewart's attorneys challenge the role and credibility of the government. They begin by appealing to basic constitutional rights for someone to "proclaim their innocence without fear of being punished by the government for their resistance," and add that the deprivation of such rights "violates basic principles of American democracy and is most disturbing." Having questioned the validity of the charges placed against Stewart, her attorneys provide the media with an avenue for conjecture about the government's motives for abandoning due process. They attack the credibility of the government by alleging that the pursuit of Stewart is a gender-biased, publicity-seeking attempt to gloss over the failure to prosecute the "real" white-collar criminals at Enron and WorldCom, those who have done actual harm to the public and the public interest but who have friends at the highest levels of the government. Essentially, Stewart's attorneys used this statement as an attempt to set the media loose on the government, portraying it as a bullying villain against a defenseless, innocent woman whose only crime is to successfully compete in a man's business world. The ideal outcome of this would be for the government to be sufficiently embarrassed by the media attack to back off from the prosecution, or at the very least for Stewart to be framed as the innocent victim of an out-of-control government in the mind of the public at large.

Finally, recognizing the tendency of the media and the public alike to rush to condemn fallen stars, they appeal to the public to withhold judgment until Stewart can prove her innocence in the courts.

This attempt to portray Stewart as David struggling in a just and valiant quest against the Goliath of government provides several lessons for those facing the loss of or damage to their most valuable asset, their reputation. Instant response is key. Even when people are vindicated by the full disclosure of facts or through prevailing in the courtroom, their reputation may have sustained irreparable damage if the real battle for public opinion has already been lost through avoidance. The tendency of the media and the public to rush to bury fallen icons is a very real problem for public figures, especially in cases such as Stewart's, where the ability of the person to argue the falsehood of the damaging allegations is delayed due to the slowness of the legal system or other impediments to timely vindication. For such public figures, it is imperative to attempt to discredit false accusations or rumors as quickly as possible by providing their own side of the story or by undermining the credibility of the accusations. In instances where, even when their side of the story is told, doubt may remain in the public's mind about the legitimacy of the claims against the person, the fallen leaders need to appeal to the public to withhold judgment until the facts can be established.

While exoneration in the court of law would have greatly aided in restoring Stewart's career, fighting the accusations made against her was even more urgent, and ultimately more important to her comeback, in the court of public opinion. On March 5, 2004, Stewart was convicted on two counts of making false statements, one count of conspiracy and one of obstruction of justice. Four months later, on July 16, she was sentenced to five months in prison and five months of home confinement. However, despite what would seem an insurmountable setback, Stewart was far from finished. Her statement outside the courtroom following her sentencing hearing, while recognizing the gravity of the situation and what lay before her, also revealed her determination to rebound. She began:

> Today is a shameful day. It's shameful for me, and for my family, and for my beloved company, and for all of its employees and partners. What was a small personal matter became over the last two years an almost fatal circus event of unprecedented proportions. I have been choked and almost suffocated to death during that time, all the while more concerned about the well-being of others than for myself, more hurt for them and for their losses than for my own, more worried for their futures than the future of Martha Stewart the person.[4]

While the courtroom battle had been lost, Stewart knew that the more important battle in terms of her comeback, the battle for public opinion, was still in process, and that this day was a vital moment in the battle. While telling of her shame in receiving the verdict and subsequent sentence, she still refutes the accusation, and now conviction, of wrongdoing, and indeed later in her statement reiterates that she will appeal. But almost immediately in her remarks, she turns the focus away from her troubles to connect with others, her supporters who are vital in retaining and rebuilding her heroic stature. She continued her remarks, connecting with those around her and telling them how much they mean to her and how they can continue to help:

> *More than 200 people have lost their jobs at my company as a result of this situation. I want them to know how very, very sorry I am for them and their families. I would like to thank everybody who stood by me, who wished me well, waved to me on the street like these lovely people over here, smiled at me, called me, wrote to me. We received thousands of support letters, and more than 170,000 e-mails to marthatalks.com, and I appreciate each and every one of those pieces of correspondence. I feel really good about it. Perhaps all of you out there can continue to show your support by subscribing to our magazine, by buying our products, by encouraging our advertisers to come back in full force to our magazines.*[5]

After extolling the virtues of her magazines and why her company should not suffer because of her legal woes, she vowed to go through the ordeal before her and then make her comeback: "And I'll be back. I will be back. Whatever I have to do in the next few months, I hope the months will go by quickly. I'm used to all kinds of hard work, as you know, and I'm not afraid. I'm not afraid whatsoever. I'm just very, very sorry that it's come to this, that a small personal matter has been able to be blown out of all proportion, and with such venom and gore, I mean, it's just terrible."[6]

Even though at the time she was convinced that she would be exonerated and still vowed to continue the legal fight, Stewart and her team were continuing to work and plan her comeback behind the scenes and to fight in the court of public opinion, the important battle, which, following the courtroom verdict, she was beginning to win.

One of the biggest obstacles to launching a comeback is uncertainty. Stewart's legal woes had already dragged on for some two years, and her company had been hugely hit by advertisers leaving in droves and the suspension of her flagship television program. However, what was driving this exodus was less the event of Stewart's conviction than the uncertainty that had been surrounding her and continued to surround her following the conviction and sentencing. She had already been strategizing about her comeback, planning two new television series with Mark Burnett, the famed producer of the reality TV hits *Survivor* and *The Apprentice* with Donald Trump, but even in the aftermath of her conviction, she was still in limbo for an unforeseeable amount of time, pending an appeal of her case. With the tide of public opinion turning in her favor thanks to her unrelenting efforts, Stewart took the unusual step of opting to take her prison term before her appeal had been heard—serving a sentence that would not have to be served if her appeal were successful—just in order to eliminate the uncertainty and be free to put the episode behind her, and get on with her life and her rebuilding process. Stewart talked about her decision process and dilemma in doing this on CNN's *Larry King Live*:

> *Well, it is a conundrum. My company needs me. I would like to get back to work. I would like this to be over. This has been a long, drawn-out process and I would like very much to go back to work. On the one hand, the business, Wall Street, advertisers—they would all like to see finality. They would all like to see an end to all of this. I, as a person with rights and with a belief in the judicial system and fairness, think that an appeal is the way to go. So what do I do? OK, if it weren't wrapped up with my company, and it shouldn't be, but it is. Inextricably. What do you do?*[7]

In the end, though, as Sharon Patrick, Stewart's friend and successor as CEO of her company, Martha Stewart Living Omnimedia, explained to us, "The uncertainty was worse than the sentence. We couldn't move forward with her comeback until the uncertainty was laid to rest. And the only way of doing that fast was to serve the sentence and get it over with."[8]

The swings in the battle for public opinion and in the public perception of Stewart and her chances of a comeback can most clearly be seen by tracking the stock market reaction to her ordeal, shown in figure 9-1. Before the initial accusations arose in June 2002, MSO (Martha Stewart Living Omnimedia) was trading at around $20 per share. From June to September 2002—as ImClone CEO Sam Waksal was arrested on securities fraud charges and speculation was rife that Stewart engaged in insider trading, culminating in congressional investigators formally asking

FIGURE 9-1

Five year chart of Martha Stewart Living Omnimedia (MSO) stock price

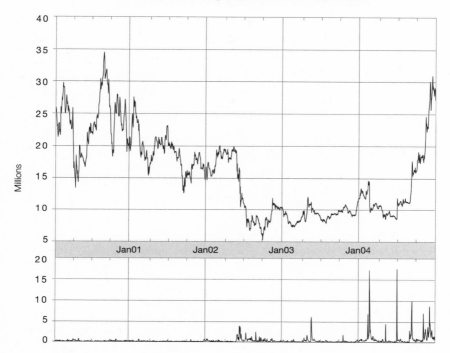

Martha Stewart Living Omnimedia as of 11-Jan-2005

Source: Copyright 2004, Yahoo! Inc., http://finance.yahoo.com/

the Justice Department to examine the stock sale—MSO stock plummeted toward $5 per share. During this period, the tide of public opinion took its greatest turn against her as her detractors were most vocal in jumping in on the speculation of her wrongdoing.

After somewhat of a recovery as speculation quieted down, the stock price went above $10 until Stewart was indicted on June 4, 2003, and forced to resign as CEO of Martha Stewart Living Omnimedia. Six days later, Sam Waksal was sentenced to seven years and three months for insider trading, obstructing justice, and avoiding taxes. The stock sank below $10 per share once again and remained there until Stewart's trial began in January 2004. In the days before the trial began, Stewart was thrust once again into the forefront of media attention, and as the public was glued to the spectacle of her trial, the tide of public opinion finally turned in her favor. During the trial, confidence rose that she would be exonerated, and MSO stock rose toward the mid-teens.

Hopes of a speedy resolution, however, were dashed with the guilty verdict, and uncertainty about Stewart's future and hopes for a comeback once again took the fore. The stock dropped immediately below $10 after the trial and continued slowly declining until her sentencing was announced. The reduction in uncertainty by the announcement of the sentence and her resolve to come back, clearly evident in her statement on the courtroom steps, revived sentiment, and the stock rebounded. However, the remaining uncertainty about her future pending the appeal and the potential protracted nature of the appeal process kept shackles on the stock as her comeback was indefinitely delayed. Stewart knew that uncertainty was the biggest barrier to her comeback and that the only way to speed the process was to decide to serve her sentence before her appeal process took place. Her decision to do this, and framing it as the beginning of her comeback, unleashed a flow of positive sentiment both in public opinion and toward the stock of her company. News of her postsentence plans—such as two television series, including a Martha Stewart version of *The Apprentice* in prime time with producer Mark Burnett—continued to fuel expectations of her comeback. Three months into Stewart's five-month sentence, Sharon Patrick told us about how Stewart was coping with prison, saying, "Martha is a very task-focused person. She knows what she has to do, and she is working hard at it. She is busy planning her comeback. She is writing a detailed diary. She knows it is going to be hard work and she is preparing. She has dropped twenty-five pounds and she is getting very fit, ready for what she has to do once she gets out. She will be back."[9]

The test of a beloved icon is what happens when you take it away. Just as The Coca-Cola Company discovered in the 1980s, when it replaced Coca-Cola with New Coke, the absence made people realize how much they loved the icon, and they demanded it back. The same was true for Martha Stewart. Her fans, far from abandoning a fallen star, rallied around her and were desperate to have her back. The astounding measure of this sentiment is measured in the stock price. Even at the midway point of her prison sentence, her stock not only had fully rebounded but was 50 percent higher than it was before anybody had heard of ImClone and Stewart's ill-fated stock trade.

Restoring reputation in order to provide the foundation for a comeback can take two broad forms. These forms can essentially be crystallized by the time orientation. One form is in protecting and dealing with the past. In chapter 7 we saw the necessity of defending one's reputation from a false and damaging accusation when that allegation may prompt a downfall or prevent a recovery. Rebuilding heroic stature, however, while resting on removing as much as possible the damage done in the past, has an essential forward-looking element that seeks to show where the leader will be in the future and communicates to a wide audience the restored trust that the audience can once again have in the leader. Part of that restoration is done with rhetoric and rebuilding or reestablishing relationships, even tacit ones—for instance, those between Martha Stewart and her many fans and supporters. While this can often be sufficient to receive the grace of the audience and build a platform for a comeback, it usually has to be shortly followed by a more solid basis on which to rebuild that trust and reputation, as the leader is asked once again to prove their mettle in a new setting.

CHAPTER 10

Proving Your Mettle

You can't con people, at least not for long. You can create excitement, you can do wonderful promotion and get all kinds of press, and you can throw in a little hyperbole. But if you don't deliver the goods, people will eventually catch on.

—Donald Trump[1]

THERE WAS NO HOPE for a comeback for the pop vocal group Milli Vanilli. The duo of Fab Morvan and Rob Pilatus, formed in the late 1980s, turned out to be a fraudulent act when it was proved that they had not even been involved with the creation of their breakthrough Grammy-winning album. The Grammy was stripped from them in 1990 when it turned out that they had merely appeared on the cover and lip-synched to prerecorded studio singers for videos and concerts. They could not prove they "still had it in them" in terms of singing talent after the scandal because they were musically hollow.

By contrast, prizefighter George Foreman was dubbed "king of the superheavyweights" when he came back out of retirement, against the odds, and regained the World Heavyweight Championship in 1995—a full twenty years after he had lost it to Muhammad Ali, who had been able to better withstand a beating. The boxing world was shocked when

Foreman, at age forty-five, defeated Michael Moorer, a twenty-five-year-old champion, with a sensational, come-from-behind knockout punch.

Regaining the trust of others through fighting unjust accusations, bringing trusted others on board, and restoring reputation are all important precursors to relaunching a career in the aftermath of catastrophic setback. Ultimately, though, the stature of the leader is only fully regained when they take steps toward relaunching their career—taking that next role or starting that new organization. It is when concrete action is taken credibly that the leader can still perform at noteworthy, if not superior, levels that final proof of the leader's heroic stature is restored in their own mind and that of others. It is not easy. As we have discussed, the fallen leader faces numerous barriers on the path to recovery, not the least of which are self-doubts in their ability to get back on top. As one fired CEO told us, "I'd never sit here and say, 'Jeez, all I have to do is just replicate and do it again.' The chances of doing it again are pretty small." However, those who are successful get over this doubt about their ability to "do it again" and set out to take action in their new role. Even when forced from familiar arenas to totally new pastures, by industry norms or other restrictions placed upon them, some leaders remain unafraid of trying new ventures. William Shakespeare penned the immortal words "Some men are born great, some men achieve greatness, and some men have greatness thrust upon them." But perhaps what marks greatness above all else is the ability to be great again—to reachieve greatness when greatness, however initially gained, is torn from our possession. It is the ability to bounce back from adversity—to prove your mettle once more by getting back into the game—that separates the lasting greats from the fleeting greats.

Recapturing Enthusiasm

Mickey Drexler was born into the fashion business. His father, a button and piece-goods buyer, had him working weekends at an early age, learning the business, taking inventory, and putting tickets on garments. In 1967 he had his first opportunity on the shop floor at an Abraham & Strauss department store in Brooklyn. After jobs at Bloomingdale's, Macy's, and Abraham & Strauss, he moved from the world of department stores to specialty retailers, joining Ann Taylor. After a very successful run at Ann Taylor, where Drexler ended up as president, Donald Fisher, founder of Gap, poached Drexler in 1983 to run the floundering chain. At the time, Gap was struggling to compete since it sold the same brands of clothing as everyone else and was caught in a pricing game. Drexler shifted the strategy to focus exclusively on Gap-branded clothing, even eventually replacing the staple Levi's with Gap's own brand of jeans. He expanded the company beyond the core Gap stores to brand extensions such as GapKids, babyGap, and GapBody, and into other complementary brands, including Banana Republic and Old Navy. From when he arrived in 1983 to 2000, Gap's sales increased from $480 million to $13.7 billion, and its stock rose 169-fold.[2] Then things began to go awry.

Drexler was known for having a hands-on management style and being involved in every aspect of the company—importantly for him—down to the details of every item destined for the stores. He had transformed Gap with a focus on the basics—T-shirts, jeans, khakis. But with an increasing array of competition in the basics, Drexler had taken Gap into more of a fashion focus, and he seemed to have lost his touch, making choices that didn't sell in the stores, with an increasing amount of the clothing ending up on the discount racks. As a result, Gap went into a slump, with same-store sales dropping every quarter for two years and the stock dropping 75 percent. Drexler recalled, "I was damned nervous. I kept thinking, 'We've got to fix it.' The press and stock market were killing us."[3] Some reported to us that Drexler had to remove several Fisher family members from the firm; at the same time chairman Don Fisher pushed him into 70 percent growth in real estate, with Fisher's brother running the construction company that built the stores. On May 21, 2002, Drexler presented the upcoming season's merchandise to the board, confident that he had come out of his slump and had a great selling line for the fall. It wasn't enough for the board, and the next morning, Fisher fired Drexler, believing that the company was now too large for a hands-on management style such as Drexler's. As a former board member put it, "Mickey wasn't so passionate about compensation committees and budgets and strategic plans. We knew the company couldn't continue to operate with a master merchant driving the brand. My own view was that there should be a transition to a more management-oriented CEO."[4] A spokesman for Fisher added, "He [Drexler] was a great partner. In 2002, the size and scope of our company required different leadership skills to move forward, and it was time for another change."[5]

Despite this major career setback, and having enough money in the bank not to have to work again, Drexler was determined to prove that the failures of the previous two years did not reflect his abilities and that he still had the fashion instinct on which he had built his career. He knew that the only way to restore this belief in his own mind, and in the minds of many others, was to return to a role where he could once again prove his mettle. Knowing that he couldn't leave his passion for clothing retailing, Drexler turned down a multimillion-dollar severance package from Gap because it contained a noncompete clause that would bar him from joining another retailer or starting his own retailing business. In the months following his ouster, Drexler worked out of office space lent to him by a former board member, John Bowes, and met with a series of clothing retailers such as Ralph Lauren and Tommy Hilfiger as well as venture capitalists willing to back him in a new venture. However, the opportunity where he saw his biggest chance to re-prove his ability came in the guise of struggling fashion retailer J. Crew.

J. Crew was founded by Emily Woods and her father, Arthur Cinader, as a catalog business in 1983. It opened its first store in 1989 and had grown into a successful, offbeat fashion retailer. In 1997 it was bought for $560 million by private investment firm Texas Pacific, which specialized in turning companies around and then taking them public. However, Texas Pacific was having trouble revitalizing the brand, having gone through three CEOs in the five years since it bought the company, and sliding further and further into the red, losing $11 million in 2001 and $40 million in 2002. Since Woods's departure with the acquisition, the management style had focused on costs rather than fashion, prompting complaints from employees. As one put it, "We'd get a list—X amount of styles, six $55 pants, seven $70 pants. We'd be picking fabrics and designing into boxes of criteria. It completely stifled creativity."[6] Drexler, however, saw this as the perfect opportunity for him to prove his worth in transforming this declining brand. Texas Pacific, meanwhile, was desperate to get someone with the hands-on management skills and instinct for fashion to turn around what was beginning to look like a bad investment, and the company was prepared to look at the whole record of Drexler's career rather than focus on the last two years.

The scale at J. Crew, with just about two hundred stores, was one-twentieth the size of Gap and consequently was much more amenable to Drexler's hands-on style, giving him greater leverage in making an impact. Drexler invested $10 million of his own money to buy a 22 percent share of the company from Texas Pacific and took a salary that was less than a tenth of what he had been earning at his former employer. "You've no idea how much it's costing me to run this company," he joked shortly after taking over the helm.[7]

In characteristic style, Drexler plunged into the details of the operation, down to the type of buttons that appeared on a shirt or a caption describing an item in the catalog. He moved the company away from trend-driven wear to the core preppy staples that were the heart of the company, interlaced with new high-end limited-edition items such as $1,500 cashmere coats. He redesigned the stores to move them upscale, closer to Ralph Lauren than Gap, and switched to higher-quality manufacturers. Rather than ensure that the stores were always abundantly stocked, which often led to frequent sales and markdowns of unsold inventory, Drexler cultivated an aura of scarcity for the products, with the aim of giving customers the idea that they had to buy the product when they saw it because it might not still be there the next time they came to the store. The results followed. J. Crew rebounded from a $30 million operating loss in 2003 to an operating profit of over $37 million in 2004. Same-store sales per square foot, one of the key metrics in retailing, rose 18 percent from $338 to $400; while in comparison, at his old employer, Gap, sales per square foot dropped 3 percent over the same period.

Now that Drexler is once again with an organization that is at a scale that responds well to his style of leadership, he has found fun in life again at J. Crew. As he puts it, "I felt like an employee at Gap. My biggest mistake was not getting out earlier. It wasn't too big for me to run, it was too big for me to have fun, to influence the product to the level that I like to. Managing managers is not as much fun as managing product and customers."[8] As to the future at J. Crew, Drexler is anxious not to expand too fast, closing seven stores and opening just nine in his first two years. That doesn't preclude future expansion—with plans to revive Crew Cuts, its brand for children, among other ideas—but being big again might not be for him. He says, "If J. Crew gets very large and remains very profitable, I'll be happy about that. I'm just not sure that I'll be the one running it at that point."[9]

While it is still early in his second act at J. Crew, Mickey Drexler has already re-proved his mettle, demonstrating that he has not lost the skills at merchandising and picking fashions upon which he built his career. Texas Pacific was in a position where it needed a masterstroke of someone unique like Drexler and was willing to base its judgment of Drexler on his overall career track record rather than his most recent lapse. Even so, there were momentary doubts, particularly given Drexler's financial security and the question of how much of himself he was willing to invest in a comeback. But these were indeed fleeting. As Jim Coulter, partner and cofounder of Texas Pacific, put it, "I worried for about two and a half minutes before I saw Mickey go to it. Does he have the energy and passion? He loves it. I call him up and he'll be worried about 48 things, and then I'll ask how he's doing and he says, 'I'm having so much fun.' "[10] For Drexler, like most such leaders who come back successfully, it is not money that is driving them, but a need to continue to create and build a lasting legacy. Coming back often means proving one's worth in what are perceived by others to be difficult situations—start-ups or turnaround situations are common. But it is in these situations that such leaders thrive on the challenge to really prove to themselves and others that they have not lost their magic touch and that no obstacle is too great to overcome in their quest for return. In proving his mettle once more and reviving J. Crew, Drexler set himself apart in an elite group of retailing legends. As Texas Pacific's Coulter says of Drexler, "There are only a handful of people in the world that do specialty retail well, and we didn't have one. Now we do."[11]

In his brief tenure, Drexler has improved the quality and style of merchandise and overhauled the chain's 167 stores. In the week immediately following its successful $367 million IPO in 2006, J. Crew shares surged upwards 37 percent on the enthusiasm for Drexler's command.

Rebuilding from the Ground Up

Virtually from the time he could walk, Donald Trump was in the real estate business, as he tagged along to construction sites with his father, Fred Trump, who built low- and middle-income housing in Queens and Brooklyn, New York. After graduating from the Wharton School, Trump returned to work for his father, who by building numerous rent-controlled and rent-stabilized apartment buildings, had become one of the biggest landlords in New York's outer boroughs. But while learning a lot from his father, Donald had even bigger dreams and a greater sense of aggrandizement. So while working for his father in the boroughs, Donald moved to Manhattan and kept an eye out for an opportunity. It wasn't too long in coming.

In 1974, the real estate market tumbled in New York. Interest rates were rising, government housing subsidies were being reduced, and New York's debt was growing to the point where people believed the city might go bankrupt. Factors that scared others away pointed to opportunity for Trump. So in July 1974, at the age of twenty-seven, he secured an option to buy two large West Side Manhattan waterfront properties from the bankrupt Penn Central Railroad for $62 million. Trump set about promoting one of the properties as a potential site for a convention center that the city was planning to build. Almost four years later, the city finally selected Trump's site and bought it from Penn Central without Trump exercising his option, with Trump receiving a fee of less than $1 million for his option. Meanwhile, however, Trump had turned his attention elsewhere and acquired an option, also from Penn Central Railroad, on the aging and money-losing Commodore Hotel, located on Forty-second Street adjacent to Grand Central Station. Trump negotiated with the city for property tax abatement, arguing that his hotel would help turn around the area adjacent to Grand Central Station, which was in rapid decline at the time. He used the same argument with the banks to get financing, partnered with Hyatt Hotels to manage the property, and in September 1980, the Grand Hyatt New York opened its doors. It was a huge success from day one. Room rates were five times higher than the rates of the old Commodore, and the occupancy rate more than doubled that of the last years of the old hotel. From his deal with Hyatt, Trump retained a 50 percent interest in the hotel.

Even as the Grand Hyatt was going up, Trump was already working on what would become his signature building, Trump Tower, right next to Tiffany & Co. on Fifth Avenue. It cost Trump $190 million to acquire the site and construct the building. While holding on to several penthouse apartments for himself, he sold the remaining apartments for $240 million and leased the retail space in the atrium to some of the world's most prestigious retailers for premium rents, earning millions more each year. The golden appearance of the building's façade was an appropriate metaphor for the golden deal it was for Trump. For the remainder of the 1980s, Trump continued going from strength to strength, with everything he touched seemingly receiving the golden Trump touch, including a major foray into the casino business in Atlantic City. By the end of the decade, his net worth was in the billions of dollars.

Then, at the turn of the decade, Trump, by his own admission, took his "eye off the ball." As he put it:

> I had taken a siesta. I had relied upon other people, many of them "highly trained and educated executives." Sure, success in business takes education and training. But it all comes down to feel and touch. I've got the instincts. That's how I'd gotten to the top in the first place. I wasn't using my instincts anymore. I'd gotten bored, taken my eye off the ball. Why, I thought, should I work my ass off when I can get somebody to do it for me? Everything had gotten too easy. My life had been a series of wins with few, if any failures . . .
>
> I got a little cocky and, probably, a little lazy. I wasn't working as hard, and I wasn't focusing on the basics . . . I began to socialize more, probably too much. Frankly, I was bored. I really felt I could do no wrong. Sort of like a baseball player who keeps hitting home runs or a golfer who keeps winning tournaments—you just get the feeling of invincibility. Ultimately, this invincible feeling, while positive at times, can be destructive. You let down your guard. You don't work as hard. Then things start to go in the wrong direction. And that's what happened to me—and I never thought it could.[12]

As real estate prices plummeted in the late 1980s and early 1990s, Trump's net worth sank into red numbers. Not only were his holdings—

primarily in real estate, casinos, and an airline—worth far less than the reported $2.3 billion in debt he held that was secured by these assets, but he had also personally guaranteed $975 million of his debt.

Of his total debt, $1.4 billion was due to his three casinos in Atlantic City, and with the recession, the gamblers declined. Also, the city had overbuilt, growing to twelve casinos, most of which were now struggling. Caught with a declining cash flow to service his debt, estimated at as much as $255 million per year, Trump was forced to miss a $43 million principal and interest payment on Trump's Castle casino debt. With this default, speculation exploded about the state of Trump's dwindling finances, with front-page articles in newspapers and magazines from the *New York Times* to *Forbes* wondering whether he was even on the brink of declaring bankruptcy. On top of this, Trump, the symbol of the conspicuous consumption of the 1980s, became in his downfall the object of derision from the media, even to the point of David Letterman dedicating one of his famous "top ten" lists on his nightly show to the "Top Ten Reasons That Trump Is in Trouble." But more serious than the damage to his ego and image from the fierce publicity—exacerbated by the concurrent filing for divorce by his wife, Ivana—was the pressure from his bankers to come up with a solution to his debt.

Just as his rise was based on his financial negotiating ability, so too was much of his rebound from this fall based on his ability to negotiate a restructuring of his debt to allow time to pass and the overall economy to recover, translating into the recovery in value of his real estate assets and improved cash generation from his casinos. Trump gathered his various bankers together and managed to strike a deal to refinance his debt, postponing interest and principal repayments for five years, gaining a further $65 million line of credit for cash flow, and agreeing that no single bank could lay claim against him for five years. His bankers even went into his personal finances and expenditures, going so far as to put him on a monthly budget for personal expenses, albeit at $450,000 per month. A few months later, Trump was forced to give up some of his ownership in the casinos to bondholders to swap debt for equity, but the restructurings reduced his interest obligations by over $100 million per year, and as the recovery began, he even took the casino business public, launching it on the New York Stock Exchange as Trump International

Hotels and Casinos, raising some $2 billion in capital. These financial maneuvers and the continued cash flow from the casino business bought Trump enough time to ride out the recession without being forced to liquidate assets at fire-sale prices, and he was able to divest himself of some peripheral holdings as good deals arose.

By 1993, things were turning around for Trump. He sold his yacht, his airline (Trump Shuttle), and some other assets but kept his principal real estate holdings. His personal debt had gone from $975 million to $115 million. Having turned the corner by virtue of shrewd financial deals and gaining time for the markets to turn, Trump saw the opportunities in the rebounding market and continued his forays into New York real estate. His most opportunistic buy was 40 Wall Street, owned for three years by a Hong Kong group who found dealing with New York contractors and tenants tougher than they could handle, to the point of being desperate to unload the building. Trump acquired 40 Wall Street, a 1.3 million-square-foot prime office building opposite the New York Stock Exchange for less than $1 million—for a building that had changed hands a few years earlier at the height of the boom for over $100 million. Trump spent some $35 million on restoring the building to its former glory, renamed it the Trump Building at 40 Wall Street, and was able to lease the offices for around $40 million per year. He was back to the height of his property development prowess.

Trump was once again able to prove his worth as a shrewd deal maker and property developer, and he continued his successful comeback, building many more Trump edifices in Manhattan, including Trump International and Trump World Tower, and developing the West Side Yards—the property where he had started his deal making. His rebound was due to many of the aspects we have talked about so far—his ability to stand up to his detractors, his ability to use his networks, his ability to rebuild the larger-than-life heroic persona and reputation—all of which gave the bankers confidence enough to believe that he could come through his setback. But Trump's successful rebound after he negotiated a second chance was also due to his ability to continue to see opportunity and prove through his deal making and real estate development skills that he still had what it took to continue to shape the New York skyline.

Just as with Drexler, Trump was able to convince others that he had the skills to flourish and turn around an ailing concern. When leaders have a significant track record of past success, as did Drexler and Trump, they can often persuade key gatekeepers to give them a second opportunity, even in the light of recent setbacks. However, even when the field is the same, re-proving your mettle and rebounding successfully is necessary not only for a successful second act but to secure a lasting legacy.

Finding New and Greener Pastures

While Drexler and Trump re-proved themselves and by so doing distinguished themselves as legends in their respective fields of retailing and real estate, sometimes the opportunity to prove yourself lies in the even greater challenge of gaining new success in an entirely different field. Another New Yorker who has proved his mettle more than once in demonstrating his ability to rebound from career setback and move seamlessly into different fields is the current mayor of New York, Michael Bloomberg.

After fifteen years of twelve-hour days and six-day weeks, Michael Bloomberg had achieved the prestigious and seemingly secure position of general partner of one of the country's most prominent Wall Street trading firms, Salomon Brothers. On a Saturday in August 1981, Bloomberg and sixty-two of his fellow partners were summoned and told that the executive committee had decided that Salomon was to be sold to a publicly held commodities trading firm, effectively taking Salomon public. Although the partners had not been asked to vote on the decision, they were not disappointed. In folders in front of them at the dinner meeting, a sheet of paper told them their payout from selling the firm. Bloomberg's read $10 million. After a celebratory dinner that Saturday evening, the next day the partners were called in individually to meet with two members of the executive committee, most to be offered new roles in the merged company. Bloomberg was not. He, along with a handful of others, was out, fired from the only firm he had worked for since business school.

At age thirty-nine, and with a $10 million payout from Salomon, Bloomberg was, for the first time in his life, unemployed. But he was not the type to mull over the past and reflect on what might have been. Instead, he thought about his options, and quickly decided that his temperament wouldn't allow him to take it easy and live off his buyout from Salomon, nor did he want to revert to being an employee in another Wall Street firm. Instead, the adventure of starting out on his own captured his imagination. But in what?

> *What would I do? Since I didn't have the resources to start a steel mill, I ruled out that possibility; in other words, I wouldn't go into industry. Having no musical abilities precluded starting a songwriting business; entertainment was out. Lack of interest in retailing excluded competing with Wal-Mart; Sam Walton's investment was safe. My impatience with government kept me away from politics; all elected officials could stop worrying. Should I start another securities trading firm and compete with my former colleagues? Been there. Done that. Maybe I could be a full-time consultant like so many forced-out executives. No. I'm not much of a bystander beyond watching my daughters Emma and Georgina ride horses. Doing rather than advising others is for me.*
>
> *What did I have the resources, ability, interest, and contacts to do? The question led me back to Wall Street. It was obvious the economy was changing and services were taking a bigger share of the gross domestic product. My talents, my experience, my financial resources, the momentum provided by the American economy—everything fit. I would start a company that would help financial organizations. There were better traders and salespeople. There were better managers and computer experts. But nobody had more knowledge of the securities and investment industries and of how technology could help them.*[13]

Like many entrepreneurs, Bloomberg started with a problem that he encountered on a daily basis for which there was no current solution. Having come out of the securities business, he knew that the biggest challenge facing everyone who selected or dealt in stocks for a living was getting the best, most accurate information available, and having the tools to analyze that data to produce information on which to base decisions. Despite the complexity of information needs, Bloomberg described his idea in simple terms:

I conceived a business built around a collection of securities data, giving people the ability to select what each individually thought the most useful parts, and then providing computer software that would let non-mathematicians do analysis on that information. This kind of capability was sorely lacking in the marketplace. A few large underwriting firms had internal systems that tried to fill this need but each required a PhD to use and weren't available off the shelf to the little guy.[14]

From a beginning in a small, one-room office facing an alley—a far cry from the plush Salomon offices—and with $300,000 of his Salomon severance placed in a corporate checking account, Bloomberg set about building his business—named Bloomberg. He recruited four former Salomon employees to join him to assess and plan the functionality of the system, and a few months later, hired some programmers to develop the first Bloomberg system. Almost two years later in June 1983, having consumed $4 million of Bloomberg's Salomon severance rather than just the initial $300,000 deposit, the firm delivered its first computer system to Merrill Lynch. Although there were still bugs in the system, the traders at Merrill Lynch were delighted by its potential functionality and the fact that Bloomberg had delivered when it said it would. Bloomberg had proved to himself, his team, and his first customer that he could deliver on his vision. In no time, Bloomberg had twenty-two terminals at Merrill Lynch, a great testing ground as the company worked together with the client to fix the bugs in the system. Through persistence, attention to detail, and a work ethic driven by the paranoia that someone else might be working harder to develop its market, Bloomberg added other names to its client roster. Soon, the buzz began to emanate about Bloomberg's machines, and orders started coming in; soon Bloomberg terminals could be found everywhere from the Bank of England, to The World Bank, to every Federal Reserve Bank, and even to the Vatican. Today, Bloomberg, still a private company, has tens of thousands of clients in 126 countries and 8,000 employees, and Michael Bloomberg himself is a billionaire, listed number 112 on the 2006 *Forbes* list of the richest people in the world with a net worth of $5.1 billion. The company not only provides an essential information service to professionals in the financial services industry, but also has its own television channel, radio station, Web site, and magazine in its media division.

In 2001, Michael Bloomberg stepped down from day-to-day operations of the company to switch careers and fields once again—this time hardly in career-rebound mode but nonetheless to prove his mettle in the entirely different field of politics. He ran successfully for mayor of New York, arguably the second-most-important elected position in the country, particularly given his election a mere two months after the terrorist attacks on the city. He won reelection to a second term four years later, after successfully mastering yet another field.

Bloomberg's story demonstrates not just that it is possible to successfully rebound in another field, but that sometimes, in order to prove you can make a comeback, you have to strike out on your own, proving that you can do it outside the protective and nurturing walls of an organization. Ultimately, though, the requirement to prove your mettle is still there. It is just that the audience may be different, whether it is the gatekeepers to an organizational position, the marketplace and those first key but wary customers, or an unforgiving and fickle electorate. Especially in a new field where your track record of success elsewhere may not count for much, it is the proof that you can succeed, and succeed early, in this new arena that is critical.

It would have been easy for someone in Bloomberg's situation, being let go from Salomon with $10 million in his pocket at age thirty-nine, to decide to retire to the beach and take it easy or, if still excited by the dynamics of Wall Street, to find a high-paying job at another firm. Bloomberg however, took a different route, discovering a heroic mission to provide better information and analysis to Wall Street, developing a market that essentially had not existed before. In the beginning, it was a struggle to create the market and persuade potential clients that they should let Bloomberg develop a system for them rather than relying on a proprietary system. In the key sales meeting with Merrill Lynch, that was the objection. The head of software development for Merrill Lynch wanted to develop a system in-house, but said it would take at least six months even if the developers were not distracted with day-to-day demands, and they wouldn't be able to start for another six months anyway. Bloomberg promised that it would develop the system in six months, and that if Merrill Lynch didn't like it, it wouldn't have to pay. This was a no-risk offer for the Merrill Lynch manager, and it gave Bloomberg the chance to prove his mettle, to see whether his heroic mission could in fact become a reality rather than a pipe dream. Bloomberg created this heroic mission from scratch but was able to do so without having to discard a tightly held life's dream. In contrast, in his prior position, although a partner in the firm, he was playing the role of someone engaged in the mission of an established firm rather than one he had created himself.

To discuss the last of the pillars of a successful rebound, we turn in the next chapter to the fundamental importance—particularly when making a career switch into an entirely new field—of regaining and redefining a sense of heroic mission. Often, successful leaders have become tightly bound to their prior mission or organization, both in their own minds and in the perceptions of others. When a catastrophic setback occurs that forcibly separates them from that mission, perhaps the biggest challenge is to redefine their mission and in so doing essentially redefine their very being, to seek what will be their next all-consuming calling, the foundation of their rebound.

11

Rediscovering Heroic Mission

IN THE LAST CHAPTER, we looked at the importance of restoring the confidence of others that the fallen person can still perform competently. There we used the example of prizefighter George Foreman's recapturing of the World Heavyweight Championship title at age forty-five, twenty years after he lost it. In this chapter, where we look at reinvention, the more appropriate aspect of Foreman's career renewal is his successful launch of his signature label on a wide variety of consumer brands, from men's apparel to kitchen equipment. Similarly, Donald Trump and Martha Stewart found media and consumer product vehicles to reinvent themselves and extend their brands following setbacks. For many, however, the notion of pursuing a heroic quest speaks to a more immortal mission than consumer goods and celebrity.

The renowned playwright Arthur Miller once noted, "One of the central elements in life is the driving need of people to define themselves, not merely as individuals, but also in terms of a function they can respect."[1] For leaders, often the only function they can respect is a place in history, endowing them with a sense of immortality—to have achieved a sense of accomplishment in creating a legacy that will last beyond their mortal existence. This legacy is not in having their names etched on an ivy-clad university building, but most often in effecting change in society through building and leading an organization to fulfill their heroic mission.

MIT professor Peter Senge refers to the essence of heroic mission as the leader's "purpose story." He describes it this way:

> *The leader's purpose story is both personal and universal. It defines her or his life's work. It ennobles his efforts, yet leaves an abiding humility that keeps him from taking his own successes and failures too seriously. It brings a unique depth of meaning to his vision, a larger landscape upon which his personal dreams and goals stand out as landmarks on a longer journey. But what is most important, this story is essential to his ability to lead. It places his organization's purpose, its reason for being, within a context of "where we've come from and where we're headed," where the "we" goes beyond the organization itself to humankind more broadly. In this sense, they naturally see their organization as a vehicle for bringing learning and change into society. This is the power of the purpose story— it provides a single integrating set of ideas that gives meaning to all aspects of the leader's work.*
>
> *Out of this deeper story and sense of purpose or destiny, the leader develops a unique relationship to his or her own personal vision. He or she becomes a steward of the vision.*[2]

Most leaders that we have profiled in this book have been engaged in their quest for immortality through their pursuit of a heroic mission before they suffer their catastrophic career setback. As we discussed in chapter 6, it is the loss of this mission that really makes the setback of catastrophic proportions in the leader's mind, since it puts at risk their lifetime of achievement. Those who have gone through such catastrophic setback, or know well those who have, know how devastating such a loss can be. On the day Steve Jobs was fired from Apple in 1985, he called a couple of close friends, including Mike Murray, to tell them the news. Murray's wife was on the phone when an emergency interrupt came through. She told the operator that it had better be important and then heard Jobs's voice saying simply, "It is." Once Murray was on the phone, Steve simply stated, "It's all over. John [Sculley] and the board have voted me out of Apple. Goodbye, Mike," and hung up the phone.[3] Murray, aware of the significance of this to Jobs, was afraid of what Jobs might do to himself and, unable to get him on the phone, went over to his house and sat with him for hours until he was convinced Jobs would not commit suicide that night. Later, describing how it felt to be separated from the organization he created, Jobs said, "You've probably had somebody punch you in the stomach. It knocks the wind out of you and you can't breathe. If you relax, you can start breathing again. That's how I felt. The thing I had to do was try to relax. It was hard. But I went for a lot of long walks in the woods and didn't really talk to a lot of people."[4]

Reflecting on the Past to Reconceptualize the Mission

Once separated from their organizations—their vehicle for the journey to immortality—leaders find that the biggest barrier to career recovery is often in reconceptualizing or redirecting their heroic mission to be achieved without the benefit of their organization. While, as we have described, support systems such as friends and family play an important role in helping the victim through such times, it is the individuals themselves who need to be able to think through their future objectives.

A week after his ouster from Apple, Jobs flew to Europe and, after a few days in Paris, headed for the Tuscan hills of northern Italy, where he bought a bicycle and a sleeping bag and camped out under the stars, thinking through the events that led to his departure and contemplating what he would do next. From Italy, he went to Sweden and then to Russia before returning home.

He contemplated a few things, including hiring a political consulting firm to decide whether he would have a future as a politician, but was persuaded that this was not for him. He even tried to be selected as the first civilian to fly on the space shuttle but was passed over in favor of elementary schoolteacher Christa McAuliffe, who was on the mission that resulted in the tragic Columbia disaster.

Within a few months, though, Jobs was beginning to clarify what his heroic mission had been at Apple and how he could take that forward once again with a new organization. He spent a lot of time wandering around the Stanford University campus, reading in the library and immersing himself in new topics, such as biochemistry, the Bay Area's other big growth industry, including a key meeting with Nobel Prize–winning biochemist Paul Berg. This time allowed him to put together the important pieces of the puzzle of his heroic mission. He described what thinking led to crystallizing his core mission:

> *I think what I'm best at is creating new, innovative products. That's what I enjoy doing. I enjoy, and I'm best working with, a small team of talented people. That's what I did with the Apple II, and that's what I did with Macintosh.*
>
> *I had a piece of paper one day, and I was writing down the things that I cared the most about, that I was most proud of personally at my ten years at Apple. There's obviously the creation of the Apple II and the Macintosh. But other than that, the thing I really cared about was helping to set up the Apple Education Foundation. I came up with this crazy idea that turned into a program called "The Kids Can't Wait," in which we tried to give a computer to every school in America and ended up giving one to every school in California, about 10,000 computers.*
>
> *I put those two together, working with small teams of talented people to create breakthrough products and education.*[5]

As a result, Jobs gathered together a few of the people he had worked with at Apple on the Macintosh project, and convinced them of his new vision of returning to the metaphorical garage to create the next great computer, designed specifically for the higher-education market. He named the company NeXT and set off with renewed passion to create a new product and regain his stature as a visionary in the computer industry.

The resulting NeXT computer was typically Steve Jobs. It was elegantly designed, technically advanced, and ahead of any competitor in terms of performance—but incompatible with the industry standard and premium priced. So while it found a small niche in some university laboratories, it was out of the reach of most students and was a commercial flop. Jobs, however, was vindicated when, in the ironic twist that brought him back full circle, Apple purchased NeXT in 1996 for over $400 million, and Jobs returned to Apple, twenty years after founding the company, becoming a few months later the CEO once again, free to pursue his original heroic mission at his original organization. Once there, he revived and reenergized the company with breakthrough, typically Jobs high-design products, such as the iMac, iBook, and iPod, and took the company into new emerging businesses, such as creating the world's largest music download store, iTunes.

Steve Jobs's new mission was born out of the opportunity to step back and reflect on what was important to him from his original mission—creating "insanely great" innovative products, working with a small team, and having a passion for education. Often, this opportunity to take a step back and reflect on the underlying dimensions of past achievements and contributions leads to the creation of the revitalized mission. Ray Gilmartin, former CEO of pharmaceutical giant Merck, had just such an opportunity in his role of transitioning out of the organization. After a decade at the helm, Gilmartin was forced to step out of the CEO role in response to the withdrawal of the drug Vioxx and the subsequent litigation. In his transition out of this CEO role, but with the board still wanting to tap his experience, Gilmartin became "Special Advisor to the Executive Committee of the Board," an elaborate title but one that allowed him to take a wider view of Merck's contributions to making the world a better place through its medications, and to experience firsthand some of the places where Merck was at the forefront of lifesaving contributions. This experience gave him a deeper perspective on his role at Merck and reconfigured his new heroic mission. As he recounted to us:

> *I ended up with the title of Special Advisor to the Executive Committee of the Board. I did not anticipate that this was a pretty valuable position from a personal standpoint in that I represent the company externally in a number of settings. I had the opportunity to go to Botswana a couple of weeks ago and spend three or four days there looking at a program that we have there with the [Bill and Melinda] Gates Foundation, Merck, and the government of Botswana in terms of dealing with HIV/AIDS in that country. Three years ago when I was there, people were literally dying in the hallways of the hospital that I visited, and we were at the early stages of getting people access to medicines. This time when I was there, there [were] over fifty thousand people on medicines, halfway towards our goal. We're adding fifteen hundred to two thousand people a month, and instead of people dying in the hallways, there are people that are healthy and waiting for the refills of their prescriptions.*

It was a good opportunity for me to see firsthand what the impact that Merck as a company has on the world, in terms of literally saving people's lives. And the drugs they were taking were drugs that were discovered by Merck in the mid-1990s [during Gilmartin's tenure as CEO].[6]

While at the time of writing, Gilmartin has a few more weeks in this special advisory role, it is clear that this experience has already set the springboard for a new life purpose for Gilmartin since he more fully understands the dramatic impact that his previous accomplishments have had. Even if a new role does not have the organizational resources that were once enjoyed, the opportunity to find a new purpose is critical in moving forward rather than wallowing in despair over past accomplishments and what might have been.

When the Peak Is Past

Many leaders, such as Steve Jobs and Bernie Marcus, are able to reconceptualize their heroic mission and reach even greater heights than they had achieved before their downfall—and also do it in the same field. Some, however, must truly start again because for some reason the door to their familiar field is firmly closed, and new pastures must be sought and a totally new heroic mission developed. This can happen when the very peak of the profession has been reached, and the realization dawns that the pinnacle of achievement in this field is in the past. In order to reemerge from being haunted by past success with no future to look toward, such leaders have to explore a new field in order to break out of that malaise. Clinical psychologist and Harvard professor Steven Berglas identified this phenomenon in Olympic gold medal winners and the aftermath of such a pinnacle of achievement.[7] He used 1992 Olympic diving gold medalist Mark Lenzi to illustrate this phenomenon. After years of devoted training, Lenzi came to the day of Olympic competition and sealed his victory with a dive that scored a perfect 10. When he returned to the United States, his achievements and instant celebrity led to invitations to be a guest on all the talk shows, from *The Tonight Show with Jay Leno* to *Live with Regis and Kathie Lee*, but he quickly became depressed on the talk show circuit as it hit him that all the comments and questions related to his past achievements. They all told him that he "was great." Past tense. Nothing about future goals and the next conquest. For his entire life, he had focused on achieving the ultimate goal of becoming an Olympic champion. Now that had been achieved, his lifetime goal had been fulfilled, and there was no heroic mission left to chase. Even though Olympic champions are not brought down from their positions in the same way that leaders are thrown out from their organizations, the void from the removal of their life purpose—their heroic mission—is the same. It is not only Olympic champions who feel the void after a successful Olympics; Olympic organizers feel the same pain. Billy Payne, the person who not only had the vision to bring the Olympics to his hometown of Atlanta, Georgia, but also made that heroic mission a reality by heading the Atlanta Committee for the Olympic Games, recognized after the games that since he had fulfilled his dream, there was nothing left that he could achieve to surpass this event saying, "Nothing I'll ever do will have the same level of public profile, the same stress, the same kind of critical deadlines, and the same enormity as what I've just done. But if my next endeavors aren't as big because they can't be, I've made peace with that."[8]

It is surprising to many, particularly those who have fallen short or still strive for the pinnacle of achievement in their career, that great success is often accompanied by a vast emptiness when the realization hits that those achievements are in the past. There is a poignant scene at the end of the Academy Award–winning movie *Chariots of Fire*—the remarkable story of Eric Liddell, Harold Abrahams, and their unlikely success in the 1924 Olympic Games—that captures this sometimes instantaneous feeling of emptiness following achievement. As celebrations by his teammates erupted in the locker room after his historic victory in the 100 meters, Abrahams is off in the corner quietly packing up his bag. Teammate Aubrey Montague shouts over to Abrahams, only to be quieted by teammate Lord Andrew Lindsay. Montague protests to Lindsay, "But he won!" expecting jubilation from Abrahams. But Lindsay chastises him, responding, "Exactly. Now one of these days, Monty, you're going to win yourself. And it's pretty difficult to swallow." The quest for achievement is a strong driving force, but once the goal is accomplished, that drive can disappear unless replaced by a new heroic mission. Abrahams transitioned from being an athlete to focusing on helping others achieve similar accomplishments, becoming the revered elder statesman for British athletics until his death in 1978. It is the ability to make peace with those past accomplishments and, regardless of the past level of achievement, reconfigure the life purpose that sets the stage for a second act. The same void that faces Olympic athletes following their athletic careers is magnified for perhaps the ultimate organizational leadership position—the president of the United States.

The contrast between the glamour of the White House in the nation's capital and a small farmhouse in Plains, Georgia, comes close to portraying the divide between being president of the United States, expecting to win reelection despite a tumultuous and highly criticized presidency, and the shock of suddenly being the former president, swept from office by a landslide of 489 electoral votes to just 49.

In the aftermath of the 1980 presidential election, in that lame duck period between the election in early November and the new president's inauguration in late January, there are the competing emotions of the continuation of the role as president, the renewed urgency to complete unfinished business—heightened for President Jimmy Carter by the Iranian hostage crisis—the creeping realization of the involuntary end of one's time in office, and the surreal experience of ceremonial functions as departure arrangements are made. During these last days at the White House, the Carters had to endure endless farewell parties, luncheons, and receptions for different groups where, as Carter put it, "We were sometimes reminded of [our impending post–White House life] by well-meaning friends: 'Don't you worry about the election. You're about to start on the most exciting part of your life.' That was not true, it would never be true and we'd rather not hear people say it. It took a lot of patience to smile sometimes."[9]

Meanwhile, the abrupt change in his time frame from "four more years" to "two more months" required an immediate adjustment to the heroic mission to which he had dedicated his efforts as president:

> *Right after the defeat, I tried to think of everything we could possibly accomplish during the few months left in the White House, and arranged the list according to feasibility, setting an ambitious schedule for myself and*

those around me. It was not easy to scale down my wish list from great and challenging dreams—such as bringing peace to the Middle East, ridding the world of nuclear weapons, and ensuring the human rights of all peoples everywhere—to those things that were possible in the time left. We had a heavy legislative agenda, and getting the hostages home was a pressing priority.[10]

Fifteen minutes after the official end of his presidency, the American hostages held by Iran for fourteen months, which had all but sealed his defeat in the election, were finally released, and the next day, Carter flew to Germany to welcome them back to freedom. But on his return, he was headed not to the White House, but to Plains, Georgia, where the reality of his postpresidency finally hit him: "Although I had not been to bed for three days during the final negotiations about the hostages, I didn't even feel the fatigue during our long trip to Germany. But I returned to Plains completely exhausted, slept for almost twenty-four hours, and then awoke to an altogether new, unwanted, and potentially empty life."[11]

The practical realities of life hit quickly. Their house, the only one they had ever owned, had not been lived in for ten years during Carter's presidency and governorship of Georgia and had fallen into disrepair from neglect. Their small home, which had seemed so spacious before, was now piled from floor to ceiling with documents and mementos from his time in office, and they could no longer merely mention a need to servants or officials and have everything taken care of—they were on their own and felt it.

Worse, before Carter had taken office, they had placed all their financial affairs into a blind trust and had separated themselves from all financial matters to avoid any accusations of serving their own interests while the president was in office. However, upon leaving office, Carter discovered that their main assets, the farmland and the peanut warehouse operation in Plains, had been mismanaged and run into financial difficulties to the point where the Carters were now deeply in debt and at risk of bankruptcy. As Carter lamented, "Just as almost two decades of political life were about to end, we found that the results of the preceding twenty-three years of hard work, scrimping and saving, and plowing everything back into the business, were now also gone. No one could accuse us of becoming rich in the White House. We had not expected to, but we had hoped at least to be able to leave with what we had when we came in. That, too, was not to be."[12]

In the following months, Carter was able to sell the warehousing business to Archer Daniels Midland Company for a sum sufficient to pay off their debts, and by the summer after leaving office, both Jimmy and Rosalynn Carter had signed book contracts. Writing his memoirs of his time in the White House was not only a financially rewarding process, but also a substantially therapeutic experience for Carter as he considered what to do with his life postpresidency. This important time of reflection allowed him to regroup and redirect his postpresidential life, to redirect his heroic mission, despite the relative absence of resources and the stature that he left behind in the Oval Office. Taking such a time to reflect is often key to rebuilding and is a common theme we heard from numerous leaders who had made a successful comeback.

Along with writing his memoirs, one of the obligations he felt as a past president was to build a presidential library to house the records of his administration. Carter had never enjoyed the role of fund-raising and was even more loath to go around "hat in hand," as he put it, to seek contributions for his library. Carter was also adamant that he didn't want the presidential library to serve as a memorial to him or his presidency. For months the Carters struggled with coming to terms with their political defeat and rethinking about the events of the past through their writings. They struggled equally with their legacy through the library as they were given architectural presentation after presentation and about what their future life work would be. Finally, while the frustrations with the library project were ongoing, Carter had his "aha" moment. As Rosalynn Carter recounted:

> One night I woke up and Jimmy was sitting straight up in bed. He always sleeps so soundly that I thought he must be sick. "What's the matter?" I asked. "I know what we can do at the library," he said. "We can develop a place to help people who want to resolve disputes. There is no place like that now. If two countries really want to work something out, they don't want to go to the United Nations and get one hundred fifty

other countries involved in the argument. I know how difficult it is for them to approach each other publicly, and they take a chance on being embarrassed by a rebuff from the other party. We could get good mediators that both sides would trust, and they could meet with no publicity, no fanfare, perhaps at times in total secrecy. If there had been such a place, I wouldn't have had to take Begin and Sadat to Camp David. There've been a lot of new theories on conflict resolution developed since that time, too, and we might put some of them into use." He talked on enthusiastically about other areas where negotiation might help—in domestic disputes and in dealing with civil laws. A center to settle disputes. For the first time since our return to Plains I saw Jimmy really excited about possible plans for the future.[13]

Jimmy Carter's new heroic mission was born. Over the coming months and years, this vision for the presidential library evolved and joined with Emory University in Atlanta, where Carter had accepted a post as distinguished professor, to become The Carter Center at Emory University, a joint venture between Carter and the university, founded on the principles emanating from Carter's middle-of-the-night vision. In the years that followed, in addition to aiding in conflict resolution, The Carter Center became a force for the eradication of diseases such as Guinea worm, river blindness, and polio, and oversaw the increase of the proportion of children worldwide immunized from diseases such as polio and measles from 20 percent to over 80 percent in its first ten years. The Carter Center also became an institution called upon worldwide to oversee and certify the fairness of elections, unafraid to speak out where it encountered electoral manipulation in places such as Panama.

Carter received numerous humanitarian awards, such as the United Nations Prize in the Field of Human Rights and the highest civilian honor in the United States, the Presidential Medal of Freedom—he was ultimately awarded the Nobel Prize in 2002 "for his decades of untiring effort to find peaceful solutions to international conflicts, to advance democracy and human rights, and to promote economic and social development."[14]

Rosalynn Carter articulated the sense of loss of heroic mission when they left Washington, saying, "I had to grieve over our loss before I could look to the future. Where could our lives possibly be as meaning-ful as they might have been in the White House?"[15] Despite this loss, the Carters found that even after a humiliating public ouster from the most powerful leadership position in the world, their "second act" could result in even higher achievement. Although Carter's term in office is still seen by many as being a failure, he is universally acclaimed as being the most successful and effective former president the United States has ever had.

Life-or-Death Struggle for a New Heroic Mission

Redirecting the leader's heroic mission is the last, but often the most criti-cal, of the lessons we learn from resilient leaders. It is often the most diffi-cult because it is an internal, mental battle that the leader must fight, and the challenge is exacerbated tremendously when it requires a drastic change from the past career. Some avoid such gut-wrenching struggles for a new heroic mission, like Bernie Marcus, who already had a vision of the type of warehouse home improvement stores he envisaged for Home Depot while he was at Handy Dan, so that his ouster freed him from the constraints to pursue that vision. For others, such as Jimmy Carter, who are not only forced from their position but also compelled to change fields, the struggle to change their whole mind-set from the single-minded attention to their old heroic mission to a new vision is the toughest of all barriers to recov-ery. It is the single-minded, passionate pursuit of a heroic mission to the ex-clusion of everything else that sets great leaders apart from the general population and is what attracts and motivates followers to join them in their heroic quest. To have that life purpose ripped from them and be prohibited from its further pursuit can leave a crushing void and doubt about their rea-son for being. Finding a new heroic mission to replace that lifelong purpose with the same meaning for the individual can be a great struggle, but one that is necessary to conquer in order to recover from the setback. For the financier who became an icon of the 1980s, Michael Milken, this literally turned into a life-or-death struggle before it was vanquished.

Many have seen Milken's life as the essence of the American myth. Born on the Fourth of July, 1946, into a modest California family, by the mid-1980s he was a billionaire and one of the most influential investment bankers in the world. He and his firm, Drexel Burnham Lambert, virtually reinvented high-yield, below-investment-grade bonds, and he became known on Wall Street as the "junk bond king," funding new ventures such as MCI and Turner Broadcasting, as well as fueling much of the takeover market by corporate raiders that occurred in the late 1980s, earning himself millions in the process. In 1987 alone, he personally earned $550 million. Eventually, though, his run unraveled with a ninety-eight-count criminal indictment and massive civil case brought by the SEC for crimes such as insider trading, stock parking, price manipulation, racketeering, and defrauding customers. Milken ended up pleading guilty to six relatively minor counts, was sentenced in November 1990 to ten years in prison, and paid over $1 billion in fines and restitution. He was also barred from the securities industry for life.

Milken could hardly believe how his life had so rapidly fallen apart, both physically, in going from a life of luxury to prison, and mentally, in going from being lauded as an icon of capitalism to being vilified for the same work. As he wrote to the judge before his sentencing, explaining how he had experienced this downfall:

I never dreamed I could do anything that would result in being a felon. These words are hard for me to write and difficult to accept . . . What I have not been able to accept, and what has been the most painful during the past four years, has been the assault on the sincerity of my beliefs, my moral systems, and my basic inner being. It has been very difficult for me to cope with. I have been forced to face the challenge that not only am I portrayed as a fraud, but everything my life stood for is called a fraud and all the principles I have spoken about my whole life are hollow. At times, this has been almost too difficult to bear.

During the past four years while I have faced continued assaults on my life's work, in addition to constant character assassinations, looking at old pictures and reminiscing about past experiences has helped to remind me of who I am and what I believed in. I began to feel that it was someone else the newspapers were writing about, not myself. It was almost as if I had stepped outside of my body. Listening to the rhetoric. Interpreting one's motives. Defining how one had lived his life. It became like two lives. A life I thought I had been living and a life depicted in the newspaper.[16]

Precluded from his profession, and with time to contemplate his future, Milken remained focused and thinking ahead to the future, returning to a formula that he developed as a nineteen-year-old college student at Berkeley and that formed the basis for his career in banking. His formula was "Prosperity is the sum of financial technology times the sum of human capital plus social capital plus real assets," or as he notated it, $P=EFT(DHC+ESC+ERA)$.[17] He had focused his life until now on the multiplier, financial technology; now he turned his attention to the human capital part of the equation, zeroing in on education. In prison, he focused his attention on inmates, tutoring those who did not have a high school education and persuading the prison authorities that it should have an education program, which was instituted with him as tutor. Within nine months, 90 percent of his charges who took the general equivalency diploma (GED) test received their high school diplomas. He spent time developing educational puzzles that inmates could send to their children. Beyond this focus on education within the prison, Milken was also thinking of how he could have an impact on the outside world once he was released. As he told a biographer from his prison cell, "One of the first projects I look forward to working on is an education entertainment channel. I had begun working on this concept a few years ago with a number of people from the entertainment industry, including Bob Pittman and Steve Ross from Time Warner. But those plans could not be fully developed and were put on hold when I began my prison sentence. What I envision is educators on cable TV teaching seven days a week twenty-four hours a day. The possibilities are endless."[18]

After serving twenty-two months in prison, Milken was released early for his cooperation with other government inquiries. But just a week after being released, he was diagnosed with terminal prostate cancer and was told he had twelve to eighteen months to live. Milken immediately turned his maniacal zeal into conquering this disease, not just in himself, but attacking the larger problem. Milken threw himself into gaining knowledge about the disease—within a week of being diagnosed he was on his private jet with his oncologist, Stuart Holden, to attend a medical research conference on the disease. He set up a foundation, CaP CURE, with Holden as its head, to fund research into prostate cancer, pouring millions of his own money into the effort and using his connections to raise further money and awareness. When researchers needed to find families with multiple sufferers of the disease, Milken decided that the best approach was to go on CNN's *Larry King Live* with fellow prostate cancer sufferer and Gulf War hero Norman Schwarzkopf and make an appeal. When Larry King demurred, Milken called CNN founder Ted Turner, the show went ahead, and the researchers found the families they needed.

On the personal side, Milken drastically changed his diet, becoming a strict vegetarian, took up yoga and meditation to reduce stress, and did what he could to fight the disease, even writing a cookbook, *The Taste for Living Cookbook*, designed for others fighting cancer. Eighteen months later, instead of being dead, as his doctors had predicted, Milken was in full remission. Instead of relaxing, though, Milken became more focused than ever, feeling that he had been given more time and that he needed to use it productively. As he remarked, "In the 1980s, I had one huge idea. Now I have two huge ideas."[19]

Besides his continued efforts against prostate cancer, Milken was determined to make his mark in the field of education. To that end, he founded an educational services company, Knowledge Universe; he and his brother Lowell invested $250 million, with another $250 million coming from his friend and Oracle founder, Larry Ellison. Ever the deal maker, Milken rapidly grew Knowledge Universe through acquisitions, from educational toy maker LeapFrog, to preschool provider Children's Discovery Centers, to CRT Group, a British information technology training and recruiting company. The mission was to put together a comprehensive company that provides educational services to people at all life stages. Within four years, Milken had acquired over thirty companies, and Knowledge Universe had revenue in excess of $1.5 billion.

Milken's reinvention and his shift in heroic mission are remarkable. He was unwilling to wallow in grief or to accept any externally imposed constraints on his desire to create and regain prominence, whether court-imposed constraints or life-threatening illness. Milken's passion for life and focus on making a positive contribution have gone a long way to ensure that his legacy will be remembered for accomplishments that eclipse his storied and controversial financial career.

Importance of the Fifth Lesson

Of the five major lessons leaders offer us for recovery from catastrophic career setback, rediscovering heroic mission stands apart from the other four. As we discussed at the beginning of the book, reputation is the most valuable possession of the leader, and protecting and restoring that reputation is therefore paramount in the leader's ability to recover from setback. In one form or another, the protecting and restoring of reputation permeates each of the other four lessons, through different means and to different audiences.

The admonition *fight, not flight* applies to those situations where the leader's core reputation is under attack and necessitates dramatic action, often through establishing the truths behind the allegations in a court of law. *Recruiting others into battle* not only provides the support of true friends and the benefits of acquaintance networks in finding new pastures to explore, but—just as Steven Spielberg and others spoke out publicly in support of Jeffrey Katzenberg on his departure from Disney—lends legitimacy to the ousted leader and helps keep reputation intact. *Rebuilding heroic stature* is most evidently about protecting and restoring reputation as the leader spreads the word of the true nature of the adversity, maintaining to a wider audience the confidence that others previously held in their ability to perform. To complement the use of words to rebuild reputation and heroic stature, *proving your mettle* concerns actions, which, as the old adage goes, "speak louder than words." In rebuilding credibility through re-proving their ability to perform in their second act, leaders are able to restore their reputation more solidly than through words, which if used alone, can prove hollow.

The fifth lesson, though, *rediscovering heroic mission*, is not about an external constituency that is concerned with reputation, but about the internal drive and redirected focus that are essential for leaders to reexamine their life's work and contribution. Whether it is going beyond past achievements in the same field, redefining what success means within that arena, such as Bernie Marcus did in creating Home Depot, or whether it is finding new pastures for building something new or conquering a new uncharted territory, as Jimmy Carter and Michael Milken were able to do, the need to find fresh purpose is the necessary ingredient that allows a leader not only to restore a past reputation, but also to go beyond past achievements and create a still-loftier legacy.

In redefining heroic mission to surpass past accomplishments, leaders achieve many successful rebounds from this opportunity to reflect on, and return to, the core of the original mission, which may have evolved along the way, providing the opportunity to go back to seek what was missed in the earlier evolution. Indeed, one of the key lessons here is that even when forced to totally reinvent yourself and refocus around a new heroic mission, most of the time the new mission springs from returning to the core of the prior life mission. We opened the chapter with Steve Jobs, who, on his ouster from Apple, reflected on the core elements of what Apple meant to him in terms of creating new innovative products with a small team, together with a love for education, which led to the mission for NeXT. For President Carter it was how he could transform the expected legacy of a presidency, the presidential library, into something that would be an active and vibrant contributor to the causes of peace that he strived for during his presidency rather than a memorial to past achievement. For Milken, it was returning to the original formula upon which he had based his prior career, but refocusing around a different variable in his equation, the human capital, as opposed to the financial capital of his prior career. Each of them reached back to examine what was fundamentally important to them, which pointed them with surety along life's journey, relegating their downfall to a mere milestone along the way.

CHAPTER 12

Creating Triumph from Tragedy—Lessons Learned from Legends and Losers

I've been a puppet, a pauper, a pirate,
A poet, a pawn, and a king.
I've been up and down and over and out
And I know one thing:
Each time I find myself laying flat on my face,
I just pick myself up and get back in the race.

—Dean Kay and Kelly Gordon, recorded by Frank Sinatra, "That's Life"

This book opened with some refrains from Frank Sinatra's classic song "That's Life" emphasizing how common failed dreams are for us all. Now we close, returning to that song's chorus, which reminds us how the core spirit of resilience is fundamental to recovery. Thirty years later, a popular youth drinking song by Chumbawamba called "Tubthumping" had the chorus "I get knocked down, but I get up again. You're never going to keep me down." As obvious as it may seem to stir up such personal confidence, it is not always easy. Sometimes the barriers are internal and some times they are external.

While the tragedies and triumphant comebacks of great leaders can seem remote stories, bordering on the mythological, to most people—especially those in the midst of facing their own tragic setback—these events enable us to draw important lessons for all who face career catastrophe. While the case examples we have considered involved largely prominent people, in tackling more familiar cases of failure, the lessons apply not only to public figures. It is easy to presume that those with more wealth, more influential networks of friends, and more recognition might find it easy to regain their footing. We selected legendary figures to show why even some truly renowned leaders may have overcome their setbacks, while others of equal resources and prominence never regained their public positions of leadership. Jamie Dimon returned to power to lead Bank One and JPMorgan Chase, Jack Bogle created Vanguard, and John Mack returned to power to lead Morgan Stanley despite each having been fired previously from leading financial institutions. Meanwhile John Akers of IBM, George Fisher of Kodak, Richard Ferris of United Airlines, John Sculley of Apple, and Carly Fiorina of Hewlett-Packard have not been able to regain their lost leadership positions despite comparable fame, integrity, and wealth.

Certainly circumstances differ, and, as we have discussed earlier, the stressors are somewhat different for a leader being fired and for those at other points in their career and their organizational level. In many ways, though, the heightened focus on the leader and their strong identity with their former role make the two key factors in restoring a positive comeback trajectory—the internal psychological obstacles to overcome and the external restoration of reputation—even more difficult to overcome. These obstacles generate important lessons that provide a structured road map for successful recovery. Indeed, for many people, the failure to come back successfully is caused by an exclusive focus on the immediate problems of dealing with the downfall—often practical and financial constraints that consume the person's energy and will.

While these are indeed important constraints and require attention, they are focused on adjusting to the downfall rather than preparing for rebound, and an all-consuming focus on these issues can lead to a spiraling down from which a person never fully recovers. Even in difficult circumstances—and several of the leaders profiled here, from Bernie Marcus to Donald Trump to Jimmy Carter, faced potential bankruptcy following their downfall—the thing that facilitated their comeback was a conscious choice not to focus exclusively on losses and adjusting to their reduced circumstances, but to focus on the future and possibilities for a comeback. The ability to look past current circumstances and construct a rebound, no matter how adverse the current situation appears, is the first step toward comeback and the first major lesson we can take away from these great leaders' stories of firing back from setback.

Lesson 1: Failure Is a Beginning, Not an End: A Source of New Success

A great pioneer of job outplacement, Frank Louchheim, the founder of Right Associates, used to always cheer up his clients after their termination by saying, "We're not undertakers, we're obstetricians!" Similarly, The Home Depot's financial backer Ken Languare told cofounders Bernie Marcus and Arthur Blank as soon as they were fired from Handy Dan's Home Improvement Centers, "You've just been kicked in the ass with a golden horseshoe." He later shared that identical advice with their successor, Robert Nardelli, just after he was passed over in favor of Jeff Immelt for the nomination to succeed General Electric's Jack Welch.

In anthropologist Joseph Campbell's inspirational book *The Hero with a Thousand Faces*, he presents the monomyth of the hero—or a career trajectory of folk heroes across centuries, countries, races, and religions. The core stages of heroic careers showed, among key stages, a separation from society, a call to adventure, continual trials through temptation, an early success spiral of dragon-slaying triumphs, and then the essential recovery from crushing midcareer defeat. It was only through triumphing over defeat that they were able to battle back against life's adversity and genuinely prove their transcendence of the forces that took down others. The genuine hero battles beyond personal and historical limitations, showing superhuman qualities, to discover a valid human solution to the community's problems and conflicts.[1]

Lesson 2: Ignore the Advice of Friends to Lick Your Wounds

We have heard this advice often, and unfortunately some friends, such as the ingenious Nick Nicholas or Michael Fuchs of HBO, took this advice—investing brilliantly, but waiting for that CEO position to return. These men, at least, dived successfully into the mainstream of board directorships and entrepreneurial investing. When financier Ken Langone felt he was falsely accused by the National Association of Securities Dealers of grabbing IPO profits due his clients, he fought the charges— with his clients at his side—and prevailed. Rather than "take his lumps," he told us, "I fought like hell because reputation matters."[2] When financial journalist Jim Cramer was falsely accused by some a decade ago of not revealing his position in some stocks he wrote about in a single *Smart Money* story, despite thousands of prior pieces disclosing his own related stock holdings, he fought to prove to the authorities and all critics that the editors of *Smart Money*, on their own, had accidentally dropped his written disclosures that one time. Some other people do retreat, "take their lumps," and may even withdraw into a world completely defined by their past greatness.

Consider Billy Wilder's film-noir classic story *Sunset Boulevard* about "behind the scenes" Hollywood, self-deceit, vanity, the price of fame, and failure. Gloria Swanson plays the character Norma Desmond, a former queen of the silent screen who, by age fifty, has been cruelly left behind in favor of younger faces and the technology of the "talkies." Now no longer a celebrity, she has withdrawn into depression, immersed in the mausoleum-like seclusion of her mansion, where she has buried herself in memoirs of a long-lost adoring public. The phone has stopped ringing with the calls of agents and producers. Her day is filled with dreaming of her comeback while she signs head shots for fabricated fans, watching her old films and screaming, "Those idiots! Have they forgotten what a star is? I'll show them, I'll return some day!" A stranded motorist, played by William Holden, who came to use her phone, observed her watching old films of herself and commented, "She was still sleepwalking along the giddy heights of a lost career! Plain crazy when it came to that one subject—her celluloid self, the *great* Norma Desmond. How could she breathe in that house surrounded by Norma Desmonds?"

Lesson 3: No Matter How Dire the Circumstances Seem, Triumphant Comeback Is Possible—As Long As You Didn't Kill Someone

While for many, the practicalities of financial and other constraints can erect seemingly impossible barriers to overcome, some of the leaders we have profiled found themselves in even more dire circumstances. Consider Martha Stewart or Michael Milken, who found themselves in circumstances they could not imagine, going from being renowned leaders in their respective fields to serving time in prison, believing they had done no wrong. Just looking at the situation, anyone would anticipate that their careers were over—the damage that being convicted of a crime and sent to prison did to their reputations, the full glare of the media giving them no place to hide, and the weight of public opinion condemning them even before the courts did. Milken had the added constraint of being banned for life from the only profession he had ever known, and then, on top of it all, being told he had terminal cancer, with less than eighteen months to live. It is hard to imagine any circumstances more dire than these, and yet both remained focused on the future and how they could rebound rather than wallowing in self-pity at the sudden change in fortune that life had thrown at them.

Now, in addition to Milken's many successful private enterprises, investments in education, and public health missions, his Milken Institute draws the world's leading scientists, economists, journalists, public policy leaders, CEOs, and clergy to focus on pressing global problems. Ivan Boesky, a fellow financier convicted at the same time, has not been heard of in public since. Similarly, Martha Stewart's media world flourished upon her return, but Leona Helmsley, another high-profile woman entrepreneur put in prison for roughly half a year, has rarely been seen in public.

Just as Austrian psychologist and Holocaust survivor Viktor Frankl recounted the horrors of the concentration camps and how the loss of a sense of meaning and purpose to life led rapidly to decline and death, he survived by imagining his life after the concentration camp and how he would bring the message of its horrors to the wider world to ensure that it would never happen again. By giving himself a purpose, something to live for and look forward to, Frankl kept himself positive and beat the odds to survive the worst atrocity in human history.

Lesson 4: While It May Seem That the World Is Against You, There Are People Who Support You and Are Eager to Help If You Will Let Them

The event of losing a job can trigger a series of reactions that tend to isolate the victim. A large part of our identity is often defined by what we do. Often, the second question asked when you meet someone for the first time is, "What do you do?" Society defines us, and we define ourselves, by our productive work lives. When they are taken away, we feel a loss of identity, not knowing how to define ourselves. This can lead to avoidance behavior as we seek to avoid situations where we will be asked that dreaded question for which we no longer have an answer. Because of the prevalence of occupation as a means to define ourselves in our society, the lack of occupation can lead to feelings of embarrassment and inadequacy, and a consequent shying away from potential occasions where we might be confronted by this unwelcome fact.

Because failure is such a taboo subject in our society, people often don't know how to confront it, especially when it occurs to others toward whom we are otherwise predisposed to be friendly. Consequently, others, particularly fair-weather friends, may also avoid the victim for lack of knowing what to say and how to address the situation, leading to further isolation for the individual. However, often people in this situation find that their true "foul-weather" friends are there waiting to be useful. Some may not offer help directly, because they do not know how they can help or even understand the circumstances in which the victim finds himself, but are waiting for a cue from the displaced individual that they are ready for assistance and what form of assistance might be the most useful. It is thus here where individuals might best use their networks of both close friends and more distant acquaintances.

Recall that in chapter 8 we saw that contrary to what most people would think, acquaintance networks are actually more likely to provide useful job leads than are close friendships because the reach of distant acquaintance ties is so much greater. Many people overlook this fact and fail to reach out to these acquaintance networks, assuming that these people have no obligation and no interest in helping. On the contrary, there is a norm of general reciprocity whereby people seek to "pay forward" help that they have received from others in the past and seek opportunities to do favors for others in their network in the same way that they hope and expect that their network would function for them should the need arise.

Strong ties with close friends are also invaluable, not only for being able to tap into them and their networks as a resource, but more particularly for the strong social support and encouragement that they can provide. Due to the self-absorption that often consumes the person facing setback as their world caves in around them, it is easy for them to overlook the collateral effect on their strong friends and family. Helping someone go through a traumatic event such as career setback can be draining on those providing support. Sometimes this can lead to the gradual withdrawal of the support they provide, not through a lack of continued empathy for the victim, but through emotional exhaustion caused by the provision of support. The fourfold increase in the likelihood of separation and divorce resulting from job loss provides a warning that the individual suffering from such loss also needs to be aware of the emotional drain it causes on those around them. The victim should bring others into the positive steps toward comeback that are being made as well as receiving the understanding and assistance from these sources of support.

Lesson 5: Get Your Mission Clear

One important lesson to take away from the comeback stories retold here is the benefit of taking time to regroup following the downfall. Even if, like Bernie Marcus, the person already has an idea of what the endgame will look like, taking time to plan the comeback and clarify the heroic mission to be pursued is a vital step to take before launching into the next thing. From Steve Jobs's thoughts as he wandered around Europe, sleeping under the stars, to Jimmy Carter's internal debates and middle-of-the-night revelation, to Jeffrey Katzenberg's discussions with Spielberg and Geffen, all took time to contemplate and discuss what their next venture would be and planned it out.

This crystallizing of the mission involves the following:

- Chart your new life interests and professional goals.

- List multiple priorities: map out all the concerns you must address simultaneously—sequential attention is not sufficient.

- Determine what financial resources do you need? Who can help? What luxuries can you sacrifice?

- Remember to consider your psychological well-being from the hurt, trauma, humiliation, and exhaustion.

- Emphasize that reputation matters and lasting impressions form fast; keep in mind the public interpretation of your situation and manage immediately.

- Secure the professional reputation you need for surrogate voices and legal guidance.

- Identify who can hurt you and what might be their motives to opportunistically seize this moment. How can you blunt their malice with ready facts?

- Consider who you most care to protect. What do they need to know to feel comfortable? How can you help them in their distress?

When things look bleak, particularly if there is financial and social pressure to get back in the saddle as quickly as possible, the result often is a suboptimal rebound at best and a second disaster at worst. While we do not advise licking wounds and retreating, tending to the situation and getting out the facts does not mean necessarily taking the first job offer that comes along. Plenty of people may try to get you at a discount price or offer you an inadequate position while you are down. The "I'll show them" approach often leads to folks "jumping from the pot into the fire." Jamie Dimon told us soon after his termination from Citigroup that he was flooded with offers—but he took more than a year to select what turned out to be the brilliant choice of Bank One after its troubled First Chicago NBD merger.

While a second downfall exacerbates the barriers to recovery, what is perhaps worse in the long run is getting into something else that is a satisfying rather than an optimizing rebound—getting stuck in a position that is difficult to leave because it is safe and pays the bills, but fails to fulfill the heroic drive that is welling up below the surface. Many of the deposed CEOs whom we talked to in researching this book had the same advice—to use the time away from work to process and reevaluate what you want to ultimately achieve and not be tempted back into the fray too quickly. As one ousted CEO said as he was still going through this time of reflection:

There's a lot of processing to do here. As I said, I've got some frustrations and anxieties and some hard feelings that I'm kind of sweeping aside, and I'll go through that okay. I guess right now I'll focus on a number of things totally separate from business. I'm just getting ready to start building a lake house. I've always wanted to get my pilot's license, and I'm going to do that. I'm going to play with the kids all summer. Basically take a couple of months off and just kind of sort it all out and regroup.

There are a lot of opportunities, and needless to say, since [my exit] hit the newspaper a month ago I've heard from more headhunters and personal financial advisers and enterprising entrepreneurs than you can imagine. But I haven't taken action on any of them yet.

I think it's safe to say I am not as far along in developing a plan of what I am going to do next—I'm not as far along in that process as probably most people would be once they have left a company and moved out of the office, but I guess the one thing that I have focused on pretty strongly is looking at other board opportunities. But in terms of other companies, what kind of start-ups I would want to do or what kind of business I would want to buy, I'm just not in a position to say that yet.

Most of the headhunter calls that I've gotten for CEO or COO positions are mostly larger companies. Basically, what I've told most of these people is that I'm not interested in jumping into a situation like that right now. I got one call from a very persuasive headhunter to be CEO of a fairly sizable company, a very well recognized name, and it had some appeal, but as I got into it and thought about it more, it's just not the kind of thing that I think I'm going to be happy with. It's just not the kind of thing that at this point I feel like I want to do. I think as I told my wife when we were talking about it, that particular circumstance came down to one that would probably be very gratifying to the ego, but probably not very fun. Not that being a fun job is the ultimate criteria. Certainly I want to do something that is going to be a satisfying job—something that I'm going to look forward to getting out of bed in the morning and go do.

A good friend of mine was CEO of a company that got sold and like most scenarios where the CEO of a company which is sold, he was not picked up as part of the deal, and his very strong comment to me was "Just take your time. Take your time. Don't rush into anything." And I'm in a position where I'm fortunate not to have to rush into anything, and so I intend to reacquaint myself with my kids for a while and spend some time doing things I want to do, and then I'll dive back in.

Oftentimes, it can take a certain amount of time to recover from the stress created by the leadership role previously held, and particularly the trauma of the events that led up to and followed the downfall. It is important to take that time to reevaluate and reformulate the heroic mission such that it is not just a reactive response to the events that just transpired, but a well-crafted and tightly held mission on which to base a sustained comeback.

Lesson 6: Know Your Story

As we have seen, for leaders particularly but also for people at all levels of an organization, retaining and restoring reputation is an essential component of a comeback. In many instances, the path to recovery is guarded by gatekeepers, such as executive search firms or others in a position to facilitate or thwart an attempted rebound. In these situations, one's reputation among these gatekeepers is essential to gaining that first step on the path to career recovery. We have seen how leaders are able to take steps to restore their reputations through rallying friends and acquaintances to the cause and by rebuilding heroic stature amongst larger audiences. All of this entails knowing, telling, and constantly retelling the leader's story, to get the real picture of past events out there, and to have an explanation for the downfall such that it enables faith in the leader's ability to rebound. One example we examined was George Shaheen, who left as CEO of Andersen Consulting (now Accenture) to head up Webvan at the height of the dot-com boom. The proud Shaheen suffered his share of teasing as his years as a consultant failed to translate into success as a CEO trying to operate a headstrong dot-com company that went bankrupt. Despite the short-lived existence of Webvan and its spectacular failure, Shaheen retained his reputation among the all-important executive search community because his experience was perceived as a no-win situation, and there was a foregone conclusion that it was headed for disaster. Although this rationalization was done in hindsight—few faulted Shaheen for leaving a premiere consulting firm for an uncertain start-up—the rationale of such a big opportunity and potential for enormous payoff enabled this rationalization to occur and Shaheen to continue to be well regarded by the executive search community, and subsequently he rebounded as CEO of Siebel Systems.

One common underlying feature of the story that explains setback but enables future rebounding is the notion of control. Even when leaders perceive outside events as having caused the downfall, it is important that the story and the leaders themselves do not portray a victim mentality, but rather reinforce the belief that they are in control of their destiny. In psychological terminology, leaders usually have a high internal locus of control, believing that they have personal control over their destiny, as opposed to those who have a high external locus of control, who would see themselves as a product of events and circumstances beyond their control, caused by the decisions of other people, chance events, or structural situational factors. Along with this psychological distinction is the overall tendency for people to attribute desirable outcomes to internal factors, but to blame external circumstances for failures. Similarly, and consistent with this tendency, previous psychological research has shown that people fail to distinguish between controllable and uncontrollable events, preferring to depend on outcomes as a guide to the controllability—positive outcomes are seen as having been controllable, but negative outcomes are due to circumstances beyond the individual's control.

A similar phenomenon is what was originally defined by psychologist Melvin Lerner as the "just world" hypothesis discussed in chapter 3. This is a person's belief that the world is in fact a just place and that in general good things happen to good people, and bad things happen to people who do bad things. The operation of luck is severely diminished, if not eliminated, from this life view, unless bad things happen to the self, whereupon external factors are once again held responsible. However, under this viewpoint, even bad things or events are usually interpreted in a positive light in an "all things work to the good of those who are good" manner.

It is essential for leaders, though, to be able to explain their story in such a way that even if external circumstances are blamed, control for rebound—and avoiding a similar fate again—rests in their hands. An illustrative translation of how dethroned leaders can interpret their downfall and position the story in just such a way to protect their reputation is the example of Maurice Saatchi, who was ousted from the advertising agency Saatchi & Saatchi, which he had founded with his brother Charles. In writing a letter of explanation to his employees, Saatchi attributed his exit to grasping new shareholders who did not understand the art of advertising, and to the fact that he was unable to control the events and personalities that forced his ouster due to their newly acquired ownership control:

> *You deserve to know the reasons [for my exit]: Saatchi & Saatchi has been taken over. No bid for the company has been announced. No offer has been made. No premium has been paid. No shareholder vote has been taken. But, make no mistake, Saatchi & Saatchi is under new control.*
>
> *The new "owners"—a group of shareholders owning around 30 per cent of the shares—have found a simple, if crude, method of controlling the Company. By threatening the Directors with an Extraordinary General Meeting—at which they could vote out others—they have given the Directors their orders: "Take your Chairman into a corner and shoot him quickly—we don't want the fuss of a public trial."*
>
> *I have watched in dismay as some of our longest client relationships have been jeopardized, the wishes of key clients ignored, and the loss of their business assessed as "a price worth paying."*
>
> *I have listened in despair as the views of leading executives of this Company were dismissed as "irritating" and "irrelevant."*
>
> *And, for the first time in 25 years, found myself in an advertising company where the term "advertising man" was being used as an insult.*
>
> *I have observed how, after seeing the value of their shares rise by 17 per cent since the spring against a 2 per cent fall for the FT-SE 100*

Index, this shareholder group nevertheless went ahead and plunged the Company into a period of uncertainty and instability.

A period in which the Directors now face a lawsuit from other shareholders for breach of fiduciary duty, and in which all shareholders lost in just five days half the share price gain we have painstakingly won since the spring.

How could I help to strengthen our relationships with our clients when, in the perverse logic of our new "owners," loyal client relationships are not understood to be the Company's greatest asset?

How could I reassure you of your critical importance to the Company, when the views of so many of the most respected among you have been ruthlessly brushed aside?

This enforced parting grieves me deeply.[3]

Here we see Saatchi stressing his values and the heroic mission upon which he built Saatchi & Saatchi—client relationships and being "advertising men," people who were valued and valued the advertising business, and saying how external forces had destroyed those values and thrown him out of his creation. Implicit in this is the value he continued to place on his employees and the loyalty he felt and expected from them, and the vindication he would receive when the new "owners" failed due to their failure to value clients and employees. Subsequently, in controlling his own destiny rather than fighting against his ouster directly, he formed a new agency, The New Saatchi Agency (held by the newly created and aptly named Dress Rehearsal Ltd.), and set about winning clients from his old firm. Within a matter of a few months, Maurice Saatchi and The New Saatchi Agency had succeeded in wresting away numerous key blue-chip clients from his old agency, which in the meantime had changed its name from Saatchi & Saatchi to Cordiant to distance itself from its founders.

Final Lesson: Comeback Is Not a Matter of Luck, It Is Taking a Chosen Path

Many of Louis Pasteur's greatest scientific discoveries came from serendipitous experiments in the field rather than from carefully controlled laboratory investigations. He wisely observed, "Chance favors the prepared mind."

What we have described in this book is not just a set of random inspirational legends of far-off leaders who came back through the good fortune of knowing the right people, of having the right resources, or just being in the right place at the right time. Nor is it the case that because these were people who had already achieved great success before their setback, they were protected from the effects of a fall through some sort of golden parachute or safety net. They faced prison time, bankruptcy, illness, public derision, lawsuits, and all manner of other ways to beat them down from their pinnacle of success and impede their path to comeback. What set these leaders apart, rather, was a refusal to be held down by these events and obstacles, and a conscious choice to make a comeback. Did they immediately see their pathway back? No, not generally. Did these obstacles sometimes look insurmountable? Yes, they were pretty daunting. Theirs was no more an obvious path to take to rebound than for anyone else. So while in hindsight recounting these great comeback stories makes it seem as if their path was obvious and well signposted, in reality they all faced difficult decisions on which path to take at every fork in the road. From the decisions to fight or take flight from accusations made to damage the reputation, to the retesting of one's mettle in a new role, sometimes the decision was the well-beaten track, sometimes the road less traveled, but always guided by a focus on their final destination. What sets these people apart is that they are what we described earlier as "bricoleurs," people who remain creative under pressure because they are able to bring order out of chaos. The creativity in finding solutions is not a random process that generates a brilliant idea, but a rational, systematic process in addressing the problem at hand and viewing it from a holistic angle, allowing creative solutions to be found by working at seeking them rather than relying on a random moment of inspiration.

What is clear to be taken away from these very different comeback stories is that there are commonalities that provide a basis for decision making for those who are facing catastrophic setback and needing to contemplate the path to rebound. Indeed, we began by examining the barriers to recovery, which break down into two main sources: external constraints—how you are perceived by others, particularly others who hold the keys to future rebound, and internal constraints—the psychological barriers that you yourself erect to forestall attempts at comeback. These barriers to recovery are overcome through fighting for and through rebuilding your reputation, through word, deed, and utilizing networks, and in overcoming the internal demons by putting aside the past, rediscovering or redefining your heroic mission, and proving to yourself that this new quest is meaningful and achievable. Our five chapters focusing on fight, not flight, recruiting others into battle, rebuilding heroic stature, proving your mettle, and rediscovering your heroic mission provide a tried-and-true pathway for the journey toward firing back from the depths of career tragedy.

Two alternative renderings of Rod Serling's *Requiem for a Heavyweight* portray how these choices over our postfailure destiny can unfold. In both the original *Playhouse 90* TV series version and the subsequent Hollywood remake for the big screen, a champion boxer is forced out of the ring at an early age. The boxer is badly battered, staying in the ring even when his own manager has bet against his lasting. His corrupt manager tries to coax him into taking a demeaning job as a fake fighter in a "professional" wrestling league, but he is repulsed by the suggestion of fraud and the idea that he no longer has any salable skills. After passing through a bar for retired boxers reliving their greatest fights of years past, he erupts, running out into the street, claiming, "That's no way—that's no way at all." The boxer then heads to an employment office, where the interviewer innocently equates him with disabled veterans looking for work, and he cries out, "I'm no cripple. I was almost the heavyweight champion of the world. I'm Mountain McClintock. Where do I write that down on your form? Then he pounds his fist on the desk, and the recruiter asks if he's hurt. The boxer replies, "Sure it hurts. Every punch along the way as you climb, you don't feel the pain then . . . but now it all comes back to hurt, and it hurts real bad!"

The difference between the two versions lies in the final scene. In the *Playhouse 90* television version, the boxer, played by a vulnerable Jack Palance, is on a train, talking excitedly to a young boy about how he is going off to become a counselor at an athletic camp and teach boxing. In the movie version, the boxer, played by an angry, depressed Anthony Quinn, having surrendered his pride and dignity, is wearing a cheap Indian costume, mechanically going through fake wrestling holds with another former boxer in a cheap cowboy outfit.

The lucky viewer who sees both versions of this saga benefits from the realization that we have choices in life even in defeat. Yes, we can lose our jobs, our health, our loved ones, and material comforts. But much can be saved. No one can truly define success and failure for us—only we can define them for ourselves. No one can take away our dignity unless we surrender it. No one can take away our hope and pride unless we give up. No one can take away our love for those others around us who believe in us—unless we elect to ignore them. No one can take away our concern for our community unless we retreat from it. No one can steal our creativity, imagination, and skills unless we stop thinking. No one can take away our humor unless we forget to smile. No one can take away our hope and opportunity for tomorrow unless we close our own eyes.

Notes

Chapter 1

1. Howard Gardner, *Extraordinary Minds: Portraits of Exceptional Individuals and an Examination of Our Extraordinariness* (New York: Basic Books, 1997).

2. Joseph Campbell, *The Hero with a Thousand Faces* (New York: Pantheon Books, 1949).

3. Jeffrey Sonnenfeld, *The Hero's Farewell: What Happens When CEOs Retire* (New York: Oxford University Press, 1988).

4. Leo Braudy, *The Frenzy of Renown: Fame and Its History* (New York: Oxford University Press, 1986).

5. David Leonhardt, "The Afterlife of a Powerful Chief," *New York Times*, March 15, 2000.

6. Felicity Barringer, "A General Whose Time Ran Out," *New York Times*, March 15, 2000.

7. T. H. Holmes and R. N. Rahe, "The Social Adjustment Rating Scale," *Journal of Psychosomatic Research* 11 (1967): 213–218.

8. Cary L. Cooper, *Stress Research: Issues for the Eighties* (New York: John Wiley & Sons, 1983).

9. Suzanne C. Kobasa, "Stressful Life Events, Personality, and Health: An Inquiry into Hardiness," *Journal of Personality and Social Psychology* 37 (1979): 1–11.

10. Amy Barrett, "The Comeback of Henry Silverman," *BusinessWeek*, March 13, 2000, 128–150.

11. Ibid.

12. Saul Hansell, "Cendant's Shares Slide on News of Breakup Plan," *New York Times*, October 25, 2005.

13. Gardner, *Extraordinary Minds*.

14. Bernie Marcus and Arthur Blank, *Built from Scratch: How a Couple of Regular Guys Grew The Home Depot from Nothing to $30 Billion* (New York: Times Business, 1999), 32–33.

15. Ibid., 34.

16. Ibid., 37.

17. Ibid., 39.

18. Ibid., 40.

19. Charles J. Fombrun, *Reputation: Realizing Value from the Corporate Image* (Boston: Harvard Business School Press, 1996); Charles Fombrun and M. Shanley, "What's in a Name? Reputation Building and Corporate Strategy," *Academy of Management Journal* 33 (1990): 233–258; Kimberly D. Elsbach and Robert Sutton, "Acquiring Organizational Legitimacy Through Illegitimate Actions," *Academy of Management Journal* 35 (1992): 699–738; and V. Rindove, I. O. Williamson, A. P. Petkova, and J. M. Sever, "Being Good or Being Known: An Empirical Examination of the Dimensions, Antecedents, and Consequences of Organizational Reputation," *Academy of Management Journal* 48 (2005): 1033–1050.

20. Peter Romeo, "What Really Happened at Shoney's?" *Restaurant Business*, May 1, 1993, 116–120.

21. Richard Tomkins, "Casinos Deal Trump a Fistful of Aces," *Financial Times*, June 31, 1994, 14.

22. Donald J. Trump with Kate Bohner, *Trump: The Art of the Comeback* (New York: Times Books, 1997); and Donald J. Trump and Tony Schwartz, *Trump: The Art of the Deal* (New York: Random House, 1987).

23. Christina Rouvalis, "A Wild Ride," *Pittsburgh Post Gazette*, July 2, 1995.

24. Calmetta Coleman, "Kmart Lures Bozic away from Levitz to Be Vice Chairman, CEO Contender," *Wall Street Journal*, November 18, 1998.

25. Michael Bloomberg, *Bloomberg by Bloomberg* (New York: John Wiley, 1997), 17.

26. Andrew Pollack, "Can Steve Jobs Do It Again?" *New York Times*, November 8, 1997.

27. Samuel G. Freedman, "Alan Jay Lerner, the Lyricist and Playwright, Is Dead at 67," *New York Times*, June 15, 1986.

28. Herbert J. Freudenberger, "Staff Burn-out," *Journal of Social Issues* 30 (1974): 159–165; and James E. Rosenbaum, "Tournament Mobility: Career Patterns in a Corporation," *Administrative Science Quarterly* 22 (1979): 220–241.

29. Barbara Gutek, Charles Nakamura, and Veronica Nieva, "The Interdependence of Work and Family Roles," *Journal of Occupational Behavior* 2 (1981): 1–16; and Mary Dean Lee and Rabinara Kanungo, *The Management of Work and Personal Life* (New York: Prager, 1981).

Chapter 2

1. Robert Marquand, "Kids Show Resilience in Tsunami Aftermath," *Christian Science Monitor*, January 7, 2005.

2. Robert Coles, *Children of Crisis: A Study of Courage and Fear* (Boston: Little, Brown, 1967).

3. Ibid.

4. "Indonesia: Signs of Resilience in the Damage in Aceh," Refugees International home page, January 14, 2005, http://refugeesinternational.org.

5. Lance Armstrong with Sally Jenkins, *It's Not About the Bike: My Journey Back to Life* (New York: Putnam, 2000).

6. Ibid.

7. "Former McDonald's CEO Charlie Bell Dies," Associated Press, January 17, 2005.

8. Harold Bloom, personal conversation with author, May 2003.

9. Bruce Dohrenwend, ed., *Adversity, Stress, and Psychopathology* (New York: Oxford University Press, 1998).

10. T. H. Holmes and R. N. Rahe, "The Social Adjustment Rating Scale," *Journal of Psychosomatic Research* 11 (1967): 213–218.

11. Jeffrey Sonnenfeld, "Martha's Recipe for Recovery," *Wall Street Journal*, June 10, 2003.

12. William Shakespeare, *The Winter's Tale*, Paulina, Act III, ii.

13. Margalit Fox, "Philip Friedman, 50, Strategist for Democratic Politicians, Dies," *New York Times*, January 29, 2005.

14. Porter Bibb, *Ted Turner: It Ain't as Easy as It Looks* (Boulder, CO: Johnson Books, 1997), 48.

15. Thomas McCann, *An American Company: The Tragedy of United Fruit* (New York: Crown, 1976), 230.

16. Logan Broner, "Obtaining Nirvana at Last," *Cornell Daily Sun*, January 29, 2005.

17. Selby Jacobs, *Pathologic Grief: Maladaptation to Loss* (Washington, DC: American Psychiatric Press, 1993).

18. Sigmund Freud, "Mourning and Melancholia," in *The Standard Edition of the Complete Psychological Works of Sigmund Freud*, Volume 14 (London: Hogarth Press, 1953), translated.

19. John Bowlby, *Attachment and Loss: Loss, Sadness and Depression* (New York: Basic Books, 1980).

20. Patricia Leigh Brown, "Silicon Valley Wealth Brings New Stresses," *New York Times*, March 10, 2000.

21. Emile Durkheim, *Suicide: A Study in Sociology* (New York: Free Press, 1951), translated.

22. Edward E. Jones and Robert E. Nesbitt, "The Actor and the Observer: Divergent Perceptions of Cause and Behavior," in *Attribution: Perceiving the Causes of Behavior*, eds. E. E. Jones, D. E. Kanouse, H. H. Kelly, R. E. Nesbitt, S. Valines, and B. Weiner (Morristown, NJ: General Learning Press, 1971).

23. Melvin J. Lerner, "Evaluation of Performance as a Function of Performer's Rewards and Attractiveness," *Journal of Personality and Social Psychology* 1 (1965): 355–360; and Melvin J. Lerner, *The Belief in a Just World: A Fundamental Delusion* (New York: Plenum Press, 1980).

24. Isabel Correia, Jorge Vala, and Patricia Aguiar, "The Effect of Belief in a Just World and Victim Innocence on Secondary Victimization, Judgments of Justice and Deservedness," *Social Justice Research* 14, no. 3 (2001): 327–342.

25. Zick Rubin and Letitia Anne Peplau, "Who Believes in a Just World?" *Journal of Social Issues* 3, no. 3 (1975): 65–89.

26. Gustav Niebuhr, "A Nation Challenged: Placing the Blame; Falwell Apologized for Saying an Angry God Allowed Attacks," *New York Times*, September 18, 2001; and E. J. Dionne Jr., "The Question of Faith," *Washington Post*, September 18, 2001.

27. Morton Beiser, "Extreme Situations," in Dohrenwend, *Adversity, Stress, and Psychopathology*, 9–12.

28. Abraham Maslow, *Toward a Psychology of Being* (New York: John Wiley, 1968).

29. Gershen Kaufman, *The Psychology of Shame: Theory and Treatment of Shame-Based Syndromes* (New York: Springer Publishing, 1989).

30. Mickey Drexler, interview with authors, August 2006.

31. Andrew E. Skodol, "Personality and Coping as Stress-Attenuating or Amplifying Factors," in Dohrenwend, *Adversity, Stress, and Psychopathology*, 385.

32. Stanislav V. Kasl, Eunice Rodriguez, and Kathryn E. Lasch, "The Impact of Unemployment on Health and Well-Being," in Dohrenwend, *Adversity, Stress, and Psychopathology*, 111–131.

33. Neil Cavuto, *More Than Money: True Stories of People Who Learned Life's Ultimate Lesson* (New York: ReganBooks, 2004), 4.

34. Neil Cavuto, personal conversation with author, October 2005.

35. Cavuto, *More Than Money*, 11.

36. Kaufman, *The Psychology of Shame*.

37. Henry A. Murray, *Explorations in Personality* (New York: Oxford University Press, 1938); and David C. McClelland, *The Achieving Society* (Princeton, NJ: D. Van Nostrand Company, 1961).

38. Kaufman, *The Psychology of Shame*.

39. Solomon E. Asch, "Forming Impressions of Personality," *Journal of Abnormal and Social Psychology*, 41 (1846): 258–290.

40. Andrew Young in a speech given at Centennial Olympic Park, Atlanta, Georgia, July 30, 1996.

41. Harold S. Kushner, *When Bad Things Happen to Good People* (New York: Schocken Books, 1981).

42. Robert W. White, "Motivation Reconsidered: The Concept of Competence," *Psychological Review* 66 (1959): 27–333.

43. Susan Chandler, "Privacy Concerns Can Limit Disclosure," *Chicago Tribune*, March 31, 2004.

44. Ibid.

45. G. Pascal Zachary, "The Survivor: She Fought Off Cancer, Then Turned a Struggling Maker of Design Software into an Industry Giant," *Business 2.0*, November 10, 2004.

46. "To Autodesk—and Beyond," *BusinessWeek*, May 12, 2004.

47. Lisa Belkin, "The Line Between Mettle and Martydom," *New York Times*, January 16, 2005.

48. Albert Camus, *The Myth of Sisyphus, and Other Essays* (New York: Knopf, 1955).

49. Viktor E. Frankl, *Man's Search for Meaning: An Introduction to Logotherapy* (New York: Washington Square Press, 1963).

50. Ibid.

51. Warren Bennis and Robert Thomas, *Geeks and Geezers* (Boston: Harvard Business School Press, 2002).

52. Peter Bell, interview with authors, December 2004.

53. Ibid.

54. Ibid.

55. Ibid.

56. Peter Bell, "Our Ultimate Business Goal: Irrelevance," *Wall Street Journal*, January 11, 2005.

57. George Eastman's suicide note, March 14, 1932.

58. Jimmy Dunne, interview with author, December 2003.

59. Steve Crofts, "Survivors," *60 Minutes*, September 10, 2002.

60. Dunne interview.

61. Ibid.

62. Katrina Brooker, "Starting Over," *Fortune*, January 21, 2002.

63. Dunne interview.

Chapter 3

1. Donald J. Trump and Tony Schwartz, *Trump: The Art of the Deal* (New York: Random House, 1987); Donald J. Trump, *Surviving at the Top* (New York: Random House, 1990); Donald J. Trump with Kate Bohner, *Trump: The Art of the Comeback* (New York: Times Books, 1997); Donald Trump with Meredith McIver, *Trump: How to Get Rich* (New York: Random House, 2004); and Donald J. Trump with Meredith McIver, *Trump: Think Like a Billionaire: Everything You Need to Know About Success, Real Estate, and Life* (New York: Random House, 2004).

2. Frank Rich, "He's Firing as Fast as He Can," *New York Times*, March 14, 2004.

3. Jeffrey Sonnenfeld, "Last Emperor Trump," *Wall Street Journal*, March 2, 2004.

4. Matthew Krantz, "Casinos Deal Chapter 11 Filing," *USA Today*, August 10, 2004.

5. Donald Trump, conversation with authors, August 2006.

6. Ibid.

7. Walter Isaacson, *Benjamin Franklin: An American Life* (New York: Simon & Schuster, 2003), 98.

8. Groucho Marx, *Groucho and Me* (New York: Random House, 1959), 6, quoted in Isaacson, *Benjamin Franklin*, 98.

9. Thorsten Veblen, *The Theory of the Leisure Class: An Economic Study of Institutions* (New York: The Macmillan Company, 1899).

10. Stephen R. Covey, *The 7 Habits of Highly Effective People* (New York: Simon & Schuster, 1988).

11. Dale Carnegie, *How to Win Friends and Influence People* (New York: Simon & Schuster, 1936).

12. Norman Vincent Peale, *The Power of Positive Thinking* (Englewood Cliffs, NJ: Prentice Hall, 1952).

13. Edmund S. Morgan, *Benjamin Franklin* (New Haven, CT: Yale University Press, 2002); and Gordon S. Wood, *The Americanization of Benjamin Franklin* (New York: Penguin, 2004).

14. Gary Scharnhorst and Jack Bales, *The Lost Life of Horatio Alger, Jr.* (Bloomington: Indiana University Press, 1985).

15. Albert J. Dunlap with Bob Andelman, *Mean Business: How I Save Bad Companies and Make Good Companies Great* (New York: Times Books, 1998); and John Sculley with John A. Byrne, *Odyssey: Pepsi to Apple* (New York: Harper & Row, 1997).

16. Dana Wechsler Linden, "Cancel That Cover Shoot," *Forbes*, January 6, 2005.

17. Ulrike Malmendier and Geoffrey Tate, "Celebrity CEOs" (working paper, Stanford University, November 2004).

18. All quotes by Don Burr in this chapter are from interviews with the authors in April 2005 and January 2006.

19. Justin Martin, "Will Air Taxis Fly?" *CEO Magazine*, March 2005, 42–45.

20. Barbara Peterson, *Blue Streak: Inside JetBlue, the Upstart That Rocked an Industry* (New York: Portfolio, 2004); and James Wynbrandt, *Flying High: How JetBlue Founder and CEO David Neeleman Beats the Competition—Even in the World's Most Turbulent Industry* (New York: John Wiley, 2004).

21. Douglas W. Bray, Richard J. Campbell, and Donald L. Grant, *Formative Years in Business: A Long-Term AT&T Study of Managerial Lives* (New York: Wiley, 1974).

22. Morgan W. McCall Jr., Michael M. Lombardo, and Ann M. Morrison, *The Lessons of Experience: How Successful Executives Develop on the Job* (New York: Free Press, 1988).

23. Sydney Finkelstein, *Why Smart Executives Fail: And What You Can Learn from Their Mistakes* (New York: Penguin, 2003).

24. Richard Reeves, *President Nixon: Alone in the White House* (New York: Simon & Schuster, 2002); Garry Wills, *Nixon Agonistes: The Crisis of the Self-Made Man* (New

York: Mariner, 1969); and David Maraniss, *First in His Class: A Biography of Bill Clinton* (New York: Simon & Schuster, 1996).

25. Robert Gandossy and Jeffrey Sonnenfeld, eds., *Leadership and Governance from the Inside Out* (New York: John Wiley & Sons, 2005).

26. Erving Goffman, *Stigma: Notes on the Management of Spoiled Identity* (Englewood Cliffs, NJ: Prentice Hall, 1963); and Erving Goffman, *The Presentation of Self in Everyday Life* (Garden City, NY: Doubleday, 1959).

27. K. H. Matheny and P. Cupp, "Control, Desirability, and Anticipation as Moderating Variables Between Life Changes and Illness," *Journal of Human Stress* (1983): 14–23.

28. Nina Munk, *Fools Rush In: Steve Case, Jerry Levin, and the Unmaking of AOL Time Warner* (New York: HarperBusiness, 2004), 292.

29. Ibid.

30. Ibid.

31. Ibid., 293.

32. Monica Langley, "Palace Coup: After a 37-Year Reign at AIG, Chief's Last Tumultuous Days," *Wall Street Journal*, April 1, 2005.

33. Ibid.

34. Peter Burrows and Ben Elgin, "The Surprise Player Behind the Coup at HP," *BusinessWeek*, March 14, 2005.

35. Neil Cavuto, *More Than Money: True Stories of People Who Learned Life's Ultimate Lesson* (New York: ReganBooks, 2004), 5.

36. Quotes from Fiorina are from Don Clark, "Fiorina Memoir Details H-P Board Conflicts Preceding Her Ouster," *Wall Street Journal*, October 6, 2006, B-2.

37. "Pretext in context: What has gone wrong in Hewlett-Packard's boardroom?" *The Economist*, September 14, 2006, 1.

38. Ibid., 7–8.

39. Ibid., 9.

40. Carol Hymowitz, "Should Top CEOs Disclose Their Troubles to the Public?" *Wall Street Journal*, February 15, 2005.

41. Diane M. Tice, "The Social Motivations of People with Low Self-Esteem," in *Self-Esteem: The Puzzle of Low Self-Regar*d, ed. Roy F. Baumeister (New York: Plenum Press, 1993), 37–53; and Bruce Blaine and Jennifer Crocker, "Self-Esteem and Self-Serving Biases in Reactions to Positive and Negative Events," in *Self-Esteem: The Puzzle of Low Self-Regard*, ed. Roy F. Baumeister (New York: Plenum Press, 1993), 55–83.

42. Herbert J. Freudenberger, "Staff Burn-out," *Journal of Social Issues* 30 (1974): 159–165.

43. Goffman, *The Presentation of Self in Everyday Life*.

44. Munk, *Fools Rush In*, 41.

45. Robert Pittman, interview with authors, March 2004.

46. Munk, *Fools Rush In*, 91–92.

47. Malmendier and Tate, "Celebrity CEOs."

48. Leo Braudy, *The Frenzy of Renown: Fame and Its History.* (New York: Oxford University Press, 1986).

49. Edward P. Hollander, *Leaders, Groups, and Influence* (New York: Oxford University Press, 1964).

50. Jeffrey Sonnenfeld, "Martha's Recipe for Recovery," *Wall Street Journal,* June 10, 2003.

51. Christopher Byron, *Martha Inc.: The Incredible Story of Martha Stewart Living Omnimedia* (New York: John Wiley & Sons, 2002).

52. Keith Naughton, "Martha's Last Laugh: After Prison, She's Thinner, Wealthier and Ready for Prime Time," *Newsweek,* February 28, 2005.

53. James J. Cramer, *Confessions of a Street Addict* (New York: Simon & Schuster, 2002); and James J. Cramer, "A Message to My Enemies," *Slate,* March 17, 2000, http://www.slate.com.

54. Nicholas W. Maier, *Trading with the Enemy: Seduction and Betrayal on Jim Cramer's Wall Street* (New York: HarperBusiness, 2002).

55. Robert Lenzner and Victoria Murphy, "Talking Up His Own Book," *Forbes,* March 1, 2002, http://www.forbes.com; and Paul Maidment, "Cramer Book to Be Reissued," *Forbes,* March 18 , 2002, http://www.forbes.com.

56. John P. Kotter, *A Force for Change: How Leadership Differs from Management* (New York: Free Press, 1990).

57. Warren Bennis and Patricia Ward Biederman, *Organizing Genius: The Secrets of Creative Collaboration* (Reading, MA: Addison-Wesley, 1997).

58. Ibid.

59. All Anne Mulcahy quotes in this chapter are from a personal conversation with the authors, January 2005.

60. John M. T. Balmer and Stephen A. Greyser, *Revealing the Corporation: Perspectives on Identity, Image, Reputation, Corporate Branding, and Corporate-Level Marketing* (London: Routledge, 2003).

61. Joseph Campbell, *The Hero with a Thousand Faces* (New York: Pantheon Books, 1949).

62. Howard Gardner, *Extraordinary Minds: Portraits of Exceptional Individuals and an Examination of Our Extraordinariness* (New York: Basic Books, 1997).

63. Ron Morris, *Wallenda: A Biography of Karl Wallenda* (Chatham, NY: Sagarin Press, 1976), 170.

Chapter 4

1. Robert Hurwitt, "Arthur Miller: 1915–2005, Playwright Defined a Nation's Conscience," *San Francisco Chronicle,* February 12, 2005.

2. Marilyn Berger, "Arthur Miller, Legendary American Playwright, Is Dead," *New York Times,* February 12, 2005.

3. Samuel G. Freedman, "Alan Jay Lerner, the Lyricist and Playwright, Is Dead at 67," *New York Times*, June 15, 1986.

4. Jeffrey Sonnenfeld and Maury Peiperl, "Staffing Policy as a Strategic Response: A Typology of Career Systems," *Academy of Management Review* 12 (1988): 588–620.

5. James E. Rosenbaum, "Tournament Mobility: Career Patterns in a Corporation," *Administrative Science Quarterly* 24 (1979): 220–241; and Harrison C. White, *Chains of Opportunity: System Models of Mobility in Organizations* (Cambridge, MA: Harvard University Press, 1970).

6. Jeffrey A. Sonnenfeld, Maury A. Peiperl, and John P. Kotter, "Strategic Determinants of Managerial Labor Markets," *Human Resource Management* 27, no. 4 (Winter 1988): 369–388.

7. Bill Gates, interview with authors, April 2005.

8. Raymond E. Miles and Charles C. Snow, *Organizational Strategy, Structure, and Process* (New York: McGraw-Hill, 1978).

9. Sonnenfeld, Peiperl, and Kotter, "Strategic Determinants."

10. Ibid.

11. Ibid.

12. David Salzman, interview with authors, April 1990.

13. George Hornig, interview with author, June 1988.

14. George Hornig, interview with authors, March 2006.

15. Robert Weisman, "Outsider Steps In at Microsoft," *Boston Globe*, March 20, 2005.

16. Ibid.

17. Patrick McGeehan, "Moving West: An Investment Banker Abandons Wall Street and Only Gets Richer," *Wall Street Journal*, May 4, 1999.

18. John C. Bogle, *Character Counts: The Creation and Building of the Vanguard Group* (New York: McGraw-Hill, 2002), 8–9.

19. Jack Bogle, interview with authors, December 2005.

20. Randall Smith, "Old Macky's Back at Morgan," *Wall Street Journal*, June 28, 2006.

21. Monica Langley, *Tearing Down the Walls: How Sandy Weill Fought His Way to the Top of the Financial World—and Then Nearly Lost It All* (New York: Wall Street Journal Books, 2003).

22. Harvey MacKay, *We Got Fired! . . . And It's the Best Thing That Ever Happened to Us* (New York: Ballantine Books, 2004), 304–306.

23. Ibid.

24. Shawn Tully, "In This Corner: Jamie Dimon, Contender. The New CEO of JP Morgan Chase Taking a Shot at World's Most Important Banker," *Fortune*, April 3, 2006.

25. Langley, *Tearing Down the Walls*, 373–374.

26. Bill George, *Authentic Leadership: Rediscovering the Secrets to Creating Lasting Value* (San Francisco: Jossey-Bass, 2003).

27. Ibid., 94–95.

28. Ibid., 76.

29. Patricia Sellers, "Home Depot: Something to Prove," *Fortune*, June 9, 2002.

30. Ibid.

31. Aixa Pascual and Robert Berner, "Can Home Depot Get Its House in Order?" *BusinessWeek*, November 27, 2000; and Dean Foust, "The GE Way Isn't Working at Home Depot," *BusinessWeek*, January 17, 2003.

32. Jim McNerney, interview with authors, November 2004.

33. Jerry Useem, "Can McNerney Reinvent GE? 3M + GE + ?" *Fortune*, August 21, 2002; and J. Lynne Lunsford, Joann Lublin, and Michael McCarthy, "Boeing Names 3M's McNerney as Its New Chief," *Wall Street Journal*, June 30, 2005.

34. Useem, "Can McNerney Reinvent GE?"

35. R. B. Gibson, "Personal Chemistry Abruptly Ended Rise of Kellogg President," *Wall Street Journal,* November 28, 1989.

36. "The Crisis at Ford as Jacques Nasser Is Ousted," *Economist*, November 1, 2001.

37. "Charitable Seductions," *Time*, October 3, 1994; C. E. Shepard, "United Way Head Resigns over Spending Habits," *Washington Post*, February 28, 1992; and M. Sinclair, "William Aramony Is Back on the Streets," *NonProfit Times*, March 1, 2002.

38. Herbert Kelleher, "A Culture of Commitment," *Leader to Leader* 4 (Spring 1997).

39. Ibid.

40. David Neeleman, interview with authors, April 2006.

41. Bill Roberti, interview with authors, April 2006.

42. Michael Dobbs, "Corporate Model Proves an Imperfect Fit for School System: In St. Louis, Some Question Whether Bankruptcy Firm's Fix Is Working," *Washington Post*, December 5, 2004.

43. Roberti interview, 2006.

44. Dobbs, "Corporate Model Proves an Imperfect Fit for School System."

45. Bill Vlasic, Mark Truby, and David Shepardson, "Nests Feathered as Kmart Failed," *Detroit News*, August 11, 2002; and Lara Mossa, "Ex–Kmart Executives to Ask for Arbitration," *Daily Oakland Press*, May 12, 2004.

46. Michael Bozic, interview with author, October 1999.

47. John H. Eyler, interview with authors, December 2005.

48. Henry Silverman, interview with authors, October 2004.

49. "Former Cendant Vice Chairman Gets Ten Years in Prison," Reuters, August 3, 2005.

50. Mike Leven, interview with authors, February 2006.

51. John Hancock, interview with author, December 2005.

52. Michel Foucault, *The Archeology of Knowledge* (New York: Harper & Row, 1972).

53. A. L. Kroeber and Clyde Kluckhohn, *Culture: A Critical Review of Concepts and Definitions* (New York: Vintage, 1953).

54. Clifford Geertz, *The Interpretation of Cultures* (New York: Basic Books, 1973).

55. Richard M. Dorson, *America in Legend: Folklore from the Colonial Period to the Present* (New York: Pantheon, 1972); and Dixon Wecter, *The Hero in America: A Chronicle of Hero-Worship* (New York: Scribner, 1972).

Chapter 5

1. Dave Kehr, "It's Not Over for the Fat Man," *New York Times*, April 16, 2006.

2. Stephanie Kang, "How Nike Prepped the Kobe Bryant Relaunch," *Wall Street Journal*, November 11, 2005.

3. Charles Elmore, "Bryant Fell Hard, but Still May Land on Feet," *Palm Beach Post*, February 19, 2006.

4. *The Oxford Desk Dictionary: American Edition* (New York: Oxford University Press, 1995).

5. Amanda Bennett and Joanna Lublin, "Teflon Big Shots: Failure Doesn't Always Damage the Careers of Top Executives," *Wall Street Journal*, March 31, 1995.

6. Burson-Marsteller, *Maximizing CEO Reputation*, 1999.

7. Rakesh Khurana, *Searching for a Corporate Savior: The Irrational Quest for Charismatic CEOs* (Princeton, NJ: Princeton University Press, 2002).

8. John A. Byrne, *The Headhunters* (New York: Macmillan, 1986), 2.

9. The data presented here is from 45 completed surveys from senior executives in high-profile executive search firms who specialize in CEO and board-level searches. We mailed a total of 101 initial surveys, for a response rate of 44.55%.

10. Sydney Finkelstein, *Why Smart Executives Fail: And What You Can Learn from Their Mistakes* (New York: Portfolio, 2003).

11. Mary Anne Ostrom, "New CEO Joins San Jose, Calif.–Area Search Engine at Right Time," *California*, August 12, 2001.

12. Ibid.

13. Ibid.

14. Bryan Burrough and John Helyar, *Barbarians at the Gate: The Fall of RJR Nabisco* (New York: Harper & Row, 1990).

15. Booz Allen Hamilton, *Strategy + Business*, Summer 2003.

Chapter 6

1. Nell Minnow, interview with author.

2. Economic Policy Institute study, 2002.

3. Anonymous quotes in this chapter are from personal interviews with the authors.

4. Harold G. Kaufman, *Professionals in Search of Work: Coping with the Stress of Job Loss and Underemployment* (New York: Wiley Interscience, 1982); M. Podgursky and P. Swaim, "Job Displacement and Earnings Loss: Evidence from the Displaced Worker Survey," *Industrial and Labor Relations Review* 41 (1987): 17–29; and J. Latack, A. Kinicki, and G.

Prussia, "An Integrative Process Model of Coping with Job Loss, *Academy of Management Review* 20, no. 2 (1995): 311–342.

5. Leo Braudy, *The Frenzy of Renown: Fame and Its History* (New York: Oxford University Press, 1986).

6. David Giles, *Illusions of Immortality: A Psychology of Fame and Celebrity* (New York: Palgrave Macmillan, 2000).

7. Braudy, *The Frenzy of Renown*, 5–6.

8. Jib Fowles, *Starstruck: Celebrity Performers and the American Public* (Washington, DC: Smithsonian Institution Press, 1992), 44.

9. Paula E. Stephan and Sharon G. Levin, *Striking the Mother Lode in Science: The Importance of Age, Place, and Time* (New York: Oxford University Press, 1992).

10. Tom Barrett, interview with authors, March 1993.

11. Steven Berglas, *The Success Syndrome: Hitting Bottom When You Reach the Top* (New York: Plenum Press, 1986).

12. Barrett interview.

13. Ralph Waldo Emerson, "Self-Reliance," in *Essays: First Series* (Boston: James Munroe, 1841), 35–73.

14. Deuteronomy 33: 46–47.

15. Gerald C. Lubenow and Michael Rogers, "Jobs Talks About His Rise and Fall, *Newsweek*, September 30, 1985.

16. Daniel J. Levinson with Charlotte N. Darrow, Edward B. Klein, Maria H. Levinson, and Braxton McKee, *The Seasons of a Man's Life* (New York: Ballantine Books, 1978).

17. Gordon A. Donaldson and Jay W. Lorsch, *Decision Making at the Top: The Shaping of Strategic Direction* (New York: Basic Books, 1983).

18. *Bulfinch's Mythology* (New York: Random House, 1979).

19. Katherine S. Newman, *Falling from Grace: The Experience of Downward Mobility in the American Middle Class* (New York: Free Press, 1988).

20. Oscar Grusky, "Managerial Succession and Organizational Effectiveness," *American Journal of Sociology* 69 (1963): 21–31; W. Gamson and N. Scotch, "Scapegoating in Baseball," *American Journal of Sociology* 70 (1964): 69–76.

21. Erving Goffman, *The Presentation of Self in Everyday Life* (Garden City, NY: Doubleday, 1959).

22. Carrie R. Leana and Daniel C. Feldman, *Coping with Job Loss: How Individuals, Organizations, and Communities Respond to Layoffs* (New York: Lexington Books, 1992).

23. Stephen Fineman, *White Collar Unemployment: Impact and Stress* (Chichester, UK: John Wiley & Sons, 1983), 108.

24. Ibid., 115.

25. Elisabeth Kübler-Ross, *On Death and Dying* (New York: Macmillan, 1969), 2.

26. Leana and Feldman, *Coping with Job Loss*.

27. T. H. Holmes and R. H. Rahe, "The Social Readjustment Rating Scale," *Journal of Psychosomatic Research* 11 (1967): 213–218.

28. Andrew Ward, Jeffrey Sonnenfeld, and John Kimberly, "In Search of a Kingdom: Determinants of Subsequent Career Outcomes for Chief Executives Who Are Fired," *Human Resource Management Journal* 34 (1995): 117–139.

29. Diane L. Coutu, "How Resilience Works," *Harvard Business Review*, May 2002.

30. J. Averill, "Personal Control over Adversive Stimuli and Its Relationship to Stress," *Psychological Bulletin* 80 (1973): 286–303.

31. Coutu, "How Resilience Works."

32. Karl E. Weick, "The Collapse of Sensemaking in Organizations: The Mann Gulch Disaster," *Administrative Science Quarterly* 38 (1993): 628–652; Claude Levi-Strauss, *The Savage Mind* (Chicago: University of Chicago Press, 1966).

33. Weick, "The Collapse of Sensemaking in Organizations," 639–640.

34. Suzanne C. Kobasa, "Stressful Life Events, Personality, and Health: An Inquiry into Hardiness," *Journal of Personality and Social Psychology* 37 (1979): 1–11.

35. Viktor E. Frankl, *Man's Search for Meaning: An Introduction to Logotherapy* (Boston: Beacon Press, 1959).

36. Ibid., 99.

Chapter 7

1. George Lardner, Jr., "Bronx Jury Acquits Donovan." *The Washington Post*, May 26, 1987.

2. Kathy Sawyer and Peter Perl, "Much of Term Spent Rebutting Allegations, *Washington Post*, October 2, 1984.

3. Kathy Sawyer and Lou Cannon, "Donovan Is 'Pleased,'" *Washington Post*, June 29, 1982.

4. George Lardner Jr., "FBI Withheld Facts It Had on Donovan," *Washington Post*, June 6, 1982.

5. George Lardner Jr., "No Intention of Resigning, Donovan Says," *Washington Post*, June 22, 1982.

6. George Lardner Jr., "No Basis Found for Prosecution of Donovan," *Washington Post*, June 29, 1982.

7. Lois Romano, "Ray Donovan Gets a Fair Sheik; 900 Pay Tribute to the Labor Secretary," *Washington Post*, October 14, 1982.

8. Lou Cannon and Kathy Sawyer, "James Baker Says Donovan Should Quit," *Washington Post*, January 11, 1983.

9. Sawyer and Perl, "Much of Term Spent Rebutting Allegations."

10. Lou Cannon and George Lardner Jr., "Donovan Resigns to Stand Trial," *Washington Post*, March 16, 1985.

11. George Lardner Jr., "Bronx Jury Acquits Donovan; Ex–Labor Secretary, Co-defendants Cleared of Larceny Charges," *Washington Post*, May 26, 1987.

12. Warren Buffett, interview with author, May 2005.

13. Suzanne C. Kobasa, "Stressful Life Events, Personality, and Health: An Inquiry into Hardiness," *Journal of Personality and Social Psychology* 37 (1979): 1–11.

14. Randall Schuler, "Organizational and Occupational Stress and Coping: A Model and Overview," in *The Management of Work and Personal Life: Problems and Opportunities*, eds. Mary Dean Lee and Rabindra N. Kanungo (New York: Praeger, 1981).

15. Kathryn Harris and Claudia Eller, "Studio Chief Katzenberg to Leave Disney," *Los Angeles Times*, August 25, 1994.

16. Kim Masters, *The Keys to the Kingdom: How Michael Eisner Lost His Grip* (New York: HarperCollins, 2000), 326.

17. Claudia Eller and Elaine Dutka, "Joe Roth Grapples with Katzenberg Legacy," *Los Angeles Times*, August 29, 1994.

18. Masters, *The Keys to the Kingdom*, 327–328.

19. Ibid., 326.

20. Ibid., 436.

21. Fred Barbash, "Britain's Major Says He Was Target of a Political Blackmail Scheme; Harrods's Owner Allegedly Engineered Plan Through Intermediary," *Washington Post*, October 26, 1994.

22. Frances Gibb, Andrew Pierce, and Philip Webster, "Libel Battle Abandoned by Hamilton," *Times* (London), October 1, 1996.

23. Kevin Brown, "Man in the News: Grilling for Toast of the Tories—Jonathan Aitken," *Financial Times* (London), April 1, 1995.

24. Nicholas Wood, "Aitken Issues Libel Writ over 'Wicked Lies,'" *Times* (London), April 11, 1995.

25. Rachel Donnelly, "Aitken Falls on 'Sword of Truth,'" *Irish Times*, June 21, 1997.

26. Stephen Castle, Paul Routledge, Dominic Prince, Brian Cathcart, and Peter Victor, "Why Cuddles and Tiny Hate the Tories," *Independent* (London), October 23, 1994.

27. Kim Sengupta, "Fayed Accused Michael Howard of Taking 1.5 Million Pounds in Bribes from Tiny Rowland," *Independent* (London), November 23, 1999.

28. Peter Preston, "Buried in Lies" *The Guardian* (London), June 21, 1997, 23.

Chapter 8

1. Rakesh Khurana, *Searching for a Corporate Savior: The Irrational Quest for Charismatic CEOs* (Princeton, NJ: Princeton University Press, 2002).

2. Joel M. Podolny and James N. Baron, "Resources and Relationships: Social Networks and Mobility in the Workplace," *American Sociological Review* 62 (1997): 673–693; Ronald S. Burt, *Structural Holes: The Social Structure of Competition* (Cambridge, MA: Harvard University Press, 1992); and Mark Granovetter, "The Strength of Weak Ties," *American Journal of Sociology* 78 (1973): 1360–1380.

3. A. Rapoport and W. Horvath, "A Study of a Large Sociogram," *Behavioral Science* 6 (1961): 279–291.

4. See http://oracleofbacon.org.

5. Jeffrey Travers and Stanley Milgram, "An Experimental Study of the 'Small-World' Problem," *Sociometry* 32 (1969): 425–428.

6. Herbert Parnes, *Research on Labor Mobility* (New York: Social Science Research Council, 1954).

7. Granovetter, "The Strength of Weak Ties," 1360–1380.

8. Ibid., 1372.

9. Michael Useem, *The Inner Circle* (New York: Oxford University Press, 1984).

10. G. F. Davis, M. Yoo, and W. E. Baker, "The Small World of the American Corporate Elite, 1982–2001," *Strategic Organization* 1 (2003): 301–326.

11. Useem, *The Inner Circle*, 50.

12. Khurana, *Searching for a Corporate Savior.*

13. Harold G. Kaufman, *Professionals in Search of Work: Coping with the Stress of Job Loss and Underemployment* (New York: Wiley Interscience, 1982); and Stephen Fineman, *White Collar Unemployment: Impact and Stress* (Chichester, UK: John Wiley & Sons, 1983).

14. E. Langer, "The Illusion of Control," *Journal of Personality and Social Psychology* 32, no. 2 (1975): 311–328.

15. Amy Barrett with Stephanie Anderson Forest and Tom Lowry, "Henry Silverman's Long Road Back," *BusinessWeek*, February 28, 2000.

16. Ibid.

17. Ibid.

18. Henry Silverman, personal interview with author, October 2005.

19. Ibid.

20. Ibid.

21. Barrett, et al. "Henry Silverman's Long Road Back."

22. Claudia Eller and Elaine Dutka, "Joe Roth Grapples with Katzenberg Legacy," *Los Angeles Times*, August 29, 1994.

23. Michael Meyer with Stryker McGuire, Charles Fleming, Mark Miller, Andrew Murr, and Daniel McGinn, "Of Mice and Men." *Newsweek*, September 5, 1994, 40.

24. Claudia Eller and Alan Citron, "Angst at Disney's World," *Los Angeles Times*, July 24, 1994.

25. Ibid.

26. Ibid.

27. Eller and Dutka, "Joe Roth Grapples with Katzenberg Legacy."

28. Ibid.

29. Kim Masters, *The Keys to the Kingdom: How Michael Eisner Lost His Grip* (New York: HarperCollins, 2000), 322.

30. Ibid., 333.

31. Ibid., 334.

32. Ibid., 335.

33. M. A. Dew, E. J. Bromet, and H. C. Schulberg, "A Comparative Analysis of Two Community Stressors' Long Term Mental Health Effects," *American Journal of Community Psychology* 15 (1987): 167–184.

34. R. Liem and J. H. Liem, "Social Support and Stress: Some General Issues and Their Application to the Problem of Unemployment," in *Mental Health and the Economy*, eds. L. Ferman and J. P. Gordus (Kalamazoo, MI: W. F. Upjohn Institute for Employment Research, 1979), 347–378.

35. Blair Justice and Rita Justice, *The Abusing Family* (New York: Human Sciences Press, 1976).

36. Carrie R. Leana and Daniel C. Feldman, *Coping with Job Loss: How Individuals, Organizations, and Communities Respond to Layoffs* (New York: Lexington Books, 1992).

Chapter 9

1. Fenton Bailey, *Fall from Grace: The Untold Story of Michael Milken* (New York: Birch Lane Press, 1992), ix.

2. www.marthatalks.com, accessed June 2003.

3. Ibid.

4. http://transcripts.cnn.com/TRANSCRIPTS/0407/16/lol.05.html, accessed July 2006.

5. Ibid.

6. Ibid.

7. Martha Stewart, interview with Larry King, *Larry King Live*, CNN, July 19, 2004.

8. Sharon Patrick, interview with authors, December 2004.

9. Ibid.

Chapter 10

1. Donald J. Trump with Tony Schwartz, *Trump: The Art of the Deal* (New York: Random House, 1987), 60.

2. Julia Boorstin, "Mickey Drexler's Second Coming," *Fortune*, May 2, 2005.

3. Meryl Gordon, "Mickey Drexler's Redemption," *New York Magazine*, November 29, 2004.

4. Ibid.

5. Ibid.

6. Ibid.

7. Ibid.

8. Boorstin, "Mickey Drexler's Second Coming."

9. Ibid.

10. Gordon, "Mickey Drexler's Redemption."

11. Boorstin, "Mickey Drexler's Second Coming."

12. Donald J. Trump with Kate Bohner, *Trump: The Art of the Comeback* (New York: Times Books, 1997), 4–6.

13. Michael Bloomberg, *Bloomberg by Bloomberg* (New York: John Wiley, 1997), 41–42.

14. Ibid., 42.

Chapter 11

1. Steven Berglas, *Reclaiming the Fire: How Successful People Overcome Burnout* (New York: Random House, 2001).

2. Peter M. Senge, *The Fifth Discipline: The Art and Practice of the Learning Organization* (New York: Doubleday/Currency, 1990).

3. Jeffrey S. Young. *Steve Jobs: The Journey Is the Reward* (Southampton, UK: Glentop Press, 1988), 412.

4. Ibid., 420.

5. Ibid., 420–421.

6. Ray Gilmartin, interview with authors, December 2005.

7. Berglas, *Reclaiming the Fire*.

8. Tom Barry, "Gold Medal Visionary," *Georgia Trend*, January 1, 1997.

9. Jimmy Carter and Rosalynn Carter, *Everything to Gain: Making the Most of the Rest of Your Life* (New York: Random House, 1987), 13.

10. Ibid., 7.

11. Ibid., 3–4.

12. Ibid., 11.

13. Ibid., 31.

14. Nobel Peace Prize announcement, October 11, 2002.

15. Carter and Carter, *Everything to Gain*, 9.

16. Fenton Bailey, *Fall from Grace: The Untold Story of Michael Milken* (New York: Birch Lane Press, 1992), 290.

17. Kathleen Morris and John Carey, "The Reincarnation of Mike Milken," *BusinessWeek*, May 10, 1999.

18. Bailey, *Fall from Grace*, 310–311.

19. Morris and Carey, "The Reincarnation of Mike Milken."

Chapter 12

1. Joseph Campbell, *The Hero with a Thousand Faces* (New York: Pantheon Books, 1949).

2. Ken Langone, personal conversation with authors, December 2005.

3. Maurice Saatchi, "To Everyone at Saatchi" *The Guardian* (London), January 4, 1995.

Index

About the Authors

Jeffrey Sonnenfeld is a professor at the Yale School of Management and Senior Associate Dean. He holds the Lester Crown Chair of Management Practice and is Founder and President of the Yale Chief Executive Leadership Institute. His AB, MBA, and doctorate are from Harvard University, where he also was a business professor for ten years. He has won multiple awards for "Outstanding Research in Social Issues" by the Academy of Management (AOM) and has served on the AOM Board of Governors and as the first president of the AOM Careers Division. He has also served as an editor of many of the leading scholarly journals in management.

Sonnenfeld has published several hundred articles on CEO leadership, CEO succession, corporate governance and board character, leadership development, and social issues. His consulting experience and public speaking are focused on CEO leadership, board governance, and leadership development. Among his six books are his prize-winning study *The Hero's Farewell: What Happens When CEOs Retire* (Oxford University Press). Sonnenfeld's commentaries on corporate leadership appear regularly in the media with frequent appearances in the *New York Times*, the *Wall Street Journal*, *Forbes*, *Fortune*, *BusinessWeek*, the Associated Press, Bloomberg, and on TV programs on CNBC, FoxNews, CNN, PBS, MSNBC, NBC, CBS, and ABC.

Andrew Ward is a member of the management faculty of the Terry College of Business of the University of Georgia, and author of *The Leadership Lifecycle: Matching Leaders to Evolving Organizations* (Palgrave Macmillan). Ward's research centers on leadership, corporate governance, and the role and challenges of chief executive officers. His work has been featured in numerous publications including *BusinessWeek*, the *Financial Times*, the *Washington Post*, *Directorship*, *Directors and Boards*, *Corporate Board Member*, and *Investor's Business Daily*. He is frequently quoted in the media on leadership, governance, and CEO succession issues.